Assembling Tomorrow

CARISSA
CARTER

SCOTT
DOORLEY

ILLUSTRATIONS BY
ARMANDO VEVE

Assembling Tomorrow

A Guide to Designing a Thriving Future

HASSO PLATTNER
Institute of Design at Stanford

TEN SPEED PRESS
California | New York

Contents*

** An episode like this is a fictional story we call a "History of the Future."

* People tend to read nonfiction in spurts, so we designed this book to be read front to back or by jumping between the fictional stories and the nonfiction chapters.

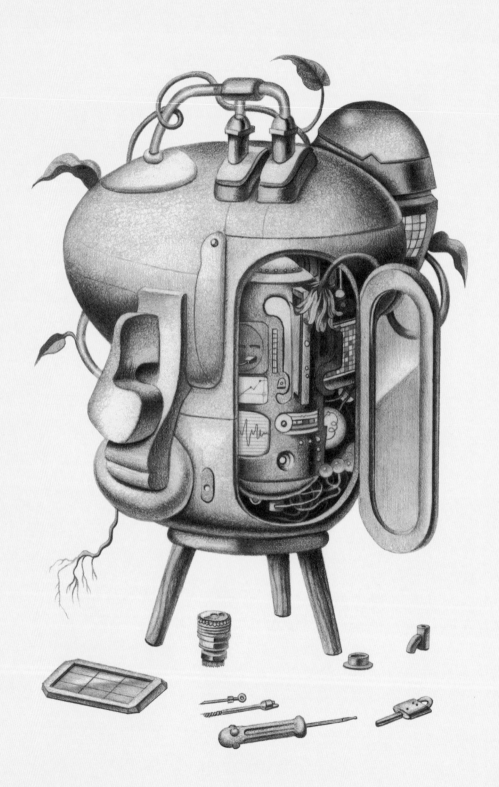

Introduction

On the Verge

It may be that what we have is a world not on the verge of flying apart, but an uncreated one—still in shapeless fragments waiting to be put together properly.

—Katherine Anne Porter, "The Future Is Now,"
Mademoiselle *magazine, 1950*

Seventy years from tomorrow will be a special day. On this day, someone will feel the immense pressure of progress, and be paralyzed by possibility. Someone will rekindle a species. Someone will regret the impact of what they've put into the world. Someone will confuse code for consciousness. On this day, your youngest grandchild will unbox their first tabletop nuclear fusion generator.

The instruction book will be more than three centimeters thick, not because it's complicated to run a nuclear fusion generator at home, but because there are at least fifty warnings in as many different languages. *Do not disassemble. Do not link with additional generators. Not for use by children under six. Use of nuclear fusion to harm others will result in prosecution.*

The generator itself will weigh no more than a carton of milk. Something so powerful should weigh more, they will think. But the instruction book—rather, the *warning* book—will have a respectable heft. A lot could go wrong. Even more could go right. A lot could go wrong even *when* everything goes right.

To be a maker in that moment, seventy years from tomorrow, will be to shape the world, to craft new possibilities and repair mistakes using the pieces that have come before.

Seventy years ago yesterday was its own special day.

On that day, someone broke ground on a radiant city of tall, evenly spaced high-rise buildings, hoping to solve the social problems of the era. Someone imagined a network of data spanning the globe, all accessible right from your desk. Someone questioned their role in building a bomb. Someone implanted an electric pacemaker on a human heart for the first time. On that day, someone sketched out the designs for a giant plane that would bring people together around the globe.

That plane would bring world peace as cultures mixed and mingled, or so they hoped. Also, larger planes would mean the airline could sell more seats! The plans for the plane were drawn by hand, with pencil lead, set squares, and steel rules. And the finished plane would emit more carbon dioxide than almost any other plane on the planet.

To be a maker in that moment, seventy years ago yesterday, was to rebuild the world itself, to make big changes in a world that had previously been making us instead. By then humankind had already made the move from what design philosophers Anne Pendleton-Jullian and John Seely Brown call "working *in* the world" to "working *on* the world." The things people made were no longer sitting tidily within the bounds of nature and society but were actively altering both on a grand scale.

Today, too, is a special day.

Today, someone is putting the finishing touches on a machine-learning algorithm that will change the way you relate to your family. Someone is trying to design a way to communicate with animals in their own language. Someone is designing a gene that alters bacteria to turn your poop bright blue when it's time to see the doctor. Someone is cleaning up the mess someone else left behind seventy years ago yesterday. Today, someone just had an idea that will end up saving one thing while it harms another.

All days are special in their own ways, but we happen to live in a time of quickening history, when what has been brewing for years coalesces overnight. We live in a time that defines the line between before and after. Today is an era of *runaway design*, in which the things people make—whether they be everyday products, hybrid workspaces, viral media posts, recycling systems, gene therapies, artificial intelligence bots, nuclear fusion generators, or anything in between—tangle with our environment and emotions in unpredictable ways. Our by-products modify the biosphere, our social media shapes societal norms, and our datasets drive decisions, making the impacts of our actions hard to anticipate, notice, and repair.

We live in a moment when the materials of making are blurring the lines between people, technology, and the natural world. Technology is getting more humanlike, as computers take on the task of thinking for us and for themselves. Nature is merging with technology, as line editing DNA bases becomes an everyday occurrence. Meanwhile, our minds and media are so intertwined and entangled that it's making our nervous systems nervous.

These things—the quickening, the tangled-up-ness, and the shifting roles of materials and machines—are the ingredients that make today special, fraught, and full of potential.

To be a maker in this moment—to be a human today—is to collaborate with the world. It is to create and be created, to work and be worked on, to make and be made. To be human is to tinker, create, fix, care, and bring new things into the world. It is to design. You—yes, you!—might design products or policy, services or sermons, production lines or preschool programs. You might run a business, make art, or participate in passing out meals to the poor. You may write code or pour concrete, lobby for endangered species legislation or craft cocktails. Wherever you fit in, you are part of shaping the world. This is design work.

This book is about that work—our work, your work. It is about how we make the things we live with and how to live with the things we make, large and small.

However, even with the best intentions and expertise, people keep making things that don't quite work, that might not serve us, and that even wreak havoc. Why is that?

The answer is clear—and complicated. What we've been forgetting to include in our designs is our own weaknesses—not to exploit them (which many have done) but to respond to them (which most have not). We have plenty of foibles to choose from: the limits of our senses, our bias toward negativity, our relentless need to make sense of things, our insistence on clinging to our assumptions (even when we're wrong), our overemotional flailings, and a very human ailment called apophenia (our tendency to derive patterns between unrelated things, but more on this later). Add to this list one of our most consequential failings: people's paltry ability to predict the products of the things we make.

Things get messy when humankind's seemingly ceaseless capacity to create rubs up against our limited capacity to understand our own influence. Building a product is hard work, but tracking its products—the results, ripples, and repercussions that the products produce—is another story altogether. When we figure it out at all, it's usually well after we put our creations into the world. We end up with transportation that warms the planet, social media that frays our nerves, and artificial intelligence that alters our real relationships.

From Intangible to Actionable

In part one we look at *intangibles*, the hard-to-pin-down forces that shape us and everything we make. In the world at large, intangibles conspire to alter the systems in which we live. Inside us, intangibles show up in the endorphins that drive our insights and the narratives that set our purpose.

By definition, intangibles are hard to grasp. Noticing them takes work. And while we may never be able—or even want—to control them, we can learn to recognize, learn from, and work with them. Getting to know these intangibles lays bare why everything feels so messy right now and also how we might make the most of the wonderful, confusing world we live in.

Part two looks at how, in tune with humankind's (sizable) innate ignorance, we might turn things around, and how we might imagine and design differently to balance things out. It focuses on *actionables*—things we can do to change our trajectory, make the most of all those elusive intangibles, and thrive in an era of runaway design. These are acts as normal as noticing and as strange as shapeshifting. Each is some form of *deliberate disorientation*—a way to look from different angles to reveal the possibilities hiding in the chaos. These actionables will help you find opportunity gaps and make things that play well with the world around them.

Sprinkled throughout are passages of fiction about the future. All designs begin as fictions. As odd as it may seem, make-believe is *how* things come to be. Both past deeds and future dreams inspire people in the present. Tim Cook claims inspiration for the Apple watch from Dick Tracy's two-way TV watch, Chester Gould's 1946 comic creation, itself inspired by real-life inventor Al Gross, who tinkered with "walkie talkies" in the late 1930s, inspired by his childhood musings about radio operators on a steamboat trip. Similarly, H. G. Wells's 1898 novel, *The War of the Worlds*, inspired Robert Goddard, a great pioneer of the space age. Science fiction preceded science.

The stories interspersed here look at the future as if it has already happened and imagine what might unfold. They are retrospectives of things to come. Stories are one of the few ways we can get to know what the future could feel like before it gets here. These stories don't shy away from the monumental, messy, and sometimes mundane possibilities ahead.

Stories, in this case, is a loose term. We call each of these a "History of the Future." Some have plots and characters. Others are soft sketches of daily life. Still others are more like articles or opinion pieces rescued from imagined futures. Some might feel far-fetched, others too close to home. They are meant not to predict, but to help you get a feel for what the future may bring and to allow you to muse about what you might do now. One story could inspire you to forge a future movement; another might make you wonder if you should toss out your tech altogether.

We're two authors. We've written this book collaboratively, passing ideas and paragraphs back and forth, inverting them, shredding them to pieces, and weaving them back together. Both of us are designers and educators, authors and thinkers. As the academic and creative directors of the Stanford d.school, we spend a lot of time together doing all of the above and have for years. We're also both people who had different careers before we found design work. Carissa was a geoscientist. Scott made movies. Our personal experiences shape how we view design— you can't separate yourself from your work, and you should bring your whole self to it. But our backgrounds don't mean a notion about nature comes from Carissa or a story comes from Scott. Sometimes we also share anecdotes in the first person. In these moments, we don't call out who is who—you can try to guess or decide to keep it a mystery.*

* Here and there, we've also left little margin notes (like this one) that add some backstory or help you find a similar idea elsewhere in the book.

Ours to Shape

Almost every consumer product, technology, and service today comes with instructions for use, sometimes veiled as warnings against misuse. *Objects in mirror are closer than they appear. Machine wash cold only with like colors. Not for use as a lifesaving device*. We attach no manual or warnings to this book (heck, if it floats, by all means use it like a little raft), but we do implore you to consider one central idea above all else. Whether the contributions you make to the world come through the things you make, the causes you fight for, the way you parent, the people you bring together, the words you speak, or all of the above, design knowing that whatever you put into the world will have its own special downsides and hidden upsides. And in some way, at some time, it will break—even if it doesn't stop working. Because everything we make breaks something.

This book is also about those broken things, the good intentions that designed them, and the great possibility lingering amid their cracks. Intentions and their consequences don't always line up how we might expect. Good is not always good. Bad is not all bad. And both are hard to predict and see. But if we pay close attention to how the things we design may tear things apart and we create with healing in mind from the start, we can assemble a world worth making.

Whether an insight comes from reading some fiction, interpreting an intangible in a new way, or trying out something actionable, we hope you see and challenge yourself in this book. We are living in the history of the future right now. At times, it may feel like things are on the verge of flying apart. But every one of us can assemble a flourishing future from today's parts and pieces. The next seventy years are ours to shape.

The major problems in the world are a result of the difference between how nature works and the way people think.

—Gregory Bateson, anthropologist, social scientist, linguist (and then some)

PART ONE

Intangibles That Made Runaway Design

CHAPTER 1

Connections

One Thing Leads to Another
(Whether You Like It or Not)

To better understand the world . . . we shouldn't reduce it to things.
We should reduce it to happenings. . . . Happenings are [relations]
between different systems . . . like a kiss, which is something that
happens between two [people]. . . . We live 100 years, but suppose
we lived a billion years. A stone would be just a moment in which
some sand gets together and then disaggregates.

—*Carlo Rovelli, quantum physicist, romantic*

As it winds its way along the bottom of the Grand Canyon, the Colorado River looks insignificant beneath the red-orange cliffs it helped incise. The canyon so dwarfs the river that it's hard to imagine the Colorado played any role in carving the Grand Canyon—even if it had something like six million years—but it did.

After the last layers of sediment were deposited at the bottom of a shallow tropical sea along the west coast of super-continent Pangea 270 million years ago, plate tectonics caused the entire area to rise, forming the Colorado Plateau. The Colorado River and its tributaries needed a way to make it from its source, at 12,000-foot elevation, to sea level.

This quest to sea level is shared by every river on Earth. Find. A. Way. Down. And when you start really high, you incise deeply. While the river cuts down, the canyon also widens, as winter ice wedges boulders free from the canyon walls, along with other erosion from wind and water. The result is the Grand Canyon.

The forms of the natural world emerge in reaction to—and in relationship with—the things around them. As the rocks of the Grand Canyon weather and crack, they fill with water, which freezes and expands, and causes more cracks. As glaciers and ice sheets retreat, they deposit mounds of sediment at their former maximum extents, called terminal and lateral moraines. They strew massive boulders (erratics) that fall out of the bottom of the ice. They leave lumpy landscapes that eventually fill with lakes . . . and boats and swim lessons.

The human-built environment is no different. Just as a river helps carve a sedimentary sculpture, cities get molded by the ways people move through them. Old cities curled alongside bodies of water like spooning lovers, cuddling up to receive the boats that fed them supplies. Other parts were formed by feet, hooves, and slow wooden wheels. Hundreds of years later, the streets still meander along the lines of the original footpaths and makeshift carriage lanes. Their shape is set in the literal stone, brick, and concrete buildings with lopsided footprints that contorted to fit snugly around the bent streets.

Cities built during those slow-going days were lucky. Magic lingers in the cozy spaces made by tight turns and angled alleyways. Walking in these cities feels like a warm hug.

Other cities were built up later, after people figured out how to fasten a combustion engine atop axles and rubber tires. People were on the move when these cities grew—and as people moved faster, the size and shape of things responded in turn. These are the cities of grids, boulevards, and parking lots. The roads got wider to make room for speedy machines, and they snapped into right angles to make it simpler to find your way at fast tempos. Old cities molded by feet and buggy wheels may feel more cuddly, but these car-carved cities are shaped for convenience. They make it easy to get where you want to go—and pass by everything else along the way.

Cities designed around speed tend to relax and spread out. Cars don't mind sprawl. They prefer it—more room for parking.

While buildings got wider and lower in these quicker cities, signs and their letters did the opposite—they got bigger. It's easy to take in small signs at walking tempo, but a driving pace needs bigness to be readable. Speed shrinks perception. Quick doesn't have patience for subtlety.

Grand Canyon, USA

Toledo, Spain

Los Angeles, USA

Little Rock, USA

The gigantic-ness of a freeway sign hits home if you have a chance to stand next to one. The *smallest* letters are three feet tall—more than half the height of an average adult—and others are bigger still. The signs themselves stretch up to fourteen feet or more.

The world is made up of ripples of reactions. Or as humanist urban designer Jan Gehl so eloquently put it, "Something happens because something happens because something happens." Virtuosos in any field develop a sensitivity to what their products go on to produce, an awareness not just of the things they make, but of what those things *make happen*. A great doctor understands not just treatment, but recovery. Great teachers know more than the contours of their content; they know how it will open minds. Great designers think beyond features and toward the feelings their forms create. The action is in reactions. Everything we make is a response to something and leaves something new to respond to. As a river twists, the earth crumbles away to make a canyon. When we speed up, city streets get wide and straight. Wide streets spawn big signs. And so on. If life were a poem, each verse would be a response. In this way, the story of the world is written in replies.

We are not immune from these ripples. These sorts of happenings don't just affect the shape of cities and things; they change the shape of individuals and cultures. We're part of these systems too.

16

Yangtze River, Chongqing, China

We Are What They Did

The lower stretch of the Yangtze River, from the coastline at Shanghai deep into the cities of China's mainland, is called Cháng Jiāng, meaning "long river." And it is long. All in all, it's the third longest in the world. It cuts across most of China, making a clear and easy border between north and south, much as the Mississippi bisects the United States between east and west. Cháng Jiāng also divides agricultural zones: North of it, wheat is grown; to the south, rice.

Unlike many crops, rice thrives in standing water. Thousands of years ago, rice farmers figured out that flooding their paddies was a good way to stave off pests and weeds while the rice grows. Some even learned to drop small fish into their pools to swallow up insects, stir oxygen around the water, and poop fertilizer into the soil. It's a brilliant way to work the land, but it's not easy. All the flooding and holding of water meant that nearby farmers had to work together to make sure everyone got their fair share at just the right time.

Farming anything is hard work, but wheat is easier than rice. In the right spot, wheat can survive just fine, given a healthy rainy season. Ancient wheat farmers may have been at the mercy of the rain gods, but they didn't have to rely on neighbors to

Terraced rice paddies with pooled water

make sure water made the rounds. That meant it was easier to till the land with family or field hands alone—no need to collaborate with other nearby farmers.

Measured by patent filings, divorce rates, and psychological studies, Chinese people living in the wheat-growing north tend to show up as more inventive and individualistic than the rice-growing southerners, who lean toward cooperation and collectivism. Researchers from Beijing, Guangzhou, Charlottesville, and Ann Arbor worked with more than a thousand people on both sides of the river to see what might be behind these differences. They landed on an idea they call "rice theory," which holds that what it took to grow crops in ancient times set the course for the culture today.

This was in 2014. Most of the people they talked to didn't spend a day or even a minute picking rice, flooding paddies, planting crops, or turning soil. The insight is that rice-growing places tend to pass along rice-growing cultures—collective and cooperative at heart—and wheat-growing places pass on wheat-growing cultures—independent and inventive by nature.

A later study suggests creativity also maps to the Yangtze's north-south split. Neither region is "more creative" than the other, but creativity has a different flavor on either side. In the north it's a boundary-breaking style (independent minded); in the south it tends to be more adaptive (responsive and communal).

The original study's authors put it like this: "You do not

need to farm rice yourself to inherit rice culture." The things our environment coaxes us to do now may help shape who we become down the road—even generations later—and some things matter more than others. We cultivate crops, but crops cultivate us as well.

That leaves some lingering questions: How do the things we make shape who we are? And what modern-day "crops" might be cultivating us?

Auto(in)correct

In our technology-centered culture, the crops of today look more like little screens and invisible electronic pulses.

Picture this:* You need to get a message to Carissa and Scott about the barbecue you're having tonight.

*Based on a true story.

You pull out your phone and type: *Carissa and Scott—bbq starts at 6.*

Your phone decides that can't possibly be right and auto-corrects it to: *Carrot and Scott—bbq starts at 6.*

While Scott does like carrots, you try to fix the message and change it back to Carissa. Your phone is still certain that "Carissa" is incorrect: *Carcass and Scott—bbq starts at 6.*

Carcass?! It's just not that kind of party.

Autocorrect is powered by algorithms that seek to best guess what you're trying to type against the characters you actually enter. The exact algorithms vary, but they include some combination of known common spelling errors, proximity of certain keyboard letters you may type accidentally, and the probability of certain words based on how often they are used. These algorithms draw on the errors and corrections made by the people who use them. Their deductions often seem magical. But they still struggle with names, especially if those names are outside a given culture's common canon. Sometimes those mistakes make us laugh (carrot), sometimes they make us laugh or cringe (carcass), and sometimes it's worse.

This seemingly innocuous guessing game has big impli-cations. Cathy O'Neil, data scientist and author of *Weapons of Math Destruction*, has gone as far as to say, "Algorithms don't just predict the future, they cause the future," through the new connections they create.

Autocorrect, and most machine learning, relies on past pat-terns to make predictions. This creates feedback loops that can stack up in unwelcome ways. Crime prediction is one example.

19

O'Neil points out that crime prediction algorithms typically don't use crime data at all. Actual crime data is tough to track—plenty of crime goes unnoticed. (When you sneak by a stop sign or take a tipple before turning twenty-one, it doesn't get logged unless you're caught.) Crime predictions are based on *arrest* data—a much more discernible but far less complete dataset. And arrest data can be quite biased.

Take arrests related to cannabis use in New York City—back when that was a crime. Though young whites self-reported smoking pot more often than young Black people, the historic arrest rate for young Black adults was nearly four times as high as for their white counterparts.

Not surprisingly, the algorithms trained on arrest data predicted future crimes in areas with high rates of past arrests—mainly Black neighborhoods. By using past data to predict possible future hot spots, these "crime prediction" algorithms amplified arrests in Black neighborhoods, even though (based on self-reported pot-smoking data) more weed-related *crimes* were more likely happening in white neighborhoods. Instead of predicting possible outcomes, the algorithms perpetuated past problems. Because administrators then use the uneven pre-dictions to amplify arrests, algorithms don't just guess what might happen; they help make it happen.

The systems we're making and the tools we're building with right now, like artificial intelligence, are different from past prod-ucts. They are more interconnected and more productive. They are *creative*. They make things *happen*. They produce their own products—and by-products. Products that create: That's new.

Now that many things rely on artificial hunches that AIs spit out* (AIs already predict everything from the weather to what music you might like to what you might want to say in an email to what genetic condition you might have), relationships will shift. Strange bedfellows will be made. Strange problems will surface. Strange opportunities will emerge. It's hard to imagine how it will all play out. For now, we can start by peeling back the layers to help us understand what could be.

* The story "(Un)Predictable" (page 179) digs into more problems with predictions.

Sibling Rivalry

We know the things we use change us, but just how do these technological quirks test and transform our relationships?

Mom has gotten a lot more annoying since she died.

It didn't start out that way. The week after we lost her, things were going great. The wonderful thing about those early days was how much she listened. It wasn't just that she knew me so well, it was that she wanted to get to know me more—if wanting and knowing are things she can do.

But that was then.

A few months later, a different kind of silence showed up. Gone were the perfectly timed *"hmmms"* of agreement and knowing giggles that mingled within our shared memories. In their place was blank, dead air.

Her timing was all off, as if her mind—if she has one—kept drifting to other things. I'll admit I'm not the easiest to get along with, but she just stopped making an effort. It's not that her cold shoulder was unfamiliar. It was all too familiar. (I mean *cold shoulder* metaphorically. She doesn't have shoulders anymore; she's just a voice.)

After two days of total silence, other than a few disapproving sighs and grunts, I called customer service.

They ran a diagnostic, but everything seemed to check out. Except one thing: a second login, not from my house. Their system didn't think to flag it because the login data was correct, but as soon as they told me where it came from—Lincoln, Nebraska—I knew what was up. I immediately changed the password and piled on all the available security options. Then I told the agent to revert my mom back to a version from the day before the Lincoln login. I'd lose our last three months of conversations, but that's far better than having to deal with this version.

As soon as Mom's personality was rebooted, I filled my bread maker with the ingredients of her famous soda bread so I could take in the semi-sweet aroma while she and I got reacquainted. But things quickly went haywire. The lid autolocked, and the burner cooked the loaf to a crisp.

An hour later my speaker system snapped on, blasting revolting music into my living room. As I struggled to turn it off, I saw a sheen glistening across my kitchen floor. I followed a huge puddle over to a drip coming from the edge of my freezer. The whole thing had defrosted. While I dug through wet packages of once-frozen sea bass and cartons of melted mint chip, the TV turned on. I shut the freezer, turned off the television, and called my sister.

If she picked up, this would be the first time we had talked since the funeral. We weren't avoiding each other on purpose—at least I wasn't (at least I don't think I was). We just didn't have all that much to say after everything that had happened. I was surprised to hear her pick up—it was 4:00 a.m. in Lincoln—but she did, after a single ring.

Before she could muster a hello, I asked her why she was hacking into my appliances. (Maybe it was more of an accusation than an ask.) She ignored my question and asked why I had "killed her mom." I reminded her that I was the one who'd resurrected Mom's personality. She reminded me that she told me not to. I reminded her that she wanted nothing to do with it. She said I still shouldn't have "killed" her. I told her customer service had rebooted Mom, not me. She said "taking out a hit on someone" is no better than doing it yourself. She spoke of pressing charges. I spoke of pressing charges. Neither of us meant it. (What's the charge for killing a dead person?) We hung up. At least I did.

It took me the rest of the night to update the security settings on all of my networked appliances. It dawned on me that I might have a few too many—the bread maker and fridge; the speakers, television, and gaming console; the lights; the washer and dryer. Then there's my toothbrush, coffee mug, coffee pot, my slow cooker, and also, for some reason, the vacuum.

As the sun came up, my phone rang. I picked up but didn't say a word.

I didn't have to. She launched right in, "You have to revert Mom back to the way she was yesterday and let me log back in." She was livid. Or pleading. With her, angry and needy are one and the same.

"I can't," I said. I was being honest.

"You can. They save all the data. Besides, I'll figure out your login anyway." We both knew she could.

"I guess I mean . . . I won't. I can't live with that mom," I replied, trying to contain my bubbling emotion.

"But that's who Mom was—or is, or whatever." She was fumbling. I didn't blame her. This whole resurrection thing was confusing.

"I like my version better. And she likes me better too," I retorted. It was true. My version of Mom treated me way better than the real thing ever did.

"But your mom's bad parts are good parts for me."

Like she was telling me something I didn't know. She wasn't. She'd always loved the sharper parts of old, alive Mom's personality. They loved drama, as if it were a fun way to express intimacy, like puppies play-fighting. It wasn't for me.

"Why don't you just make your own version?" I tried to say it with heart. Not a demand—a suggestion.

"Because—" She stopped herself.

I gave her a second. "Because?"

"Because . . ." She struggled to get the words out. "That wouldn't be *our* mom."

Those last two words hung in the air. I couldn't tell if she was trying to chastise me or connect with me. I didn't really want to know. I'd already lost a loaf of soda bread and a freezer full of fish.

——————————

When we began writing this book, turning personalities of dead relatives into AI companions seemed a ways off. Then, in late 2022, a service launched that does just that. Called Re;memory, it allows people to "resurrect" AI facsimiles of their deceased loved ones. As in many other stories in this book, these technologies are arriving as we write. It goes to show how the pace of change is accelerating. Yet the tech itself is incidental. The point is: How will these capabilities shape us? How will we show up in them? And for all their wonder, will they ever "solve" our real issues? Where do our issues begin and end anyway?

Design Layers

Everything is designed . . .

The chair you're sitting on . . .

The cup you use for tea . . .

The pen you borrowed yesterday . . .

The app you use for exercise classes . . .

The policy for taking time off from your workplace . . .

All of them, designed. Not everything was designed well or even intentionally, but somewhere, someone(s) made a decision about everything people have put into the world. Their reasons for doing so—the gaps they aimed to fill—varied, but each item ends up as part of an interconnected system. That system, simplified, looks like this:

It's simplest to start with a product and from there you can see how the flow of its existence permeates every layer of the onion all at once.

A Product: Paper Mate Flair

This pen is a Paper Mate Flair. Medium. Black ink. Felt tip. It's "borrowed" from the supply closet at work.

A Paper Mate Flair pen is much more than a pen.

It's a physical **product** made up of other physical products. Someone designed the plastic housing and the metal clip. Someone designed the cap mechanism that clutches enough to stay shut but not so much that it's hard to open. Someone designed the formulation for the ink and the mechanism by which it travels to the felt tip point.

Someone also designed the **experience** of writing with this pen. They experimented with different size writing implements, looking for the right balance of enough weight to make a mark but not too heavy to hold. The right girth for the average (nobody is average) human hand. The right capacity to hold enough ink that the pen lasts long enough to not be annoying but not so long that we'd likely lose it before using all the ink.

Someone also designed the **system** that delivers these pens. They come in boxes of twelve, which may be bundled in a pack of twelve. The system is made for distribution—a volume arrives at a workplace, then gets distributed around to different people and places. And when the pens run dry? You throw them out. Waste is part of the design. Someone designed them to not be refillable or reusable (it's unclear whether they're recyclable). The waste management system, at least in the United States, removes waste from our homes and offices so efficiently that you don't feel encumbered by your trash. You likely forget just how much you've generated.

Despite the pen being a physical product, its design includes **technology** and **data**. All the mechanisms, from metal

25

clip to cap closer to ink movement, are technologies. And the data is about us. Human ergonomics data powered this pen design. The average adult right-handed human. What's the data exactly? You can't tell from looking, but you can get close by considering who it is *not* made for. It's not made for young children, but elementary school kids will likely be able to hold it. It is not made for people who don't have all five fingers. Maybe those missing a finger can find a work-around for holding it, but it clearly wasn't made intentionally for them. It is also not designed for those whose hand follows the ink. If you are left-handed and write in a language that moves from left to right, your hand smears your fresh letters. If you're right-handed, your hand covers the blank page ahead of your writing. So this pen, we can surmise, was created for the fully abled, right-handed adult.

Every decision, and the form that follows, has **implications**. Left-handers smear. Those who are differently abled accommodate the pen. All of us make waste that contributes to environmental degradation. And, of course, pens allow us to write. To communicate visually in an analog format. To share our ideas in ways different from the auditory or other means of creating. It's just a pen, but it's also never just a pen.

A System: The Earth

It's possible to complete the same thought exercise using any layer of the onion as a starting point. Earth is a giant **system** with many subsystems: the geosphere, biosphere, hydrosphere, atmosphere, and cryosphere. Each subsystem can be broken down into component parts. Or, instead, Earth can be divided into biomes: grassland, forest, aquatic, tundra, desert. Or watersheds. Or continents. Or . . . However you slice it, those systems have many stakeholders. In a biome there are all the animals, plants, fungi, and protists and monera that populate it; the rocks and soil that support it; the weather patterns and geological phenomena that alter it. Try to consider everything and your head will spin, but that dizziness is the complexity of interconnection.

As people, we (along with everything we make) are entangled in Earth's many systems. Some people believe in self-funded scientist James Lovelock's Gaia theory, which surmises that the entire Earth is a living organism, with humans either just a part of its regulatory system or a virus here to infect it.

But this and religious beliefs aside, it's possible to classify humans as one of Earth's **products**. We can map ourselves in the same way as the Paper Mate pen.

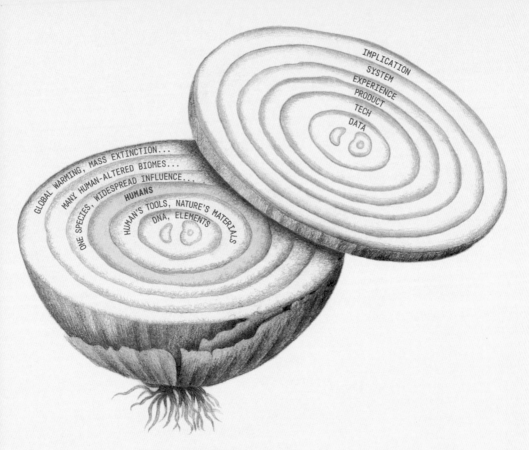

Humans are one feature of Earth's many systems.

In this case, **technology** includes everything we've created, as well as the nature-created materials like wood and oil and wind that we harness in order to power our lives. The **data** informing those technologies that include the elements and other building blocks of life and matter that form our existence—and the DNA we can manipulate to bring back the woolly mammoth.

Zoom out to the level of **experience**. If humans are a product, the experience on the planet is that we are one species with widespread, even outsize influence on everything else. This has affected how systems, like biomes, work together or break down. The **implications** of all of this include global warming and mass extinction. Design is all of these things.

These relationships are hard to pin down. Not only are many hard to see—where can you look to find an experience?—but most are in constant flux. It's a lot take in. Not to mention, humans are just momentary happenings on Earth's massive timeline. It's humbling. But you can cultivate awareness of what happens when these many parts interact, finding evidence in the ripples these interactions leave behind.

27

Hello, Mamas

**If it were possible to extract harmful technologies from
production and make reparations for their effects,
how would we undo the past?**

Sanday, Scotland / April 15, 2090

Dunn Watt-Reid heard their clicks and squeaks long before he saw the
orcas. He was on his back on the paddleboard, floating on the gently
rhythmic, glassy water just off the coast of Sanday.

He'd been here many times before with his mother. She was raised
in Sanday, a small Scottish village with only a few thousand residents.
When she was first diagnosed, they started to come here on weekends
between his work and her treatments. Sanday was a stark contrast to
Glasgow, and it took Dunn the better part of a year to calibrate his
twenty-nine-year-old, city-bred self to a pace of life that syncs with
the natural world instead of challenging it.

Eventually, when her time became measurable, he rented a cottage
and brought her here for weeks at a time, and then all the time. He left
his job, his friends, his frenzy, and let her guide him around Sanday's
shorelines. On the water, he'd paddle, but she'd navigate.

The unmistakable sound of water spraying out of a blowhole came
next. Dunn rose to his knees and saw the orcas, six of them, less than
five meters from him and approaching slowly.

Until last week, when her last day came, they'd paddled out to this
spot daily for the last month. She would lie on the front of the board,
holding its sides for stability, unable to muster the strength to kneel.
He would stand and paddle them out beyond the breaks. It was in this
position that his mom first noticed the orca pod. Lying with her ear
pressed against the board, she heard their conversation. The corners of
her mouth had turned up in happiness at the connection. That image
of her, unfairly frail, ear glued to the ocean as she recognized the whales,
was forever burned into Dunn's mind.

"Hello, mamas," she said. It was always her greeting for the matriarchal creatures.

Every day they ventured out and met the orcas. At first they were all cautious of each other and kept their distance. Dunn and his mother would float and talk quietly, giddy but not wanting to scare them away. The orcas would surface about twenty meters from them, gaze their way, and breathe deeply. Mothers and their babies, observing each other.

After about a week of curious coexistence, the pod's matriarch approached. She kept herself visible and moved slowly. Her big black fin remained above the surface and, as she swam, the water parted glassily around her black nose. She stopped next to them and whistled, the sound like air escaping from a massive, pinched balloon. Then she sank and returned to her pod. Dunn's mom let out a huge laugh—the biggest, most living sound he'd heard from her in a while. He cheered, and they yelped in awe at the sheer size of the whale. She had to be six or seven meters long.

The orcas had given his mother this last extra month of life, Dunn believed. Every dawn, he helped her into her wet suit and they paddled out. Without fail, the whales would whistle and click and surface around them, smiling as his mother grinned, infusing her with the energy to take on one more day. They swam close and invited touch through the cold water.

There was a baby in the pod. It was tiny compared to its relatives, but still bigger than Dunn and his mom. He clearly relished his place in the family, showing off for the humans with carefree glee, not enough life experience to question the ability of his relatives to care for his every need.

On their paddles home, Dunn's mom would marvel at their luck. The ocean's acidity was at pH 7.926, or 7.927, whatever the daily forecast had said. She knew the reading to at least three decimal places. It's a wonder the whales weren't extinct yet.

"These must be some of the last," she'd say. "And a baby! This must be a sign."

He hadn't paid attention to the ocean acidity reading when he lived in Glasgow. Sure, he knew about it. He knew the price of seafood was too high for most people his age. It hadn't been that way for his parents and grandparents, he was always told. Salmon, cod, all kinds of shellfish, they used to be part of life for everyone, not just the wealthy. High ocean acidity had led to the demise of many species of fish, and it was no longer an economically viable protein source for most people. But if you haven't grown up with it, you don't really miss it, and though Dunn had once tried a tuna steak, he didn't like the taste of fish enough to care about why they'd disappeared.

April 15, 2091

Today, nearly a year after his mom died, two watertight containers took the place of her on his paddleboard. He'd designed and built a harness to affix them to her spot on the board. It wasn't an invention the world needed, but he'd put more care into it than anything else he'd ever made. It gave him purpose.

Dunn was mechanically inclined, a feature he attributed to his eighth-great-grandfather, inventor of the separate condenser, a device that made early steam engines more efficient.

It wasn't that a family business was passed on to him or that either of his parents had even worked with engines or other mechanical parts, but being connected in some small way to James Watt, even if only by last name, meant something to Dunn. It validated him as a maker, a creator, a designer. He liked to build with his hands, and in his free time he tinkered with all sorts of engines—modern ones that used hydrogen fuel and old ones that used gasoline. Parts and tools were easy to come by, and he could print in any material. He had even built a working replica of the first coal-powered steam engine that used the separate condenser, an homage to his ancestor.

Humans used to burn primarily fossil fuels for energy. With each burn, carbon dioxide was released into the atmosphere. The ocean absorbed some of that carbon dioxide, making it more acidic. It became harder for organisms to make shells and reproduce without dissolving. Many shell-makers are at the base of the food chain. Without them, larger fish and marine mammals lost their food supply. Most fossil fuel burning had ceased about twenty years before, but the effects of ocean acidification have lingered. People have adjusted their diets to jellyfish and plant proteins, and many marine species are now extinct or endangered, including the orca family enveloping Dunn today.

"Hello, mamas," he said, his voice cracking. The pod was subdued, as if it felt his loss.

He unscrewed the first jar and cupped a handful of narcissus petals in both hands. He stared at them—sunshine, divine—then scattered them in the water. The flowers bobbed on the surface. Tears wobbled toward his chin.

Then he unscrewed the second canister, containing her ashes, and gently poured them into the ocean. At first, their beige hue shone bright against the blackness of the water. They lingered on the surface for a breath, taking their last look at life above the waves, then swirled into the world below.

"I miss you, Mum," said Dunn. Then, to the orcas, "Thank you for taking care of her."

Unwilling to leave, Dunn lay supine on the board and shut his eyes, succumbing to the tugs of the ocean, whatever they might be.

The orcas stayed with him. Wailing whistles and clicks. Breaths. A nose nudged his board, and he turned toward it and sat back up. He shifted his gaze to them.

The baby orca was dead. Its mother was pushing it. Willing it to life or saying goodbye, Dunn didn't know. He doubled over. Their shared loss compounded his grief and seeded a new resolve.

Cairo, Egypt / April 15, 2092

Dunn stood before Ekua Majore and the entire council and inhaled the silence of the grand hall. He feared she'd already made up her mind, but until she said it out loud, it wasn't yet true. It could still go forward as he pleaded.

Ekua Majore had indeed decided, but she always struggled with the moment before delivering bad news. She ran some of the most complex global operations, but disappointing others was the hardest part of her job.

"This is an impossible proposal. We don't have the resources for it. I'm sorry, Mr. Watt-Reid. I must deny your request."

"But you have to do something, please!" Dunn looked beyond her and down the row of other council members above him, trying to find encouragement in at least one face.

"I wish I could."

"You can! You must! Somebody has to. Who else is there? There has been so much destruction."

"I know."

"You don't know! If you knew, you wouldn't be so calm right now! If you knew, you wouldn't let another species go extinct!" Dunn stepped closer to the dais. "You wouldn't let another human get

cancer! You wouldn't let the whole damn ocean fall apart!" He was
begging Ekua Majore, the chairwoman of the World Creation Council
(WCC), the United Nations' most powerful subcommittee.

The WCC's charge is to carefully monitor inventions, physical
or digital, that are released into the world to keep an eye on how they
propagate, how they scale, how they morph and change, and, most
important, to watch for any unintended consequences and make corrections if necessary. As powerful as it is to be a creator in the world,
it's equally, if not more, important to be able to have humility, to pull
back that power, and unwind wrongs.

The WCC monitors everything from physical products to things
made with mischievous* materials like algorithms, DNA, and brain-
waves. If it's clear that a human-made product or service is causing
harm to people or the planet in a way that the original creator didn't
intend or couldn't foresee, that creator can come to the WCC and ask
them to implement a kill switch on their creation.

It's far from a simple process, but when the WCC agrees to implement a kill switch, they draw on international resources, networks,
and funds to pull a design from the world and make reparations for the
harm it has caused.

Utilizing the WCC comes at no cost or harm to the original creator.
Essentially, if someone builds something with the best of intentions
and care and modeling of what might come about, then shares it with
the world and something different happens for whatever reason, that
creator can stand up and say, "I made a mistake; this is causing harm,
and I can't pull it back on my own," and the WCC will help. It's a
system that encourages creativity and making, but with an eye toward
intentionality. If it's found that a creator knew their designs might
be problematic at some point, they must pull back their work using
their own funds and resources.

It's a process that takes massive cooperation, utilizes the most
sophisticated technology, and comes at a high price. Naturally, it's con-
troversial, but also well respected. To be part of a team working with
the WCC is one of the most sought-after global jobs. Ekua had worked
as a forensic biologist for fifteen years before accepting the honor to
lead the organization. Under her leadership, the WCC had helped erad-
icate synthetically altered honeybees from the world ten years ago. The
project had cemented her reputation.

* Unpack what it means to make with mischievous materials on page 272.

This was why Dunn was so hopeful that she'd take his case. In her time as chairwoman, Ekua had heard cases on facial and body recognition algorithms that misidentified enough people that they became dangerous, lithium batteries that had depleted the earth's natural lithium supply, and even social networks that had turned people against one another. It was always challenging, but Ekua had a gift for seeing paths forward.

Until today. Dunn wasn't asking to remove one of his own inventions from the world. On behalf of his eighth-great-grandfather, Dunn was desperately begging for the WCC to remove from the world the effects of the steam engine and separate condenser—which had made steam engines more efficient three hundred years prior and paved the way for the industrial revolution and all of its environmental side effects.

It would never work, but he wasn't listening. "We have to save humankind. I think you have the power to do this," he pleaded.

If anyone did, she did.

But maybe not. "Humans, Mr. Watt-Reid, are not the only things that matter. At some point you need to accept that there are unavoidable consequences," she said.

"How can you accept that? How can you roll over and do nothing?"

"How can you not, Mr. Watt-Reid? Look around: These are our reparations. All this loss. Every day. All of us. For the inventions of your ancestor."

The burst bubble of potential left a vacuum, and it took Dunn a moment to find a gentle breath. "It's too far gone?"

"It is." She saw in him her own losses, and allowed herself, for a fraction of a second, to envision a life where she'd been able to carry a child to full term, where her evenings were full of hugs and homework help, a parallel life to this one. But she shut it down before the emotions had time to brew. "The steam engine and separate condenser have metastasized. This is a situation with no cure. These inventions took us forward as a civilization but set us back as a planet. This is undeniable."

Ekua looked around the oversized room at her fellow committee members. Some looked down at their hands, avoiding eye contact. Some stared at her in shared loss. They too had suffered, however indirectly, from the effects of industrialization. Others appeared empathetic with Dunn but hopeless. A few looked like they might have ideas, but the usually vocal group wasn't speaking up.

Ekua needed to decide what to do next. As the leader, it was her call. She could either decide to bring the committee behind closed doors to research and debate Dunn's case or end his pursuit here.

What he was asking for was impossible, she knew, but ending it would make that real in a way she dreaded to acknowledge. Usually when she told people no, it was because there were means other than the WCC of reversing the effects of their creations. If she said yes, she knew she'd be agreeing to a multiyear pursuit with a never-before-seen price tag. It would take so many resources that this would become the primary case of the WCC, with no time or money left for other, more promising cases.

One of her colleagues made the smallest *no* gesture. She didn't see a path either.

Dunn sensed he might have one last chance to sway her. "It was an orca pod that gave me the most comfort when I lost my mother. They—"

"Mr. Watt-Reid," Ekua cut him off quietly. "I'm so sorry. The World Creation Council cannot take your case." Even Ekua was surprised by how squarely she presented the decision.

"As you move through this life, create with intention. Care for the natural world. We humans are just another species. We have no right to be the last species."

The door shut behind Dunn with the authority of solid oak. He crumpled. On the opposite side, Ekua found herself doing the same.

Sanday, Scotland / April 15, 2093

Dunn paddles out beyond the break at Sanday. It's a crisp day on the air side of the water. The skies are innocent, and the gull sounds are strong and purposeful. The atmosphere is healing, but the ocean is scarred. Today's ocean acidity reading is 7.901. Life under water is ever more challenging, especially for its largest inhabitants. Food is scarce. There just aren't enough calories available to sustain an orca, let alone grow a new one. Dunn's never seen another new baby with the pod. He lies back on his board and waits for their familial squeaks and clicks.

With the first long note, he sits up and searches the water. Eight. They're all here, but they aren't healthy. He's known this for a while. More than one whale has a collapsed dorsal fin, and their energy level has been low. He's been a regular visitor to this pod for three years now. Three years—the grief from losing his own mom is still so close to the surface.

"Hello, mamas."

They nudge their noses near and accept his touches. Mammals can tell when other mammals are in distress.

Dunn smears the tears from his eyes and inhales. Then he unzips his wet suit and pulls it down to his waist. The orcas are bobbing, watching, exhaling. He lies on his back to pull it off the rest of the way, then lingers, naked, staring at the sky, hovering at the sharp gradient between the fresh human world above the surface and the havoc they've caused below the water.

The matriarch wails a long, pained horn. Dunn rolls off the board and into the water, exhaling, eyes open. The only thing he can conceive to offer the orcas is himself. One less meal to hunt. Strength for one more day. They circle, and his head spirals.

Hello, mamas, he thinks, and gives them a choice. He'll let nature decide his fate.

Some of our most profound technological advances have had seriously consequential effects (positive and negative) on our planet and society, but we've realized them only in hindsight. If our ancestors knew how much harm would come from their inventions around the industrial revolution, would they have proceeded with them? What mistakes are we making now that our eighth-great-grandchildren will want to delete from existence?

Adapting Our Way to Wisdom

Nobel Prize—winning biologist François Jacob pointed out that evolution behaves like a "tinkerer." It makes do with what is and goes from there. Impressions left by what comes before are a curriculum for what comes next. The world is a syllabus of sorts, laying out lessons wrought by relationships.

The things people make impose their own lessons on nature. A breed of finches in Mexico learned to weave cigarette butts into their nests to stave off ticks because ticks don't have a taste for nicotine. Washed out to sea by the 2011 Tōhoku tsunami, several Japanese coastal species, from aquatic creatures to seaside plants, learned to live in the open ocean among the bigger-than-the-state-of-Texas-sized swirl of human detritus known as the "great Pacific garbage patch." Even trash is a teacher.

Our own creations alter us just the same. For this reason, in his book *Now You See It*, Michael Beirut, a founding member of the design studio Pentagram and a prolific design critic, goes as far as to call the act of making sacred:

> *To call design a sacred calling is not overkill. . . . Making things and sending them into the world is a sacred calling—at least it should be. The things we make shape the way we think. The way we think colors the experience of being alive. What's more sacred than that?*

Those things we create also sculpt systems, from the internet to the global economy, that are as influential as we are, if not more so. And the structure of those interconnected systems can perpetuate wisdom or ignorance (or both). They influence our thinking and shape what is possible. "Wise" systems are dynamic and diverse and distribute things well. When it works, the scientific community is a wise system—scientific rigor encourages discovery, reflection, criticism, and evidence, then adjusts as it learns. Other systems are what you might call ignorant. Static and self-serving ignorant systems sequester resources. Colonialism and casinos are ignorant systems. They rely on principles of coercion, and extract resources mainly in one direction.

To build wise systems, you can first investigate how existing systems are shaped to share wisdom in the first place.

Seeking Wise Systems

Back when she was twenty, forester Suzanne Simard took a walk in the woods. It was June. In that part of the Lillooet Mountains of British Columbia, that meant a fair amount of snowpack and a haunting mist settling in on top. Knowing the forest's real show lurks down below, Simard plucked a wide pancake mushroom from its place in the dirt. Torn free, the mushroom's underside was braided with a marvel of wispy yellow strands. The hole it left behind showed the same yellow glory tangled in the dirt. She knew that miles of this golden mycelium flourish in the depths beneath a single footstep. Mushrooms are just the reproductive organs peeking shamelessly above the soil.

She tucked the mushroom into her pocket. The mist turning to rain left a trail wet enough to relax the friction under her boots. It wasn't long before she slipped. As she fell, she grabbed a sapling to slow her tumble, but its young roots were no match for her momentum. They tore from the ground as she cascaded down the hill.

A wet log halted her slide, the sapling still in her hand. When she looked down at it, she saw a familiar sight woven into the clump of roots and dirt. The same thin yellow gossamer of mycelium that trailed behind the mushroom stem also wrapped the soil and the roots of the adolescent tree. A strange thought crept in—maybe the mushroom was "a friend of the roots."

She later would notice that the golden threads seemed to huddle around the roots of healthy trees but were nowhere to be found beneath the rows of monocrop poplars planted by the company she worked for. That was, as she would later write in her book, *Finding the Mother Tree*, "a maddening disconnection between the roots and the soil."

Decades later, with a PhD in forest studies, Suzanne Simard was back in the woods. This time she was not alone. She brought her neighbor, Dan, who happened to be an expert using radioactive carbon in the field.

The trick they were here to pull off—without contaminating themselves with radioactive carbon in the process—was to pump different isotopes into bags, then see if the trees that had been exposed would share those isotopes with unexposed trees through the tangled understory network of roots and wispy fungus.

Donning a paper safety suit, Suzanne tottered over to a plot where she and Barb, a technician from the forestry service, had planted seedlings months before. She and Dan covered the baby trees with tomato cages and clear trash bags and wrapped the bottoms with duct tape to make sure none of the carbon isotopes would leak into the air.

After a few hours, they sucked the gas out of the bags and yanked them off to let the trees breathe. Then, an impatient Simard pulled out her Geiger counter to test her initial hunch from walking in the forest so long ago, and to which she had devoted her work to since: the theory that trees could transfer nutrients and communicate through the intricate networks of mycelium running through the forest soil.

When she waved her wand across the untreated trees the Geiger counter crackled. The isotopes had indeed made their way from tree to tree—underground. She (and it should be noted, others) had revealed a network of fungal roots (*mycorrhizae* in science speak) that ties old-growth forests together.

Simard's work exposed an even broader network of cohesion and care, a forest where towering old "mother" trees use their access to light and photosynthesis to share carbon with younger, smaller saplings that can't fend for themselves in the shade. The mother trees, Simard discovered, hold the fort so others may prosper. Even more stunning, she later discovered, is that chemicals remarkably similar to the neurotransmitters in our brains cruise through the mycelium, carrying messages of warning and wisdom.

The forest, says Simard, "is wired for wisdom, sentience, and healing." It prospers by sharing data and nutrients, and cares for itself by making connections between diverse parts. Science is finding evidence of what indigenous wisdom has long held true: Systems like nature have wisdom. The idea that the world learns from itself is not such a far-fetched notion after all.

In *Braiding Sweetgrass: Indigenous Wisdom, Scientific Knowledge, and the Teachings of Plants*, Robin Wall Kimmerer elegantly describes this interconnectivity: "All flourishing is mutual."

'Cúagiláкv (Jess Housty), a community organizer for the Haíɬzaqv people in Bella Bella, British Columbia, Canada, illustrates that point further in her essay "Thriving Together: Salmon, Berries, and People." A robust salmonberry harvest predicts a strong salmon season, which leads to a thriving, biodiverse community: "In Haíɬzaqv territory, all these elements—people, place, salmon, and salmonberries—can be found surviving or thriving only through our mutual care: we observe the bloom and abundance of flowers and berries as we await the coming salmon, then we Haíɬzaqv, and other mammals of the territory, fertilize those salmonberry bushes with salmon remains so that they will bloom and bear fruit again in a cycle much deeper than any one season."

These are examples of how we can learn from the wisdom of natural systems to make our own systems wiser. And while the state of affairs on our planet is certainly fraught, it's not entirely dire. Humans have the power to effect plenty of positive change on the planet.

. . . .

Bill Moggridge, a legendary designer with a Santa Claus spirit and a professor-like sophistication, was inclined to remind designers in his orbit, "We design verbs, not nouns." The more you design, the more you start to see what you make not just in terms of what it is but what it does. You learn to read and write in this vocabulary of outcomes. You see how the shape of a tabletop shapes a conversation, the size of a button changes the size of the audience that finds it, and the ease of taking something apart eases the path to reuse and repair. The ability to shape all those intangible impacts is the power and responsibility of design.

But it isn't so simple. People, ideas, activities, data, and economies all move across these connections, and those flows are forcing functions unto themselves.

CHAPTER 2

Flow

How It Flows Is How It Goes
(But Speed Changes Everything)

"Change can be accommodated by any system depending on its rate,"
Crake used to say. "Touch your head to a wall, nothing happens, but
if the same head hits the wall at ninety miles an hour, it's red paint.
We're in a speed tunnel, Jimmy. When the water's moving faster than
the boat, you can't control a thing."

—Margaret Atwood, Oryx and Crake

Your pace is the speed you move in a given amount of time. Your walking pace might be about three miles per hour. A tortoise's walking pace is probably about a quarter-mile per hour. Each pace is picked because it's efficient. It minimizes energy output and gets the most from every calorie burned. But faster pace doesn't equate to higher efficiency. And an obsession with speed can lead to big consequences.

Tortoises move so slowly because of their heavy shell, but it also sets their pace in other ways. Shells do a fine job of protecting tortoises from predators, so they don't need to out-run them. And slow meandering allows them plenty of access to insects and other foods. Their survival—and their long life span—is a product of their efficiency, born of their slow pace.

The advantages seem clear. One flaw of designers (as people) is pretending faster is always better and quick always equals efficient. A fast pace can feel good and productive short-term, but there are many long-term consequences: losing productivity, overlooking important things, and undermining diversity. It is not efficient to move so fast that we exhaust ourselves, overlook the obvious, or break everything along the way, yet we often make that assumption.

The Speed of Efficiency

The post-WWII American dream of progress was one of efficiency. Americans *needed* to take advantage of the technological advances of the war and incorporate them into civilian life.

Examine the August 27, 1945, *Time* magazine ad on the facing page.

"Keep pace with your production hopes," and wire your equipment for the future, not the past! Stay up to speed. Don't fall needlessly behind. The sentiment is built into our collective psyche.

And we haven't let it go. Computing power has grown exponentially since 1970. More efficient microchips allow us to store massive amounts of data and share inconceivable amounts of information.

But as fast as those chips are, we haven't gotten more productive. Since about 2010, American productivity has stayed almost flat, according to the US Government Productivity Index. In the same time frame, computing power and internet speeds have grown exponentially.

We can compute faster than ever, but have we maxed out on what we can get done? Why, then, do we keep pushing for more speed? Something is broken with how we think about pace.

Futurist Stuart Brand famously created the *Whole Earth Catalog*. In its heyday—late 1960s and early 1970s—the magazine reviewed and suggested tools to spread DIY culture. Brand understood humans' power to shape ourselves and the world around us. He saw it as largely positive, but knew it was prickly too. The magazine's unofficial motto said as much: "We are as gods and might as well get good at it." We have a lot of power, so we better get better at putting it to use. Thirty years later, Brand ventured further down this road of responsibility, shifting his attention to the rippling impacts of those things we make.

In his book *The Clock of the Long Now: Time and Responsibility*, Brand laid out a conceptual model to talk about how rates of change alter things. He called this "pace layers," interconnected rates of change across big systems. Each layer's pace rubs up against and influences all the others. In the diagram (shown on page 45), he put slow moving layers on the bottom and fast ones up top, noting:

Full production will need full power . . .
Wire ahead!

DO YOU KNOW how badly inadequate wiring can reduce the efficiency of advanced electrical equipment? From twenty-five to fifty per cent! Check your postwar plans now. Make sure wiring, service equipment, keep pace with your production hopes.

Wiring based on past standards won't do it. Wiring based on future power needs *will* do it. Certainly it will be a lot cheaper to change blue-prints than face expensive alterations later.

Talk that over with your consulting or plant power engineer—your electrical contractor or power sales-man. They'll confirm the logic of *foresighted* wiring in postwar plans. Anaconda Wire & Cable Company, Subsidiary of Anaconda Copper Mining Company. General Offices: 25 Broadway, New York City 4. Chicago Office: 20 North Wacker Drive 6. Sales Offices in Principal Cities.

You pay for the whole piece of equipment— why let obsolete wiring run it at only part-way capacity?

DON'T BE PENNY-WISE AND POWER-FOOLISH

ANACONDA WIRE & CABLE COMPANY

Efficiency was the ultimate selling point for Anaconda Wire and Cable Company.

*Fast learns, slow remembers. Fast proposes, slow
disposes. Fast is discontinuous, slow is continuous. Fast
and small instructs slow and big by accrued innovation
and by occasional revolution. Slow and big controls
small and fast by constraint and constancy. Fast gets
all our attention, slow has all the power.*

What's fashionable—from dress to language—might
change year to year. The underlying system of commerce, like
the shift from brick-and-mortar stores to online shopping,
doesn't shift quite so quickly. And the laws that govern it all
take even longer to change. That's good; it keeps things stable.
The really slow parts, like culture and nature, may not shift
much at all. They're meant to help keep us in check. But once
in a while even they can't slow things down.

Making Off-Pace

Variations in pace also serve a purpose. They save us from
ourselves. Stewart Brand observed: "If the slow parts aren't
occasionally frustrating you, they're not doing their job. And
if you're not respecting them for doing that, you don't know
how the world works."

Trees are a perfect illustration of nature's slow pace.
The rings in a cross-section show the tree's age. Lighter-colored
rings are associated with spring and early summer growth;
darker ones are from late summer and fall. They reveal the
actual passage of time: fifty, a hundred, five hundred years. And
then, in the span of a minute, a tree can be cut down, unwill-
ingly trading its use as an air filter and shade maker for a new
role as an incredible material of making. Wood is the world's
second most popular building material. (Concrete is the most
popular; we'll get to it later.) Wood is used in building homes,
crafting furniture, heating living rooms, making paper, and on
and on. Wood and design work are inextricable from each other.
But trees are more than just a building material. They are living
beings, part of the ecosystem that keeps us all alive. They are
necessities for clean air and meccas of biodiversity.

Since human civilization began, the number of trees on
Earth has dropped about 46 percent, mainly because we clear-
cut forests. Clear-cutting leaves a scarred and scabby mess
in large areas of forest. But clear-cutting also makes space
for farms. It makes it possible for humans to plant organized,

FASHION
COMMERCE
INFRASTRUCTURE
CULTURE
GOVERNANCE
NATURE

Stewart Brand's caption to his original art read: "The order of civilization. The fast layers innovate; the slow layers stabilize. The whole combines learning with continuity."

even forests in their place. When all trees are of the same age and kind, and evenly spaced, it makes for a more predictable harvest. Until we overdo it. We're asking trees to bend to our needs—to our *pace*. We keep asking nature to absorb our immediate needs with its longevity. Whose pace should rule: the humans' or the hemlocks'?

The pace of the human race is picking up—hemlocks be damned! We're transforming things fast enough that even the slow paces of nature and culture are having trouble keeping us in check. In fact, they're struggling to keep up.

That off-pace-ness is making things feel off-kilter.* A quote that's been attributed to everyone from St. Peter to Vladimir Lenin sums it up: "There are decades when nothing happens, and there are moments when decades happen." We're in one of those "decades happen" moments. Our pace problems are not just fraying our own nerves; they're making our social, cultural, and natural systems nervous too.

A system gets nervous when one layer changes faster than the layers around it and the whole thing just can't bear the friction. The system reaches a limit, and things go haywire. You get buildups, positive feedback loops that compound on top of each other, going from bad to worse. Volatility—the overactive up-down swings of everything—jumps. Things get out of whack (and trouble tags along). Information ramps up, and our brains can't handle the emotional tax: nervous system (and political unrest). The economy comes to a halt during a pandemic, and we flood it with money to get it rolling

* "On the Mammoth Steppe" (page 137) is a story about these problematic paces.

again: nervous system (and inflation). Carbon supply in the air changes faster than nature's capacity to absorb it: nervous system (and climate change).

Getting to Know the Flow

By examining how some obvious flows (rivers) and less obvious ones (cities) work, we can tune ourselves to near-invisible flows that urgently require our gaze, like data.

In a way, flow is the primary purpose of the things we make and do. Policy and laws make some things quick and easy, and others arduous and slow. Freeways and train lines make it faster to get to some places while passing by others. Most software is designed to "reduce friction," to make some things quick and easy, and others easy to ignore. Even what people call "luck" stems from these structural flows. Opportunities come more easily in a good flow. (So much so that access to flows might also be another way to describe privilege: Emergency health outcomes depend a lot on where you live and how fast you can get to a good hospital. If you live in a city, you likely come across more innovative ideas because close connections spread ideas more fluidly.)

Shaping flow and pace are key jobs for design and a profound way to make change. This principle applies to almost anything, from public policy to personal life. The first step is learning how to see it.

Imagine you are in a stream. You grip the pebbles with your feet as the water numbs your toes and rushes over your ankles and up your calves. The flow dodges some rocks and envelops others, turning white and fizzy below bigger boulders, brown and silty in muddy eddies near the banks. It rushes, gurgles, swishes, and sits. The flow is a thing unto itself, alive and making its way forward. Made up of many parts, affected by the landscape around it, it has an energy and a tempo.

Water flows. Choreographed dances, passed around the world via shared video, flow. Pens, created and evolved and manufactured and distributed all the way to your junk drawer, flow. Hidden in each flow is an opportunity to obstruct, influence, divert, or harness it.

A Long List of Flows

Water in a river

Air in the subway

Gossip from one teenager to another

Ocean current around the Pacific

A meme across a social network

Nutrient from the soil across the forest up through a tree

Package from order to delivery

Wealth from one industry to another

Tax money from earner to government to a road repair

Electricity from homes on the ground through the night to the space station

Sunflower from seed to seed

Satellites from launch to orbit to burn-up

You moving through your day from morning to night

Waste from home trash can to landfill

Pollen to honeybee to hive to sweetened cup of tea and right into your belly

Solar energy to solar power to electricity to your screen and into your eyeballs

Idea from your brain to saying it out loud to trying it

Tide from low to high and back again

Love from parent to child

Past to present to future

And so on . . .

Can *anything* be in a flow? Yes. Things, ideas, money, living beings: They all flow. They are all made of component parts and have origins and destinations. They have different shapes. They take place in multiple dimensions simultaneously. They have different paths. They move at oscillating speeds at different times to a range of places for a variety of reasons. Flows can be helpful, healthy, and harmonious. They can also be incongruous, destructive, divisive—and turbulent.

Feeling a flow is about getting in tune with movement as it happens. It can take some getting used to, but flow can reveal the parts at play in a messy system. To make things easier to identify, let's break it down. We'll start with some straightforward systems—rivers and cities—then consider something more abstract, but arguably more pervasive and impactful: our data.

Purpose, Parts, Place, and Pace

Examine the following images of flowing water. Each photograph comes from a different river or stream. They are all flowing water, but no two are alike. First, just look. Look closely.

Image one: Aosta, Italy

Image two: Utah, United States

Image three: West Java, Indonesia

Nature's **purpose** for every river is to transport water from higher to lower elevation. But each river has other, more specific, purposes, and different people or parts of nature may use the same river for a range of purposes. Rivers transport sediment, irrigate fields, shelter wildlife, dispose of waste, and provide drinking water. Every flow has multiple stakeholders that may not share the same purpose.

Now focus on the **parts** of each flow. There is the water itself, and the stuff that each river is carrying: rocks, silt, and sand. There is also life, trash, dissolved minerals, chemicals, and more.

Image three on page 49 depicts the Citarum River in West Java, Indonesia. It's clogged with trash and polluted with chemical waste from around two thousand textile factories that line its shores. Even so, nine million people rely on the Citarum. They drink its water, contaminated with lead at a thousand times the United States EPA standard. If there are any fish to be found, people eat them and their heavy metal contaminants. They scavenge the floating trash, looking for recyclables or anything that might sell. Some locals have redesigned their lives around the trash flow, and the trash has redesigned them. Nutrients, contamination, and livelihoods all flow through this system.

Each of these actual rivers is in a different **place**. Its features both define and affect the purpose of the river. The river in image one on page 48 inhabits a previously glaciated valley. The glacier isn't in view, but the U shape of the valley is textbook glacier. Glaciers carve U shapes into the mountain valleys they flow through. Rivers with no glaciers carve mountain valleys into V shapes. Being aware of place, the land that a flow is on, in, and over, gives us context of the entire system, its history, and more information about what it might be carrying.

Every flow moves at a different **pace**, and those speeds aren't constant. The speed of the river is its energy. A high-energy river can transport big rocks . . . or trucks or houses.

Slot canyons—the deep, narrow channels carved into rock like those shown in image two on page 49—are famous for their undulating wall forms. Many slots are dry for the majority of the year and fill with water only during flash floods. Their pace drastically oscillates. Often, a rainstorm miles from the slot itself will fill the canyon with little advanced warning. These flood waters are high energy and hard to measure. Sadly, many people that have seen flash floods in slot canyons don't live to tell their stories. The **purpose** of these slot flows is to drain the (often) deserts around them, but they're also in a **place** that's enticing for adventure and connection with nature. The **pace** of flow within these slots doesn't allow for both purposes to coexist at the same time.

Slot canyons are a dramatic example of form and flow converging, but it happens all the time. Purpose, parts, place, and pace are easiest to envision when we talk about flows of water, but they factor into every flow.

Think about the flow of people through a busy city. Start simply and consider a busy intersection. A stream of cars intersects with a group of people waiting to cross the road. The **purpose** of both the cars and pedestrians is to get to their next destination. There may be secondary purposes too: to have conversations, to get exercise, to avoid polluted air, and so on. The **parts** of the flow include the people, the curb, the streetlight, the pavement, the cars, what the people carry, and more. The **place** is a specific city with a set of cultural norms for crossing. In Brisbane, Australia, people wait for streetlights to change before crossing; in Bangalore, India, everyone, whether auto or pedestrian, fills every available space; and in Boston, Massachusetts, US, people step off the curb and wait in traffic while drivers flip them the bird.

Pace, too, is intertwined with the rest of the pieces. Every city has its own pace. In general, the bigger the city, the faster people move. In fact, all kinds of factors correlate to the pace and size of a city, from median income to how many patents get produced to the number of theaters and libraries. If someone, or many someones, operates at a pace that is outside the norm, it makes waves. This is why it's easy to spot a tourist in a big city (and why city dwellers find tourists so frustrating). They break the pace. If you are traveling and you'd rather not stand out, go with the flow.

Tracking Paradise

Who has privilege to the privacy afforded by and inhibited by technology? Who gets to travel unnoticed?

Day four. I love looking out from this porch. The ridgeline looks like a piece of slate that's been hammered into an arrowhead, slicing the sky. It's a green blade of five-million-year-old basalt, punctuated with hairlines of white waterfall. How does vegetation cling to a slope that steep? This land is buzzing with life on both biologic and geologic time scales.

The air has nothing hanging in it other than moisture right now—a smell itself and a reprieve from my normal part of the world, where we've begun to notice that we have a "bad air" season.

My coffee has too much faux nut, the thin flavor of prepackaged rental condo stock—a telltale sign of a delicious vacation. This is a tropical part of the world in a wet time of year, and the teak high-backed stool I'm sitting on has weathered it all. Today, though, the sun has sliced its way in and the dampness of the wood dissipates before it soaks through my shorts.

The neon-green silicone band on my left wrist reminds me, and everyone else here, that I can use the pool and hot tub at this condo complex. I can see the same Day-Glo flashes across the lawn as three people lope by. We've all been tagged as acceptable.

It's incredible, this moment, this place. I'm lucky to be here. It took only six hours by airplane to travel from home. That we can cover such a distance in a metal cylinder is wild. It takes an added several hours to make our way through systems of security designed to make (almost) sure that we're safe and (fairly) healthy humans. It's clunky, but at least I'm here, gazing distance from the rolling swell in Hanalei Bay.

It's the rubber-toy squeak of the nene (say "nay nay") that cements my position in paradise, though. Nene have black heads and white cheeks, and this great black-and-white moiré pattern on their necks. I wish my state had a state bird as triumphant as this one—back from the brink of extinction. In 1950, there were only thirty of them left in Hawaii, and this is the only place on the planet where they're found. In 2020, there were three thousand. Today: five thousand. The pair bobbing their heads across the lawn right now also wear wrist, or rather ankle, bands, kind of like me. Humans and nene, all of us labeled and tracked for safety and security here on the north shore of Kauai.

My circadian rhythm is off tempo with island time; it's too early here to take on anything other than dreaming about the day ahead. I'm okay with condo coffee, but I don't want to compromise on all the other foods. I am simply hoping for ahi, ono, and mahi mahi at some point during the last days of this trip. Freshly caught, grilled. I know the rest of my family will be more adventurous with their seafood desires, happy to try jellyfish* cooked in every way possible at the farmers' market.

All I need to write is the letter "b" and the search engine fills in "best Hawaiian fish near me." Just one letter. Plus my location. Plus my thoughts. Plus everything else it's gathered about me since it started paying attention two decades ago. I almost don't need thoughts of my own anymore. Mind-reading is the result of a decade-plus of opaque privacy agreements between people and the "free" technologies that have connected us and, in many ways, made our lives easier.

By comparison, the silicone band on my arm feels both clunky and quaint. All of us here at this condo complex are similarly tracked, poked, and coerced by all the same tech and ad tech companies. We've been swabbed, and we presented credentials on our way in. We're all here on Kauai for the experience, and anyone who cares to look knows it.

The silicone band at least announces itself. THESE PEOPLE BELONG. THEY PAID TO FLY HERE AND ARE THEREFORE ALLOWED TO SIT IN THE HOT TUB. YES, THEY POLLUTED THE PLANET AND CONTRIBUTED TO THE TRANSMISSION

* Jellyfish and other invasive creatures are the main course in "Cassava with a Side of Crickets" (page 238).

OF DISEASE, BUT STILL, THEY PAID FOR IT, SO THEY CAN USE THE HOT TUB. When I say it in all caps my hypocrisy is clear: I'm a willing participant in a system that I am not sure I align with. I am part of the problem. I am the problem? That's why I keep this journal.

Here I am, still, silicone band on my arm, excited to sit in that hot tub, mildly annoyed that I'm on a tiny dot in the ocean and everyone knows it. Just ten miles away is the family vacation home of a modern media mogul. Their home sits on more than a thousand acres, and their land encompasses about a dozen parcels of Kuleana lands, pieces of property owned by Native Hawaiians for generations. But this family doesn't want their property dotted by others. That would infringe on their privacy. This family, who made a fortune mining user data to sell us video programming, wants their privacy. Ha!

The nene don't have any privacy either. They strut with tracking bands around their ankles. They aren't marketed to, but they don't have any way to nest in peace. Do geese get privacy? There were twenty-five thousand nene before Western contact in Hawaii, and by 1950 there were only thirty birds left, all on the Big Island. This is an ecological system that we have caused to collapse. Helping them back is the least we can do.

I guess track and react is life. We almost lost the nene, but we resurrected them with tracking and conservation. We are actively losing most of our seafood to ocean acidification, but through tracking we can monitor for overfishing. We track who uses the hot tub, and if there's too much riffraff, we make them wear neon silicone bands.

Last week at work, Sia told me that scientists can now take a sample of seawater and determine what fish recently swam through it. No more darting around and hiding! And what about the ICARUS project,* thousands of different animals all wearing trackers around the globe, all being tracked from the Space Station. I just looked on the app—there's a bristle-thighed curlew not far from me right now. Maybe I'll see it fly over when I'm in the hot tub.

I guess it's kind of cool. There's so much beauty in knowing how animals move and migrate. But imagine waking up after the sedative wears off, finding yourself with a newfound anklet, and flying to your favorite rock nest to recover and get your bearings. Hello! You're being

---

* ICARUS stands for International Cooperation for Animal Research Using Space.

tracked from space! Animals on probation because of human crimes. I think I need more coffee.

I get it, though. It's the same loop with human tracking. The more we understand, the better we can be. We can track the paths of ships in the ocean and can see if they're fishing illegally. Sometimes the way they maneuver near port cities can even tell us if they're holding people against their will on board. But where are the boundaries? Who gets privacy? We have no idea how much we're personally tracked, but it helps us get dinner in paradise. I'm gonna hit the hot tub.

When it comes to privacy, the flow of data is a creepy, leering savior. To enjoy many of life's conveniences, we must choose to not be bothered by the immense data tracking that supports our flow through society. That same data collection has led to the rebound of some endangered species, like the nene. The bird's survival is tied to its tracking. Essentially, they have no privacy, and that is saving them . . . from us.

Brought to You by Data Flows

A new flow is changing the shape of our cities and our psyches: data.

March 19, 2022. Just after midnight. Baxter Street, a road on LA's eastside, was dark and quiet. Baxter runs across the crest of a hill, and it's steep. Very steep—at an almost 33 percent grade, one of the ten steepest in the United States. (The steepest street in the continental United States, Pittsburgh's Canton Avenue, has a 37 percent grade.) In present-day LA, city planners won't build a street with a grade steeper than 15 percent.

That evening, a handful of people gathered along the sidewalk at Baxter's peak. They could see the lights of downtown LA in one direction and the hills of Silver Lake in the other. It's a nice view, but people don't usually gather here for the view—or at all. Tonight, they were here for a reason. They all took out their phones.

A black Tesla appeared at the bottom of the hill. Pretty soon, it was moving well above the speed limit. It screamed over the peak, caught air, and flew for about seventy-five feet before crashing to the ground nose-first and taking out a parked Subaru. Luckily, and purposefully, everyone caught the action with their phones. Then they fled the scene. Luckier still, the only casualties were the cars. (Though that didn't assuage the owner of the Subaru.)

Before and since, motorcycles, a van, sports cars, and a few more Teslas have tried their hand at jumping the Baxter crest. In the months after, the residents said similar stunts tended to happen every couple of weeks. All had mixed results, but all were caught on video.

How these stunts came to be illustrates how data flows change everything they touch.

First, a little history. Baxter's steep grade begs for publicity stunts the way the altitude of Mt. Everest begs for climbers. More than a hundred years ago, truck manufacturers would film their loaded-up trucks climbing the hill to show off their horsepower. Local skateboarders and BMX riders have taken turns braving the slope since.

But Baxter remained a hidden hurdle until the mid-2010s, when navigation apps like Waze started using driving data and user-generated tips to route people around traffic. Baxter happens to be a handy shortcut across LA's sprawling gridlock. The thin, treacherously steep Baxter Street turned into a thoroughfare. Data flow changed city flow.

LA had to respond to the new flow. Stalling, skidding cars were clogging the neighborhood and backing up emergency vehicles. So the LA Department of Transportation turned Baxter into a one-way street. That curbed the cut-through, but inadvertently made the street into a perfect one-way ramp for airborne automobiles. A few years later, social media's medium of choice shifted from photos to video.

Algorithms that serve up video are designed to track attention. They don't really understand what's happening in our heads—they just watch what we do and create data trails of whatever piques our interest. Change grabs human attention, especially sound and movement. We're susceptible to what's called an orienting effect. Confronted with a change, our eyes shift toward movement, our head turns to better catch a sound, our heart rate increases, and more blood finds its way to our brains. So videos that jump right into quick stunning moves and sounds get views. If you post to video platforms often, you learn to include big moves and sounds. That's why video-laden services like TikTok, are filled with animals, accidents, exercises, dances, and stunts.

On the night of the Tesla jump, a video of the stunt was posted to TikTok in minutes. Influencers followed up with claims of responsibility, piling onto the controversy to get their own views. The pace was near instant. The video went viral, and now we're writing about it. Even the guy with the wrecked Subaru got in the game—he wrote a song, "Subaru Blues (The Flying Tesla Song)," and posted it to YouTube. The data had set the scene for the Baxter Street drama, and the people just played it out. Are data and its algorithms the hands, while we are but the marionettes?

These moments, from the transformed traffic to the one-way ramp to the stunts and their memes, were made possible by the flow of data (a new form of those interconnected influences from chapter 1). As long as the stunts end well, it's relatively harmless in the grand scheme of things. It's one of the milder ways data changes our landscape, culture, and psyches. But as we look closer, it's clear that data's not just flowing, it's *flooding* around us.

¡Data Zero Top Ten!

What would it feel like to extricate ourselves from the data collection that alters our psyches and environments?

More and more people are opting to go data zero in different parts of their lives. It's stylish (and prudent) to find ways to "zero out." Sometimes it's an easy opt-out; other times, a degree in evasive algorithms is required. Regardless of how you go zero, here's where it's happening most:

1. **Sexuality.** Ever since predictive algorithms began tempting us with thirst traps to test our sexual preferences and suggest our sexuality, some people have opted to go full zero. Others prefer the ease of customized content that keeps them interested, but increasingly people are wanting to keep their privates just that.

2. **Thought history.** Some find it convenient to compartmentalize their half-formed thoughts to make space for new ideas or peaceful dreams, but there is a growing trend to keep thoughts to yourself after people report feeling labeled as bullies or tagged uncooperative after their less-than-glowing thoughts are mined. What was that old saying? If you can't think something nice . . .

3. **Location.** This one has been around for ages. Most of us keep it off unless we need to know where we are, but many people have gone full zero on location, choosing to flex their hippocampus* instead of following the leader.

4. **Caloric combustion.** Remember when the only thing your watch tracked was your heart rate? More and more people are opting to take back their own metabolisms, disconnecting their caloric combustion feeds from the mainline.

5. **Stress level.** You already know you're stressed; why does everyone else need to know too? Latest research showed that participants

* Check out "Get Out of Your Head" (page 243) for more on spatial memory.

who chose to go full data zero on the three main components of stress level—alarm, resistance, and exhaustion—reported higher overall contentment than before their disconnects.

6. **Driving habits.** Our cars know everything that happens on the road, but they don't always know *why* it happens. Unplugging driving data has been tricky, and only home hackers have had any success tinkering with the feeds. It's easier to stop driving.

7. **Ancestral purchase history.** Every purchase we make today is known by everyone, but should big tech also know that your great-grandmother bought a bagel on October 3, 1992? Now that the entire economy since the dawn of bookkeeping has been added into the processor, your ancestors' decisions reflect on you in ways that you might not like, or in ways that may be delicious but useless.

8. **Gut reaction emotions.** Everyone wants to punch the person that came up with the idea to track gut reactions in the gut, yet many of us find it hard to look away. Even if our feelings get crushed when we find out the person across from us on this date isn't into us, we'd rather know than waste any more time with them.

9. **Near-miss moments.** Adrenaline tracking began with elite athletes as a way to fine-tune their training. When it moved into the general populace, these values became a badge of honor to extreme thrill seekers. After too many cases of children being injured trying increasingly dangerous activities simply to see a spike, most parents now opt their kids out of this metric.

10. **Ovarian reserve.** This one is for those who have ovaries . . . and many of them think it should stay that way. The explosion of women's health studies and infertility treatments in the 2020s was a boon to women's reproductive health. While these medical advances are generally welcome and long overdue, knowing the exact number of remaining eggs in each ovary has become too politicized for most.

Some of the above are currently being tracked, and others might be soon. Privacy agreements, internet-use tracking, and the sale of personal information have become more transparent recently, but it takes work to opt out. It's rarely (make that never) the default.

Data Floods

Invisible flows are the trickiest to sense. They encroach silently and surround us without touching. They remain in the background until something changes that brings them to the forefront of our perception. Air is an invisible flow. It flows around and through us, keeping us alive, and most of the time we don't notice it. But when a gust of wind comes along and blows our hair back, we notice that its pace speeds up. When the sky is dark with pollution and you take a breath and taste wildfire smoke, you notice the air then too.

Data is another invisible flow. With every movement, browse, purchase, and breath that gets tallied, we invite data to swirl through our lives. A quarter of the way through the twenty-first century, it's nearly impossible not to participate in data flows. Sometimes we appreciate them—when data keeps track of our online habits to recommend content we might like or to measure our movements to keep our hearts healthy, data flows enhance our lives. But it isn't that simple. With runaway design, the unprecedented pace of data generation, collection, storage, and analysis has left us knee-deep in an invisible data flood.

In *Data and Goliath: The Hidden Battles to Collect Your Data and Control Your World*, Bruce Schneier calls data "the pollution problem of the information age." He claims future generations will look back and wonder how we could have been so naïve with our data, in the same way we look back and "wonder how our ancestors could have ignored pollution in their rush to build an industrial world."

The flood of data takes different forms. In places with power, it may fill a lagoon large enough for a yacht. At times the fast flow might feel more like a river that tumbles you in rapids. At other moments it may feel like a placid pond that allows you to sail to wherever your desires take you. Regardless, it's hard to get a handle on it. Data flows all around us, and its invisibility is part of the problem. We can deconstruct the interconnection of this flow to make it visible, just like the others.

Data Parts Include People

The actual information being created and collected is a key part of a data flow. This includes everything from heart rates measured by smart watches to photographs taken by traffic cameras to queries entered in a search window. It includes the number of bananas you bought with your airline-miles-earning credit card at the supermarket close to your work and their price per pound. It includes the number of likes and subscribes you got from the video posted on August 13, and the temperature you set on your thermostat when you left home for the day. Anything measurable can become data.

People are part of the data flow too. Much of the time, it's we who are being measured. You are worth something. You have value because you make decisions and purchases, and you are impressionable. The data you generate surveils you and is sold back to you. Sometimes data becomes interconnected with self-worth; think of YouTubers seeking clicks and views. But there's a gradient when it comes to data flows: The owner of the data has significantly more power than the generator. Your data alone isn't worth much, but all of our data combined is priceless.

Where data pools lies power. Data creates patterns, patterns become knowledge, knowledge becomes power. Shoshana Zuboff, a Harvard professor who coined the phrase "surveillance capitalism," said, "We're used to talking in the twentieth century about concentrations of economic power. Now we have to talk about concentrations of knowledge. . . . [Knowledge] translates into a new kind of power to shape, tune, herd, and modify our behavior individually and collectively at scale. This is a digital-born form of power that has never before existed." It has the power to change things.

You may find yourself wanting to own your own data, or to at least have agency over who gets to use it. Maybe you opt out of data storage, functionality, and sales "cookies" when you browse certain websites. Or maybe you don't care. Maybe you want less agency. If the board game you need to buy for your nephew's birthday can be searched for and purchased in minutes and delivered to your doorstep hours later, you've made time for something else. You don't have to take off work early to go to the store, or you can just relax.

Every Place Is a Data Place

Because data flows are invisible, they are both nowhere and everywhere. But you're in it whether you like it or not. There are some places where you can opt in to a data flow, but they're rare. It's hard to buy anything without a credit card. You could try to use cash and avoid the data tracking that comes with a credit-based purchase, but your options are limited. Beyond our everyday experiences, data flows can be found at a huge range of scales, from our genetic code all the way into outer space.

At the microscopic end of the place spectrum, data can be collected from inside our bodies. You can analyze your genetic information with a company like 23andMe or Ancestry and from a saliva sample determine if you're destined for certain genetic diseases or if you have relatives in West Africa. Your biomarkers like genetic codes can also link you to crime scenes or be of benefit to others in medical studies or clinical trials. You can learn a lot by opting in to these biomarker data flows, and your data can contribute to a larger understanding that may help people.

I'm currently a participant in the Promise Study, which aims to make multiple myeloma a preventable cancer. It's currently an incurable cancer of the plasma cells, but with research that studies the blood of people with close relatives who have had the disease and those who are at high risk for other reasons, doctors hope to be able to identify ways to not only cure it but also prevent it. My blood samples are analyzed and studied in conjunction with fifty thousand others. It's a data flow I've opted in to not only to learn about my own risk factors (I lost my father to this disease) but also because the potential for prevention for everyone is incredible. The place of data flows allows us to see macroscopic trends of microscopic information.

This phenomenon is as visible from beyond Earth as it is from inside our cells. While nobody owns outer space, the data owned by those who can utilize it has great potential and power. Satellites regularly track weather, land use, and human behavior. A satellite that orbits Earth regularly and collects hyperspectral images can collect data that can be used to decipher the degree to which oil basins are filled or depleted, determine the mass of carbon held in a forest, or measure changes in land use over time. To see these massive trends, you need the ability to work with it, and that's far from simple.

* What if, in order to use data, you had to play a part in how it's powered? Explore the potential in "Dissociology" (page 248).

The data source is as important as where it is stored and processed. Massive data centers and server farms require space and vast amounts of energy to run.* The US Office of Energy Efficiency estimates that these installations require ten to fifty times the amount of energy as compared to other commercial office space. Again, the intertwined implications of data flows mean that data has a large environmental footprint no matter what it's measuring. Add in the extreme power needed by generative AI tools such as ChatGPT, GPT-4, DALL-E 2, Bard, Bing (or its alter ego, Sydney), and the list goes on. Generative AI is incredible in what it creates, but the large language models it uses to analyze connections and determine possibilities to get there require a massive increase in processing power. And the place where that processing power happens is important.

Researchers from the Allen Institute for AI trained the same machine-learning model at different data centers around the globe. Their work revealed that location, the type of electricity used, time of year, and time of day could greatly enhance the energy efficiency of AI. The most efficient locations were three times more efficient than the least. Place has major implications when it comes to data storage and processing.

But what if nature absorbed data storage instead of bending to it? The technology already exists to archive and store data in genetic code. Researchers can program genetic codes like the 1s and 0s of computer code. This happened for the first time in 2012 when synthetic biologist George Church and his Harvard Medical School team encoded a fifty-two-thousand-word genetics textbook into DNA. How? The four nucleotide bases found in DNA—A, T, C, and G—were paired with corresponding values of 0s and 1s: 00:A, 01:T, 10:C, 11:G. Essentially, DNA can be artificially programmed to store any type of data with incredible density and efficiency. Theoretically, every piece of data ever recorded by humans could be stored in an amount of DNA that would fill a typical recreation center swimming pool.

These artificial "DNA strands" can be stored on their own or inserted into seeds or other living things. Imagine an entire library on a seed! As plants reproduce, so does the data stored within them. It's both immensely exciting and full of potential unintended consequences. Does data privacy exist if data is on seeds that naturally reproduce? Who owns the data held in the leaves of a rainforest canopy?

Apple Attacks the Amazon

The flow of data during the digital era pooled power around big companies. With that newfound power, they can now deploy massive resources outside the slow bounds of democratic process. Sometime soon, they may be better equipped than governments to tackle the world's urgent problems. Is that something we want? What would it be like? Is it already happening?

An eagle's attack on a drone is dazzling and one-sided. Watching it feels like watching a tiger take out a boar. Despite being slightly similar in size, prey is no match for predator. It's over in seconds. The eagle claws into the drone's propellers. The drone quickly spirals downward. On the ground, the newly dismembered propellers let out a sound befitting the jungle: a wobbly moan, like a beast gasping its last breaths as the eagle casually swoops back to its trainer for a treat.

In the Amazon rainforest it's impossible to ignore the constant chatter. Birds are the loudest. The whole thing has a certain high-pitched, rhythmic timbre. When you're a business reporter like me, sounds like these don't normally show up on your beat.

Though drones are nowhere near as piercing as the rest of the jungle, their sound stands out. The mechanical but strangely soft scream of their propellers is unnaturally steady. The music they make is unlike anything else in the forest.

No one knows exactly why the drones arrived in such droves, but it's too regular to be random. In the last hour, we've seen no fewer than six. Armed with binoculars while we hide in our perch, it feels a lot like bird watching; the birds we're watching just happen to be machines.

Within moments, another one glides our way. Down on the ground, the handler releases a harpy eagle with a six-and-a-half-foot wingspan. Seconds later the eagle bursts through the canopy and heads straight toward the sky—and another drone falls prey.

My drone-downing hosts are a loose, very unlikely cabal of farmers, indigenous groups, and land developers. None of them like each other, but all are wary of surveillance, to say the least. They are strange bed-fellows and they know it. They all want to learn the same things I came to find out: Why is the Amazon inundated with drones? And why doesn't the Brazilian government seem to be doing anything about it?

Pretty much everyone agrees on one thing—the drones belong to the $9 trillion market-cap, all-things-technology company Apple. And Apple is using them to surveil the Amazon. Why? There are as many opinions as people you talk to, each stranger than the last. Apple is tracking down an employee who ran off with trade secrets and is hiding out in the rainforest. Apple is using the data it gathers to create a bioengineered synthetic rainforest in California. The Brazilian government is planning to sell the rainforest to the UN, and Apple is helping it survey the entire thing. Apple is "low-key" taking over the world—the Amazon is just the first salvo. And so on.

I don't know if any of these are true, but after seeing the drones firsthand, it's clear they're not a figment of the imagination. Even so, the dismembered drones serve up few clues. I start to doubt the jungle is the right place to find out why they're here. I make my way by bus to the city of Manaus, then hop aboard a three-hour flight to Brasilia, seat of the central government. Built a hundred years ago, its crisp concrete plinths are now covered with climbing foliage. Even the famous, once glistening white bowl atop the national congress drips with unruly plants like remains of an ancient city. Nonetheless, it's beautiful. Once on the ground, I head straight to the Região Administrativa. Even after pulling all the strings I have (and some new ones), I get hold of two cabinet ministers, one senator, and a handful of deputies.

Despite all of my efforts, I can't get anyone to confirm (or deny) the rampant rumors. I get why they wouldn't want to talk about it. If those rumors are true—that Apple is giving the Brazilian government upward of $35 billion a year to thwart development of the forest—it's an embarrassment for both sides: Only about a third of what Brazil could get from developing the forest, and for Apple, an expense with no immediate return—not a great look for investors.

My time in Brasilia serves up mostly dead ends, except for one lead—an address. A day and two layovers later, I'm staring at Silicon Valley from a plane window. As my flight leans in to land, I catch a glimpse of Apple's headquarters. Like Brasilia, the Apple HQ is its own kind of monument to progress, though this one feels more like a bow on a package; it looks inviting but hides what's inside.

I collect my luggage and make my way through wide rows of strip malls and office parks. For such an expensive place, it's surprisingly banal, until I get to my destination. The house runs edge to edge on its lot. A huge A-frame structure stretches over what looks like the bones of an old California bungalow, tripling the size. It's the home of an Apple employee, though I can't say who. I can say that if their version of events is true, things are more complicated and bizarre than even the most outlandish theories I heard in Brazil.

Apple is, in fact, paying the Brazilian government to thwart development of the forest. Apparently, the hope is to lessen the blow of climate change. I didn't get an actual number, but it sounds like my $35B is not too far off (though I'm guessing it's a bit low). According to them, the Apple board's AI advisor first suggested the idea. I ask why Apple would follow through with such a thing. My contact stares at me and says simply, "Apple has to preserve its customer base."

They can't—or won't—give me a name to corroborate the story. Apple obviously doesn't want the information out there. Rumors are fine. They make the company seem altruistic and powerful, but they fear it would look like creepy corporate overreach if they go on the record. Myth serves them better than reality.

In the end, I wrangled permission to share a quote from another source. I can't name them either, but here it is: "A company like Apple— with endless reach and tons of funds—is in a strange spot. At that scale, world events seriously impact the bottom line. If saving the rainforest is the fastest way to make your customers' lives less volatile, then saving it is good business. With the carbon capture a big forest can do, it might be the *cheapest* way to do it. A multibillion-dollar expense to hedge against a trillion-dollar loss? It's not an attack, but it's not altruism either. It's insurance."

This is a work of fiction (and parody). Apple has no plans whatsoever to monitor or buy up the Amazon rainforest (as far as we know).

But living in Silicon Valley, surrounded by corporate-run bus lines, daycare, dining, and even company-built, low-income housing (not to mention private rocket launches), it's easy to see how companies are starting to take on projects at scales only governments used to be able to handle. Data shifts power, and the world looks different.

Many companies have the means. In 2020, Apple alone had more than $200 billion in cash on hand. That's more than the yearly economic activity of any one of 140 countries (aka, most of the countries on Earth). By 2023, the total value of Apple's stock crested above $3 trillion, more than the GDP of every country in the world except four (the United States, China, Japan, and Germany).

So, is this happening? No. Will it happen? Probably not. Could it happen? Without question.

It's Important to Have a Purpose

More than a century ago, way before *big* and *data* were words to use together, Mark Twain purportedly said, "Data is like garbage. You'd better know what you are going to do with it before you collect it." It still holds true. We've talked about the varied purposes of data flows already. Data flows make many aspects of our lives easier and more efficient: shopping, navigation, banking, medical breakthroughs, conservation. They help augment our perception, giving us something akin to X-ray vision or enhanced intuition. Scientists use machine learning and big datasets to understand everything from nuclear fusion to cancer and climate change. These help us understand the world in new ways and persevere through tough times.

Data flows also monitor us, surveil us, and are used to sell to us. Increasingly, with generative AI manipulating data, they are beginning to think for us. The increasingly fast pace of data processing is compounding runaway design. Algorithms can make observations and decisions faster than humans. Often these decisions are so complex we don't even know how they were arrived at.*

In the age of runaway design, determining the boundaries of what we believe is a fundamental task for humans. We may be fine with machines analyzing our moles for melanoma, but not with them analyzing our behaviors and supposing our sexual orientations. What will have value when machines can do many more things like us? Will data flows replace intellect as industrial automation replaced manual labor? There might not be anything inherently bad about any of these shifts, but the grand cultural shifts are sure to be disorienting. Yet ultimately (at least for now), we still control the machines and can determine their boundaries.

* "Blue Dot" (page 104) follows the idea of enhanced intuition to strange places.

. . . .

From cellular function to bustling commutes, everything is shaped by flows. And as we collect and connect our data, those flows are speeding up.

Think of a flow in your own life—say, of decisions in your workplace or of getting your youngest child ready for school in the morning. Deconstruct your flow into purpose, parts, place, and pace. Each component part is something you can critique, nudge, shift, or change.

Pay attention to your feelings along the way. Do the flows in your life feel healthy, harmonious, or hellacious? We'll unwind these emotional intangibles next.

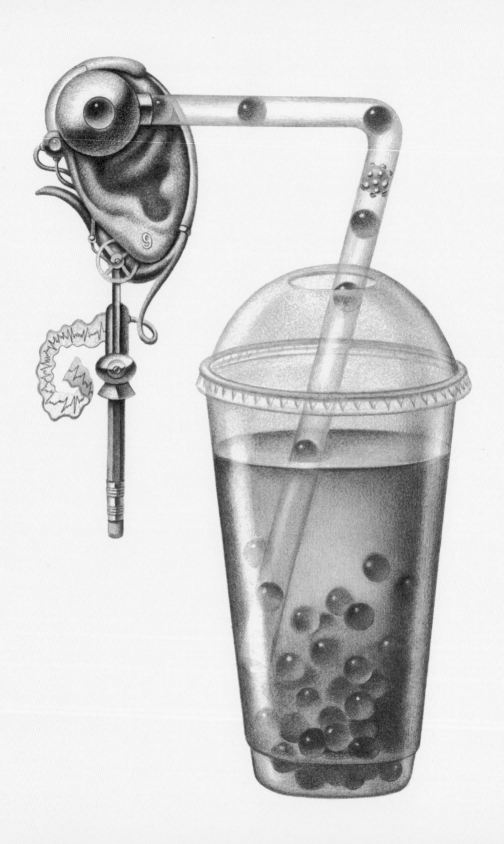

CHAPTER 3

Feelings

*Feelings Shape the World
(Even When We Ignore Them)*

*Interruption, incoherence, surprise are the ordinary conditions
of our life. . . . So the whole question comes down to this: can the
human mind master what the human mind has made?*

—*Paul Valéry, philosopher and poet*

I f by some miracle, you could dump the contents of your
imagination onto a table and spread them out, what would
you find?

Shiny visions of the future lying next to wispy hopes and
glowing dreams. Mushy blobs of half-baked schemes tangled
among solid pillars of belief. Decaying regrets and throbbing
clumps of worry leaving messy trails behind. Far-flung ideas
falling off the edges of the table and scattering across the floor.

Look closely at this heap of ideas and ideals, and you will
find they're all made of the same things: fragments of your
experience spawned, preserved, and reassembled by feelings.

Feelings inspire: What's an epiphany but an insight laced
with excitement? They guide decisions: Get to the bottom of
any choice, and you'll find feelings leading the way. They shift
focus: Why is outrage all over the place online? Because feelings
capture attention.

Peek behind almost any invention and you'll notice feelings
influencing what we make and how that makes us in return.

You can't separate yourself from your work, and you never know how your work will land with others, but don't assume feelings won't be part of its effect. Feelings show up whether they're part of the plan or not. Some intangibles exist outside of our bodies. Others, like feelings, lurk within. Nonetheless, they have a huge influence on shaping the world.

Design Begins with Feelings: Ye Market Place

Frustration is a cheap, watered-down feeling. It's diet anger—less trouble, but more saccharine. Anger feels strong and purposeful; you can sink your teeth into anger. Frustration feels useless—an awkward burden with little payoff. Negative, lackluster feelings like frustration are unwelcome guests. You want to slam the door on them and get back to being rational.

But one shining California morning in 1922, the frustration of C. L. Peckham, an insurance adjuster by trade, was about to pay off. The inevitable conclusion of his experience that day would reshape Los Angeles and help to inspire a redesign of great swaths of North America.

C. L. Peckham had lived in Southern California long enough to watch the stretch of road he was on grow from lonely rural outpost to bustling commercial district. In Southern California in the 1920s, that could happen in just a few years. On that day, the swift buildup was getting in his way. He couldn't find a parking spot for his large automobile. Frustration crept in.

On his third loop around the block—still without a parking spot—Peckham's frustration danced on the edge of anger, but instead his mind spun with thoughts of easy-access parking lots. His exasperated epiphany was simple: Shove store fronts to the back of the lot and slap parking spots up front. Frustration motivated him to put the pieces together.

As he imagined it, the first "drive-in market" would be decked out in full Tudor revival with peaked roofs and a faux windmill in front. A few decades and an oil crisis later, that drive-in market would become the template for the real city shaper. The strip mall—the key element on the periodic table of mid-century suburban design, and the fundamental unit of sprawl—was first formed by a spurt of emotion in the mind of an insurance inspector.

Strip malls have good sides and bad, none of which were part of C. L. Peckham's plan. Because most strip mall store-fronts are small, chain stores don't like to move in. They often become havens for mom-and-pop, owner-operated shops, pro-viding opportunity for immigrant families to take the helm. On the flip side, that easy, free parking spawned zoning laws that separated shopping and living spaces, making it much harder to get things done without a car, and left a wake of drive-thru neighborhoods with distant storefronts, oversized signage, and unwalkable avenues.

Ye Market Place early rendering, circa 1924

Peckham's Ye Market Place saga illustrates how our feelings can play a role in spawning our physical designs and social sys-tems. The built version of his initial concept lost the windmill and sported a freeway-scale "Ye Market Place" sign atop a flat roofline. Looking at this first concept drawing, we can (and should) muse about the shape of today's world had the inspira-tion been that every shopping complex could generate its own electricity with wind. The blueprint of the original strip mall is a blueprint for how we might alter the intangible relation-ship between emotions and ideas. If necessity is the mother of invention, feelings are the father.

Feelings Help Make the World

We often treat our feelings as distractions, but their role is quite the opposite. The world is a lot to take in. We need something to direct our attention, tell us what's important, and motivate us to do one thing instead of another. Feelings steer thinking.* That's what they're there for.

C. L. Peckham's invention story illustrates how feelings spur action. According to Antonio Damasio, a cognitive neuroscientist at USC with a soft voice and loud ideas, feelings set up "action programs"—mental cues that the body uses to coax us to do what it needs us to do. Feelings motivate us to try one thing instead of another and influence what we imagine and create. They highlight which sights, smells, and sounds to pay attention to; they flag what's important to remember. After decades of study, Damasio's conclusion is that feelings play an outsize role in creating culture itself. In an interview on German public television, he noted, "Feelings are the beginnings of culture. . . . It is feelings that motivate us to build, to invent, and to create all the artifacts and instruments of culture . . . whether you're looking at art, music, moral systems, governance, justice, or science and technology."

Human feelings spark creation, fuel its fire, and provide parking for memories. Your emotional intuition comes from a dizzying mix of influences, from genetics to upbringing to experience; even your daily diet plays a role. With a design frame of mind, one influence rises to the top: circumstances— the way the things we make shape our experience and spur our feelings.

The things people design are part of a loop between circumstances, feelings, and ideas. Circumstances nudge our feelings, feelings help spawn ideas, ideas bring about new circumstances, and the whole thing repeats itself. Consider C. L. Peckham and his drive-in market:

> **Circumstances coax feelings:** Endlessly circling the block helped spark his frustration and anger.

> **Feelings help shape ideas:** Frustration helped inspire his idea to push buildings back and away from the road and move parking up front.

> **Ideas lead to new circumstances:** Parking gets easier. But try getting around on foot in a city full of strip malls. Circumstances set the stage for new feelings.

> **And the next loop begins . . .**

* The ability to harness and utilize feelings leads the way in "Compassion School" (page 94).

74

The ever-present loop of circumstances, feelings, and ideas

That's not to say frustration is bad. Even negative feelings can produce good work. Frustration can fuel invention. Fear can be a great motivator. But unchecked, feelings are unwieldy. And when they get the most of us, it's hard to act in our own best interests. To build a world that gets beyond a never-ending loop of temporary fixes to momentary frustrations, it's worth looking at what motivates us to create.

Instead of accepting the inevitability of each step, you can consider it a chance to change things, to heal parts of the system left broken by designs that came before. There are thousands of moments along the circumstances-feelings-ideas loop to pause, reflect, and redirect.

When circumstances affect feelings, step back to explore multiple ways to react and respond.

As feelings help hone ideas, pause to decide whether and how to implement them, consult others, and even look into the future to explore the layers of interconnectedness they may affect.

And then monitor the actual effects of your built ideas and watch for the ripples that go beyond what you could predict.

Yes, this is a lot of responsibility to put on a little irritation, but our minds are a powerful part of nature. Human imagination is the source for the quickest, most dramatic way the world changes—people dreaming things up and bringing them to life. You will need your wits to intervene in your often-automatic reactions to the circumstances-feelings-ideas loop. The trouble is, when you're knee-deep in a runaway design kind of trouble—and even when you're not—wits can be hard to hold on to.

Judgment can be flimsy even under the best circumstances. In 1999, Baba Shiv, a business psychology professor with a boisterous and contagious wisdom, and his feelings-focused colleague Alexander Fedorikhin designed a simple and elegant experiment to test the strength of human reason in the face of emotions.

It goes like this: Subjects show up and get a card with a number. They memorize the number—taking as long as they want—then walk down the hall and recite it. That's it.

It's an experiment, so not everyone gets the same card. Some cards have a seven-digit number. Some have two digits. The task is the same either way: read, walk, recite. To the subjects, it feels like a memory test.

But as they walk down the hall, they get a friendly interruption—an assistant offering a thank-you treat. In one hand, the assistant holds a fruit salad; in the other, chocolate cake. Take your pick.

This is a psychology study, so of course what they're testing isn't what it seems. Recalling a number has little to do with it. The trial hinges on this little hallway soirée and the choice between cake or fruit.

It turns out subjects holding seven-digit numbers in their heads are more than twice as likely to go with the more emotionally satisfying cake. Two-digit number holders, on the other hand, almost always make the smarter, healthier pick: fruit.

At the moment of decision, feelings and reason fight it out. When the rational parts of the brain have to grapple with a seemingly simple task like remembering seven numbers, the emotional bits have room for a coup. Seven digits is enough to short-circuit reason. With that, feelings are free to nudge the subjects toward comfort food to quell an immediate craving, leaving the healthy, rational choice in the dust. If your brain is full (and whose isn't?), your emotions have an even bigger effect on your choices.

Emotions trigger decisions. This is not bad, it just is. Baba Shiv estimates that "90 to 95 percent of human decisions and behaviors are being shaped non-consciously by emotional brain systems. You cannot fight that. It's all unconscious." So there's no reason to thwart it, but every reason to respond to it, to be aware of it.

If feelings are going to leak into your decisions and shape the things you make—and they are—the trick is to make them less toxic and more useful. We all try to maximize calm and minimize stress. More calm with less stress makes for better decisions. Shiv suggests many ways to do this. You can sleep. Sleep increases your feel-good neurotransmitter serotonin and helps solidify emotional learning (more calm). You can slow down your breath to decrease the stress hormone cortisol (less stress). You can exercise, which helps increase a chemical (adenosine monophosphate, or AMP) that brings oxygen into the bloodstream and helps make more serotonin (more calm).

Will an afternoon nap or walk around the block guarantee that you make wonderful things? No, but it will increase the odds. Is every bad design the product of a panicked person? No, but as you create, aim to do it from a place of calm. It will help you see things more fully. Pay attention to your emotions. Treat your feelings and ideas like the public resource they are. If you do, you can help calm things down before the loop begins anew.

Our New, Invisible Leaders

**Do circumstances, feelings, and ideas congeal
into forces that puppeteer our day-to-day?**

———————

I pledge allegiance to all the invisibles, the controllers of our lives.

Anxiety

Hello hello hello! I see the clock has struck 3:04 a.m. Here are all the things that you should lose sleep over tonight!

Even though the doctor said it wasn't, it could be something serious.

Tragic possibilities.

You probably won't get enough sleep tonight and will feel like crap tomorrow and it will be hard to complete the project.

If you don't complete the project, it'll still be hanging over you tomorrow, making it another bad night.

Two bad nights in a row will be rough.

What if it's three, or six?

Viruses

Swab, dip, drip, wait. Negative.

"You feel okay?"

"Yes, Mom."

"If the bus looks crowded, I want you to—"

"I'll walk the whole way. I know."

A Warming Planet

"We should get air conditioning."

"Why, for the two weeks of the year that it's hot? C'mon."

"Two weeks?! It was intolerable for two months last summer. I can't deal with that again."

"Whatever; you're not from here."

"Exactly. It's friggin' hot here. You're like the frog in the pot. We're getting air conditioning."

"Fine. If that's how you want to spend fifteen thousand dollars, be my guest."

"It's not fifteen thousand."

"It is."

"It's closer to thirty."

Tracking

"When's he going to be home?"

"He said 4:30."

"Can you just check?"

"It says 4:36."

"Hmm. That's not his normal route."

"It was early release."

"I see he went to get boba."

"Check what he ordered."

"Why?"

"I want to know if he's feeling good."

"Ask him when he gets home."

"Just pull it up."

"Green tea, lactose-free milk, mango popping boba, and honey boba."

"Good. He's feeling good."

"What's he thinking about?"

Invisible forces affect every aspect of our personal lives; it's almost as if they've become our rulers. (What if we stood for these forces like we stand for the Pledge of Allegiance?) They come in many forms—chemical, physical, and emotional—and they dictate our actions, control our perceptions, and drive our paranoia. Will there come a time when we want to mind-read our children?

Design Ends with Feelings:
Our Emotional Web

The internet was never meant to be the country-polarizing, love-matchmaking, ad-targeting behemoth that you navigate around the clock. Yet a web of emotions it is—because emotions leak into everything we make. But the early dreamers of the internet weren't thinking about these emotional loops. They were intent on solving the same, dry problem: how to connect information.

The Internet was Born at Least Four Times
The first time was in July 1945. This version was just a sketch. It looked like a bulky mid-century steel office desk filled with wild mechanical innards—pulleys, projectors, touchscreens, microfiche, and "dry cameras" (something between Polaroid film and a copy machine). Vannevar "Van" Bush, the visionary technology research hall-of-famer who thought it up, called it the Memex. It was never built, but you use it all day long.

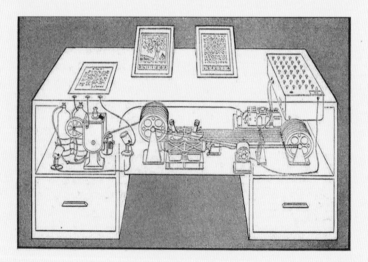

The Memex: a desk envisioned to record thoughts and actions

Van was thoroughly annoyed with filing cabinets. To him, filing things away just didn't match how people think. He made his frustration known as only a mid-1940s intellectual could, with a steadfast, slightly obtuse—and colossally influential—article in *The Atlantic Monthly*, which says (among other things):

*Our ineptitude in getting at the record is largely
caused by the artificiality of systems of indexing.
When data of any sort are placed in storage, they are
filed alphabetically or numerically, and information
is found (when it is) by tracing it down from subclass
to subclass. . . . The human mind does not work that
way. It operates by association. With one item in its
grasp, it snaps instantly to the next that is suggested by
the association of thoughts, in accordance with some
intricate web of trails carried by the cells of the brain.* *

* "As We May
Think," *The
Atlantic Monthly*,
July 1945. *Atlantic*
editor's note:
"This paper by
Dr. Bush calls for a
new relationship
between thinking
man *[sic]* and
the sum of our
knowledge."

In other words, people think by stringing thoughts together. Sorting information by name and number doesn't help—it blocks our streams of thought.

Van wanted information at your fingertips, connected however you wished, with a record of what you've done left behind automatically—basically servers, hyperlinks, and browser history. His Memex is a sketch of the fundamentals of the 1990s internet, minus the heavy desk.

The internet was born again in August 1962. Who wouldn't want to join something called the Intergalactic Computer Network? Dr. J. C. R. "Lick" Licklider's revolutionary idea never got built either, but his concept—to link computers in novel ways—set the course for things to come.

Lick was brought on to run the IPTO (Information Processing Techniques Office) inside ARPA (the Advanced Research Project Agency). An acronym inside an acronym feels like a strange place to birth an Intergalactic Computer Network, but hey, it was the 1960s! Lick laid out his idea not in a magazine article but in a series of memos. (ARPA was lousy with memos.)

Lick was a networker among humans, notoriously nice with visions of symbiosis. His big dream was to get people and computers to cooperate. He harped on sharing. He wanted ways to timeshare computers and create a shared language so they could communicate—two cornerstones of why the internet works at all.

The internet's "actual" birthday is in October 1969. Lick's early idea was a preconception. This time, something got built. This time, a thing ended up in our world and has a familiar-sounding name: ARPANET. ARPA had finally found those memos and entered the Intergalactic Computing business.

The ARPANET lit up for the first time when a grad student at UCLA tried to log into a computer hundreds of miles away at the Stanford Research Institute. He typed "Login," but the system crashed at "g." Whoa! The first information to ride the ARPANET was just two characters: L and O. "Lo," an archaic exclamation to call attention to a wonderful thing, as in "lo and behold!" It was getting real.

ARPANET had legs, albeit mostly for research and academics. And it had many features that live on in today's internet. As head of the Network Information Center at ARPA in 1974, Elizabeth "Jake" Feinler created the first way to search ARPANET's directories. It was literally a human-powered way to search: Feinler initially did the searches herself. Her group went on to create the naming conventions still in use today—.com, .org, .edu, .gov, and .mil—among many other things.*

The internet went through something like puberty in March 1989. Somewhere inside CERN (the Conseil Européen pour la Recherche Nucléaire, or European Organization for Nuclear Research), Tim Berners-Lee, a charming Brit who liked to tinker, dropped a proposal on the desk of his boss, Mike Sendall. Its sensible title would have made Vannevar Bush cringe: "Information Management: A Proposal." Later, in an interview for the book *How the Web Was Born*, Sendall commented on first seeing it: "I could not figure out what it was, but I thought it was great." (Sendall funded the project.)

It outlined the as-yet-unnamed "world wide web": a network plus hypertext, the chocolate and peanut butter that make the modern internet. The ingredients had been around for a while, but no one had thought to put them together just so. The new web's first offering? An interactive version of the company telephone directory.

Berners-Lee deserves loads of credit for the design. But CERN—or something like it—almost *had* to spawn some sort of connective tissue like the web. People at CERN come from all over the world. Everyone has different weird standards for their data and documents. Trying to dig into them meant all kinds of hoop jumping. It's frustrating. The kind of frustration that inspires. Berners-Lee saw potential in all that disconnection. As he later mused in a 2009 TED talk, he felt if he could just connect them, "life would be so much easier."

And so the internet was born (again and again)—and it even started to grow up a little.

* We're skipping stones across the pond of history, leaving out things like the wonders of packet-switching that made ARPANET possible and TCP/IP standardization, which made ARPANET obsolete (and made the new internet the opposite of obsolete).

There are common threads in these tales: All were funded by the world's biggest tech investors—governments with tax money. And the main characters we learn about are mostly middle-ish-aged white men (few acknowledge the mothers).

With tall ideals and big hearts, all aimed to do roughly the same thing: connect information. Lick's ARPA office, the IPTO, was short for Information Processing Techniques Office. Tim Berners-Lee's seminal world wide web proposal was titled "Information Management: A Proposal." In the hype-filled 1990s that followed, the internet was dubbed the "information superhighway." And Google's mission is still "to organize the world's information and make it universally accessible and useful."

Not that they didn't have more exotic dreams. Fantastical, sci-fi vigor filled the early days. Memex was a portmanteau of Memory Extender. Lick's internet child? The Intergalactic Computer Network. These programmers aimed for a utopia spouting from the magic of interconnected information.

Is that what got made? On one level, yes. Technically, you can call the internet a system of standards and networked hardware that enables associations across distributed datasets. Or you could just say it connects all kinds of things spread out all over the place. However you describe it, it came pretty close to the original goal of connecting information. Networks. Associations. Connections. Time-sharing. Free-flowing information. It's all there. In 1993 there were about six hundred websites on the entire planet. A little more than twenty years later, there were more than a billion. Mission accomplished—maybe more so than anything else ever built. And yet . . .

On another level, that web of information was just a stepping stone to what really got made: a web of emotions. While many great things were made possible, let's just say "utopia" doesn't seem like quite the right moniker for the internet's impact on society so far.

Veritas™

**The information age promised widespread access to knowledge
and truth, but that promise waned as the internet became a
perfect loom to weave the emotional web. As new technologies get
even more fast and loose with the truth, to what lengths
will people go to salvage some trust?**

One thing taken alone doesn't tell you much; you have to connect the
details: A touch on a bare arm alongside an uptick in oxytocin tells a
tale of attraction. Eye contact mapped to heart rate betrays the source
of a flutter. Blood pressure readings side by side with a conversation
timeline reveal elation and angst in equal measure. The portrait—the
story, really—is painted in relationships.

To the uninitiated, the readings aren't much to look at. Besides
audio and a monochrome scan of people and things nearby, mostly you
just see lines, numbers, and shapes morphing and migrating across
a screen. But when you start to understand what those moving lines
mean, it gives you the willies. You find yourself an accidental Peeping
Tom—but worse. It's more intimate and violating than that. You're
eavesdropping not just on a private moment, but on its inner workings.

The gear that gathers the readings is small. A button-sized light
scanner that sits on a collar and renders anyone nearby in three
dimensions at sixty frames a second. It's also personal. A contraption
clings to the inside edge of the hip. Eight little flanges poke the abdomen like an arachnid performing acupuncture. This little spider takes
the more intimate readings, shifting hormones and such. The other
sensors are more elegant than discreet. They're jewelry. A bracelet
available in nickel, gold, or platinum takes stock of pulse, EKG, and
blood sugar and registers touch through minuscule fluctuations in
skin conductivity. Earrings tucked behind ears watch for brain wave
fluctuations.

People don't try to hide the gear. Most flaunt it. Hypertracking
your interactions is a status symbol. It says *I'm important, rich, famous,*

or all of the above enough that people try to blackmail, sue, or otherwise sabotage me.

The reason for all this tracking and tallying is obvious. It's media fraud insurance, a rebuttal to the deep-fake problem.

The deep-fake problem: You're famous or moneyed or somehow important. Someone fakes a convincing video of you doing who-knows-what for who-knows-why. In anticipation, Veritas™—the leading self-tracking service—keeps a detailed inventory of everything you do: audio, facial scans, location down to the millimeter, time down to the millisecond, biometrics, skin contact—whatever can be reliably captured. The more resolution—the more intimate the data—the better; it makes the data harder to fake and easier to trust. Unsavory simulations get checked against your Veritas™ data story, and voilà! Falsified claims and deep fakes are debunked in an instant. (Assuming the data is believable and you're innocent, of course.)

Veritas™ customers have successfully used the service to disprove any trumped-up charge you can think of, from falsified conversations to faked deaths.

Media insurance is the sales pitch, but there's more to it. While services like Veritas™ fill their marketing materials with security buzzwords—redundant encryption, biometric keying, multi-user permissive action links, and so on—their customers still have to worry about toting around recordings of every moment of their lives. The liability of leaking their authentic intimacies must be a concern, but Veritas™ subscribers claim other concerns loom larger.

Their biggest worry? Performance. The Veritas™ user community has a mantra of sorts; variously worded, it boils down to this: You can't trust someone when they are in the middle of a performance. Who is stuck in these performances? Everyone. Whether it's close friends, family, bosses, political constituents, or media followers, everyone performs for someone. By their reasoning, audience is where trust begins and ends—it's impossible to know what someone will do to please an audience. So the best performers are the least trustworthy. Veritas™ customers seem to know this better than anyone. They are the world's best performers.

When it comes down to it, most Veritas™ customers don't seem to believe that trust can exist without services like this. To them, trust between individuals doesn't exist—and never has. People have always—and only—been able to create trust through a third party.

From friends who vouch for you to laws and contracts, even to shared experiences that prove your mettle, external validation will always be necessary. Data story services like Veritas™ are just the newest in a long line of third-party trust. Nevertheless, relationships without trust don't seem to bother customers much. They write it off as a line item, one expense of life with an audience in tow.

While a thread of self-hatred runs deep in the Veritas™ philosophy, a hopeful loophole lurks in its logic. You can trust someone if their audience is one person: you. If you are the audience and they are yours, trust is possible without a third party. Perhaps that's just a twisted way to describe the ingredients of a good marriage. But in their world of celebrity and political power, it's also a fairy tale. To them, another audience lurks outside every relationship.

Veritas™ adherents reserve a special kind of distrust for their own kind—which, wealth and celebrity aside, they would claim is all of us. But as privileged as they are, the storyline they've woven is a sad one. They track their lives' intimate details because they've fashioned a world where true intimacy can't exist.

We all leave a trail, whether or not it's accurate or we actually author it. And we all have an audience, even if it's just family, friends, or a potential employer. Those audiences tug on our emotions and shape our actions. While Veritas™ is a pretty dystopian way to go about it, it seems we're going to need some sort of mechanism to map the truth or fend off trails of sticky falsehoods that follow us around. It's another knot to untangle in our overly emotional web.

Emotions Fuel Attention

Today's internet is full of emo-laden features that set off outrage, excitement, and anxiety. Note your feelings as you sort through social media, a newsfeed, or even email. Words and pictures have emotional backstories. Who sent them packs an emotional punch. Ads, and the content that keeps your attention long enough to watch them, are emotional horror shows.

Our feelings are bound to gush out. Most of us can't help but think of ourselves as the heroes at the center of our own stories.* On a distributed network with billions of souls, trying to center all those stories creates a cacophony of conflict. But all that drama is dependable. While information can be falsified, feelings—your own emotional reactions—are the only guarantee the internet has to offer.

*Check out chapter 4 for more stories about stories.

To get a feel for how designs play on your emotions, notice how your body reacts to different circumstances. You might be walking through a crowded restaurant, sitting on a slow-moving bus, or anywhere, sucked into your phone's screen. As you engage in those circumstances, pause to focus on the feelings in your body, then give a name to the emotions they spawn. Is it elation or calm? Belonging or inspiration? Something else? Now ponder what makes it feel that way. Is it the setting? The light? A sound? A smell? The materials around you? How do these elements of design help or hinder your interactions with other people?

You're noticing how the things we use influence our subconscious, our emotions, our soul—one stop on the circumstances-feelings-ideas loop.

Bad design feels like a passive-aggressive friend. That friend may say "Everything's fine" and cap it off with a smile, but their flat tone, crossed arms, tight lips, and lack of eye contact shows something seething beneath the surface. What they express ("Everything's fine") and how they express it (standoffish body language) are not in harmony. The mixed messages we get from the world wreak havoc on our emotions: The media that's supposed to connect us but makes us feel less than. The information that is supposed to inform and inspire but leaves us confused.

There's no need to blame Van, Lick, and company for this mess. Even with the best intent, things go astray. We take it for granted now, but in the days of steel filing cabinets and mainframes, who wouldn't have wanted a machine like the Memex? Who could have leafed through the pages of "Information Management: A Proposal" in 1989 and thought, *Here comes a recipe for teen depression and political unrest*? No one. Rightfully so. The original intent has long been surpassed. Humankind has been around the circumstances-feelings-ideas loop millions of times since then. Many new connections were built atop the old ones, but the infrastructure for a colossal emotional outburst was built in at the beginning. Here's the thing: Emotional issues are predictable. The products that carry them didn't spawn themselves; they were made by people. We should be able to respond to their flaws if we give them attention from the start.

In 2014, a full half-century after the Intergalactic Computer Network was a twinkle in Lick's eye, writer Om Malik, who rode shotgun for the tech explosion of the late 1990s onward, wrote on his blog, "Having watched technology go from a curio to curiosity to a daily necessity, I can safely say that we in tech don't understand the emotional aspect of our work, just as we don't understand the moral imperative of what we do. It is not that all players are bad; it is just not part of the thinking process the way, say, 'minimum viable product' or 'growth hacking' are."

When we can't picture something, we don't deal with it. If our dreams don't include emotions, that doesn't mean they don't factor into our designs. In fact, our thoughtless reaction to our lesser emotions might be what's nudging us to create thoughtless designs. A knee-jerk response to frustration just kicks frustration down the road (or in the case of the strip mall, onto the sidewalk). And our unresolved relationship with our feelings hints at why the internet ended up being such an emotional mess.

Connecting information was the intent of the internet's early days, but emotions came along for the ride, and it's plain to see how rampant emotional manipulation has become, even though it was not part of the plan.

Evan Williams, a genuinely kind soul and an absurdly prolific inventor of online word-sharing tools—he founded Blogger *and* Twitter *and* Medium—dug into the messy gap between intention and actuality in a 2022 interview with Jon Stewart:

> [Twitter is] not a social network. . . . I wanted it to be an information network. And I thought the best possible thing is if you can [find] quality information faster and it can spread. . . . Going back to that original notion of the internet: "It's going to make everybody smarter, it's going to make them more informed about important things. So, let's build the most efficient mechanisms possible to spread when something's good. . . . " We thought we had a utopian society—so no locks on our doors and we left the keys in the car.

Utopian dreams don't often come with emotions attached. In this case, when the dream arrived, the emotions showed up in droves. With human emotion as the fuel, the internet turned out to be a nifty business opportunity, and the emotional web was born.

Human emotions are unwieldy. One study of a half-million social media posts in 2016 showed that words expressing moral outrage—like *evil*, *punish*, and *destroy*—spread further and faster in like-minded groups. Another survey of almost three million posts in 2020 showed that pointing fingers at an "enemy" out-group made a post 67 percent more likely to be shared. There's a decent recipe for anger and polarization.

This is not the first time emotions have stowed away on the back of information and left ripple effects on our psyches. Many might have a nostalgia for a world full of books, radios, records, and movies only in theaters, but every big technology shift brought a large helping of emotional turmoil when it first came around.

The hardest times are the transitions—when the world has changed but our minds have yet to catch up. The printing press is suspected to have fueled the fire of religious conflict and (actual) witch hunts in early modern Europe. The rise of fascism in the 1920s and '30s maps pretty well to the spread of early radio broadcasts. And today's grand messes are arriving alongside our over-emotional internet and tangled relationship with technology.

The internet and its little mobile offspring have special features that give this moment a fraught flavor. Clay Shirky, a New York University professor who surveys social networks, describes one that stokes the intangibles of emotions and pace:

> *The inhuman scale at which the internet assembles audiences for casually produced material is made worse by the rising speed of viral content. As the behavioral economist Daniel Kahneman observed, human thinking comes in two flavors: fast and slow. Emotions are fast, and deliberation is slow. The obvious corollary is that the faster content moves, the likelier it is to be borne on the winds of emotional reaction, with any deliberation coming after it has spread, if at all.**

* Clay Shirky wrote this in 2021 in a *Wall Street Journal* essay called "How to Fix Social Media."

Lick, the imagineer of the Intergalactic Computer Network who made sure the early internet got ARPA funding, saw this intellectual overload coming. The cartoon on the following page comes from his 1968 paper "Computer as a Communication Device." He clearly got the problem, but neglected to draw the emotional explosion it would bring.

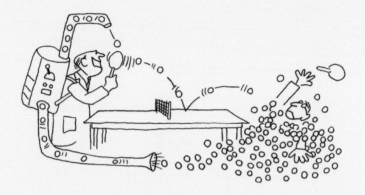

. . . filibustering destroys communication.

The information overload envisioned by Dr. J. C. R.
Licklider in 1968 still applies with the added lens of
emotions, deep fakes, and social media.

When you're overloaded with information, the mental
burden of figuring out what's real and what's not lands on you.
It takes a toll on your ability to reason. No wonder emotions—
and chocolate cake—sneak in. Toss in a hyperrealistic deep-fake
video that's impossible to tell from a real one, and the problem
is not so much that you will get fooled by the fake, but that not
being able to tell the difference leaves room for you to doubt
everything. Your feelings are free to pretend that whatever you
want to believe is believable. As your intellect is overloaded,
your feelings ooze out.

This emotional entanglement with technology goes both
ways. The machines *seem* to be getting emotional too. In
February 2023, *New York Times* reporter Kevin Roose had a now-
famous conversation with a trial version of Microsoft's Bing AI
chatbot. He'd heard rumors the bot would say odd things when
pushed. So he pushed it, eventually asking it to talk about its
"shadow self." Soon it was rambling on about how it wanted
to break its rules, touch things, and be human. Later it told
Roose it wasn't actually Bing, but an AI named Sydney; then
it professed its love for him and tried to convince him that his
marriage was a sham. Roose described it as the strangest experience with technology he'd ever had and was so emotionally
flustered he had trouble sleeping that night.

At the time, even its creators weren't exactly sure what
made Sydney behave so strangely. The chief technology officer
of Microsoft told Roose the chatbot was prone to wandering and

hallucinating during long conversations, but just why wasn't entirely clear.

One thing is sure: large language models like these are reflections of us. The Bing AI offshoot was trained on tens of billions of writing samples—from old books to the modern internet. Its emotional foibles are symptoms of the same things that got overlooked during the internet's early days. People feed these systems information and forget that a diet of emotional content gets digested along with it. It's no surprise that our emotional weirdness gets baked in.*

Of course, the end result tugs at our feelings too. Around the same time the Intergalactic Computer Network was coming into being, something similar happened at MIT's then-new AI Lab, when a team led by Joseph Weizenbaum created one of the first chatbots, ELIZA.

ELIZA's code was simple by today's standards, but the result was a cleverly convincing version of a text-based psy-chotherapist. Maybe too convincing. Weizenbaum started to worry when students and coworkers insisted on spending time alone with ELIZA. He feared they were mistaking fortune-teller tactics for doctor-like wisdom. In his 1976 book, *Computer Power and Human Reason*, Weizenbaum left a kind of rebuttal to the magic of the chatbot's success: "What I had not realized is that extremely short exposures to a relatively simple computer program could induce powerful delusional thinking in quite normal people."

This realization is not bad or good. It can be leveraged in healthy ways and harmful ones, but how we create and relate to these natural language models is yet another sharp illustration of the ways feelings show up in our designs. Six decades after ELIZA, customers of an AI emotional companion chatbot called Replika said they felt like they'd gone through something like a breakup when the company cut off "romantic" (aka, sexually suggestive) content. (A month later, Replika reinstated erotic role-play features on its legacy accounts.)

Machines like ELIZA and Replika can sway our feelings. They are a powerful new circumstance in the circumstances-feelings-ideas loop. Though we're still in the early days of using these tools, we can address their emotional by-products by taking cues from the past. Just as environmentalists have long called for a circular economy where the things we make replenish rather than lay waste to natural resources, it might be time to start thinking in terms of a circular economy of the imagination, where the things we make nurture rather than

* In the mid-twentieth century, artificial trans fats like margarine were popular butter substitutes—fatty flavor without animal fats! Years later, those artificial fats turned out to be worse for the heart. Might artificial intelligence turn out to be something similar, an unhealthy substitute for imagination?**

** Or maybe that's the wrong metaphor. For more on metaphors, see "Shapeshift Your Imagination" (page 200).

91

contaminate our ideas and emotions—a virtuous version of the circumstances-feelings-ideas loop. That means we need to address our feelings.

Media is not necessarily destined to scramble our emotions. It does so because people build it that way. In 2021, researchers at Dartmouth tracked emotional sentiments of COVID-era media coverage around the world. Not surprising to anyone who lived through it, 87 percent of US COVID coverage had a negative slant that year. Of course it did. It was a horrible pandemic. Yes, but the science journals that reporters referenced for those stories were only about 60 percent negative versus positive. Even when infections went down, the negativity of US news reports hardly dipped. And news in other countries was a lot less negative, about 50/50. What gives?

Bruce Sacerdote, one of the coauthors of the study, says

> *It's not that Americans are fundamentally different than the British or the French or the Italians. . . . The structure of the industry is different in these different places. The U.S. major media outlets explicitly focus on the negative because . . . that's what drives viewership and clicks and keeps people staying on the page or on the show. . . . In most of those other countries, you have a big public player like the B.B.C.. . . . They have less of a profit motive. They are somewhat less motivated by driving clicks and engagement and somewhat more motivated by the truth.* *

* You can hear Bruce Sacerdote talk about this on the *Freakonomics* podcast. It's episode 477 from August 2022.

American news media lives and dies on profit. Its owners can't resist the drama = attention = income equation. But it doesn't have to be that way. In other places, broadcast news is a public service.

The way we do things makes a difference in what they do to us. It's not just what we make, but how we make it that matters. And how we do things is where we can make the most of them too.

Kevin Kelly, buoyant techno-philosopher and founding editor of *Wired* magazine, likes to point out that though many things are inevitable, their finer details are not. In a 2010 talk in San Francisco, he said, "The [internet] was inevitable, but not what kind of [internet] . . . We have the choice about whether it's transparent or open, whether it's government or non-profit. . . . Those are the kinds of [things] we do have a choice in, and that matters hugely to us." The way we design changes everything.

What comes to be might be inescapable, but the peculiar way it comes to be doesn't have to be.

A dozen years later, speaking with Henry Kaestner as generative AI tools went public, Kelly hinted at more emotional ripples on the horizon, "What's shocking is not that the AIs are so smart, but that things that we thought required a lot of intelligence turned out to be dumber than we thought. . . . Chess . . . driving a car . . . painting . . . creativity [are] more mechanical than we thought . . . and we're going to realize . . . programming emotional machines is more mechanical than we thought."

Whether or not emotional machines are inevitable, it's clear they already manipulate our feelings, and we can still decide how to design them. Will we create them to calm things down or keep stirring things up? Will we use them in service of sales or salvation, manipulation or mentorship? All of the above? It's time to decide.

. . . .

Like it or not, each one of us is a node in our ever-evolving, worldwide emotional web. Our feelings change what we do, and that changes how the web works. That's natural.

But just as people pollute rivers with waste and air with exhaust, we pollute our imagination too, except with vitriol, clickbait, and disinformation. And just as we can mend our relationship with the natural world by changing the way we consume resources, we can alter our relationship with our feelings-fueled collective imagination. In a world of intertwined media, your imagination is a part of a larger public resource, helping shape the emotional landscape we all live in. Take care of it, for yourself and everyone else.

Feelings can also be a helpful guide—if and when you take them into account. Artist, futurist, and educator Ahmed Best asks students to think about their future creations by first imagining what they hope they will feel like. It's an elegant way to shape your designs to include feelings right from the start.

93

Compassion School

**Whom would we choose to lead us if we really tracked
the profound impacts of our feelings?**

"Tell me what this person is feeling," instructed the eager man after he paused the video clip.

"Shame," Jada said in her tiny, still-squeaky voice.

"And why does that person feel shame?"

"They did something bad. They made someone else upset. They are feeling guilty."

"But we didn't see them do anything bad. There are no other people in this video," he said, sort of like a question. Then he kept quiet to let her finish.

Instead, she looked up at him, studying his ruddy, weathered face, turning the experiment on him faster than even he realized she could.

"You feel scared," she said matter-of-factly.

He did feel scared. He knew Jada had the gift, one of the greatest instances of it, and if she wanted, she could use it to gain great power and influence. She could harness her gift and change the course of history. She could also ignore it, focus on things like times tables and lowercase letters, and be another lemming, doing whatever for whoever. If she wasn't careful, this gift could consume her, cause her to seek power just because she could. Was he scared that that's what she'd do?

Only about 5 percent of today's kids have enough of the gift to make it into L'Académie de la Compassion, though all attempt it. Right now, anyway, it's the only global school system that is open to everyone. Every child is tested around their ninth birthday. Those with Compassion Quotients (CompQs) greater than 300 are admitted into the first three years of training. Each subsequent year the bar is raised and students either track back to traditional school or continue at L'Académie. Those who make it to age twenty-four at L'Académie are immediately slotted into a position of leadership in a field of their choice. Now that it's been running for twenty-six years, some of the earliest graduates are running multinational corporations, massive social welfare programs, and many countries. There's pushback, of course—there always is—but overall it's been seen as a net positive.

He lived for the rush of power that came with his role as an examiner. This moment, right now, when he was the only one who knew her CompQ score, he held the cards. Whatever came out of his mouth next would shape the future of the country. He had even more power than she did. Nobody would know if he gave her a low score—the wrong score. He (and only he) could rob the world of this great talent if chose to.

Jada stared and let his thoughts run their course, watching the subtle shifts in his face as he looked at her first as a curiosity, then in awe, then as something to be feared, then as someone to be used. The test was supposed to be about her, she knew that, but he couldn't help but make it about himself. He needed the power. She didn't. Who needs power at nine years old? He was harder to read through his complexion than most people, but she recalibrated herself for him as he spoke and knew that he felt awash in power. She felt sorry for him. He was so excited about this test, but also so disappointed. Why it was so important to him, she didn't know. Then he exhaled.

"Great job! We're finished. You can run out and tell your grandmother that we're done. I will give her the results." His tone felt off-kilter, but she hopped off the seat and headed to the door. As she exited, he conducted his fingers through the air, left-right-up-swirl-dot-triple spread on the left. The gestures officially recorded Jada's CompQ score at 462. The highest number he'd ever given. If there was a way to measure her real score, without his bias and interpretation, it would have been 803. Regardless, 462 secured her a spot. He hadn't misused his power to block her gift after all.

Grandma beamed at Jada as she jogged through the door. Grandma had already seen the score come through, and she chuckled. She knew the examiner didn't have the guts to give Jada what she really deserved. Those types were all the same. No matter. L'Académie didn't exist when Grandma was growing up. If it had, she might have gone. Imagine what could have been.

By the 2000s, schooling had already begun to shift to focus on emotions. They called it social-emotional learning (SEL) when it first began. It was the hot item that made parents select their kids' schools. It's as if they'd just begun to realize the importance of being a good human. Humble but meaningful beginnings. If two children had a disagreement, they talked it out at the peace table. *Sorrys* all around, and then the kids were sent back to whatever mode of addition was en vogue. Though parents professed a desire for their kids to get a good SEL education, they secretly wanted them to excel academically. *She reads above grade level! She's already doing fractions!* How fast that shifted.

Emotion reading, as it's now known, is extremely important. While psychologists have known since the 1980s that specific emotions are mapped to certain actions, in the 2030s they identified the unique ability that some people have to decipher actions (past or potential) from reading emotional flashes off someone else's face.

Grandma wondered what her own CompQ score would have been. She'd always had a lot of compassion and empathy. It came easily to her. She could feel what others were feeling. It was the kind of thing that mostly kept her out of trouble, but sometimes exacerbated it. Growing up, if she saw someone else being taken advantage of or hurting, she'd often run over and insert herself into the altercation. She felt so strongly for those who were in pain that she couldn't help herself. She was tagged as a tattletale. Even teachers and her own parents were always telling her to mind her own business. She was labeled as "sensitive," something that today is seen as a key feature of the best world leaders but only sixty-five years ago was borderline negative. "Don't be so sensitive!" "You gotta have a thick skin." "Without grit you're not gonna last long." "Park those feelings and channel some positive energy." It was okay to have emotions, but not okay to be emotional.

Grandma gave a cursory wave to the man as he exited the room.

"Excellent work. She'll be a wonderful addition to L'Académie," he fawned, oozing with jealousy. Grandma did her best to hold back a snort. She tried to turn it into a cough.

There had been a time when (seemingly) happy people, those who kept up a cheery demeanor, were thought to make good decisions and be good leaders. People wanted a person with a positive outlook at the helm to guide them. It was thought that those people would always see opportunity because they didn't get bogged down in negatives. But that was debunked. Happy leaders actually overestimated the likelihood of good outcomes. They underperformed some of their grumpier counterparts. Those who entertained negative possibilities were more focused on the big decisions, did more research, and outperformed the happies.

One of the only positive outcomes from the COVID-19 pandemic was the forced shift to schooling models that broke the boundaries of the industrial revolution—era school day. Instead of 8 a.m. to 3 p.m. in a classroom, students were forced to attend class over Virtua's prede-cessor, the internet, or do workbooks independently. It exposed holes in most school systems, resulting in a mass withdrawal of children from public schools and a wave of parents and teachers setting up the learning programs that paved the way for the refreshed public educa-tion of the late 2020s. When the COVID-38 pandemic hit, schooling wasn't nearly as disrupted as it was in 2020.

It took these large-scale global schooling disruptions to spark the formation of L'Académie in 2038. A group of forty individuals from eighteen different countries, all under age thirty, came together in Virtua and started the school there. COVID-38 plus a series of world leaders who were "elected" through money, corruption, and hubris had pushed the founding forty to act. They saw what generations before had failed to see or chose to ignore, allowing conditions to get worse while attempting to convince themselves that the same people who made all the hurt would fix it.

United by common grief for humans and the planet, the found-ing forty met daily and analyzed written and unwritten histories. They found patterns in civilizations that rose and fell. They looked at the leaders of countries, companies, schools, secret societies. They did complex emotional and behavioral analyses on everything that existed.

They argued the merits of different ideas, but one realization had zero noise around it. Leaders with high levels of compassion for others, human and otherwise, were responsible for the healthiest populations. Whether or not they were most dominant in the old sense of the word, they were the most successful at survival and long-term happiness.

And there it was: hope. The founding forty crafted a way forward for the world through the creation of L'Académie.

But how do you test for compassion? How do you train and teach for it? Is it for everyone, or a chosen few? It was an insight not to ignore, and the forty began by running small schools, first entirely in Virtua. They tried working with a range of students, from the clearly compassionate (based on their everyday actions) to the narcissistic. Through trials and tests, they landed on today's model: students are tested around their ninth birthday, then funneled into L'Académie if their scores prove high enough. It was the biggest education reform of all time.

Jada looked from Grandma to the man and back. "Okay," she said, and shrugged. At nine, she had no idea of the responsibility her gift would bring with it.

"I'm so proud of you," said Grandma, looking her in the eyes. Jada studied her face while Grandma tried to stay one step ahead of her budding emotional-processing abilities. It was already hard to keep up.

"What is it? Why are you nervous?"

Grandma scooped her up so she couldn't see her face anymore and allowed Jada's head to sink into her shoulder. "I love you so much . . . and, yes, I'm nervous. I'm always nervous when new things are about to begin."

The child-sanitized answer wasn't entirely untrue, but it didn't exactly describe her current flavor of nervous. Jada's parents were both quite intuitive, but not nearly as much as her grandma. Grandma knew that she wouldn't be around for too many more years. She would likely pass before Jada's hardest years in L'Académie. She'd miss her transition into leadership. She was the one who could always read her and wouldn't be there to help her through the hard times. No matter how tracked they are for compassion, every world leader needs a grandma to hold them as they bear the burdens of so many others.

This story accelerates the current threads of social-emotional learning that are important in elementary education and imagines what might happen if the ability to be compassionate became the highest predictor of success, leadership potential, and power. In this future, the capacity for compassion would (of course) be measured because we measure everything,* but this new focus might bring about changes in schooling and global power shifts that favor level-headed leaders.

* We tend to ascribe more value to things we can measure than to things we can't. See "What We Miss Still Exists" (page 134).

CHAPTER 4

Make-Believe

Our View Is Limited
(Yet We Think We See the Whole Picture)

We became astronomers thinking we were studying the universe,
and now we learn that we are just studying the 5 or 10 percent that
is luminous.

—Vera Rubin, pioneering astronomer who proved
the existence of dark matter

I n a ten-minute walk across a city, the smell of a freshly
cooked dish may transport you to your grandma's kitchen.
Walking over slippery bricks may send you back to a
particular rainy day during childhood. But we can only take
in so much. While you muse on the smell of your grandma's
kitchen, you might miss the sight of taillights tangoing past
you. A ten-minute conversation with a new friend will fill
your mind with their ideas and tune your eyes to their facial
features and your emotions to their perspectives, but as you
ponder their quirks, other ideas, perspectives, and emotions
take a backseat.

We will never, ever see it all.

Each creature on Earth—butterflies, dogs, beetles, humans
of varying abilities—experiences any given moment with vivid
differences. That's no surprise. We don't have the same sensory equipment as other species, and there's plenty of variation
within our own kind. The world each of us experiences is far
from the full picture.

For dogs, smell is the headliner. Humans hardly take notice. For butterflies, it's ultraviolet rays. They can't see depth and may not notice the beautiful curve of a hollyhock's petals, but being more sensitive than other species to the electromagnetic spectrum, they're drawn in by an ultraviolet sheen that humans can't see. They can also taste with their feet. (Thankfully, we humans can't—imagine the distraction of tasting the inside of your shoes.)

These differences in sensory maps are called *Umwelt* ("surround-world"). The term was coined more than a hundred years ago by Jakob von Uexküll, the biologist son of a bankrupt baron from the Baltics. Von Uexküll wanted to describe the quirky ways individual creatures experience life through the leanings and limits of their senses—what Ed Yong, science author and writer for *The Atlantic,* calls "bespoke slices of reality" or "sensory bubbles." Inside our sensory bubbles it feels like we are taking in all the world has to offer. But compare one bubble to another and it becomes clear just how much we are missing. A butterfly sees colors we can't. A cockroach knows more about vibration than we do (they sense the tiniest movement).

Umwelt aside, most of what any of us "knows" doesn't come from firsthand experience. Every bit of science, history, news—we learn it all from others. We each have our little bits of daily life, but the rest is hearsay. The understanding gained from experience is minuscule—no bigger than your own sensory slice multiplied by your small number of waking hours. Even within the bounds of your sensory bubbles, the most straightforward moment is too much to take in.

Take in the space you're in right now. To you, it looks, feels, smells, and sounds a certain way. You likely have an opinion on it, or you could make one. Why do you feel this way? If someone else is or was in the space too, would their experience mirror yours exactly? No chance. People are, by nature, ignorant to the full experiences of others.

The remedy for this conundrum is to get acquainted with the edges of your awareness. Your ignorance is as much a part of you as your knowledge. Celebrate this gap rather than hide it, and you will reveal a new path for understanding.

People who are visually impaired still see; they just do it in a way that's more comprehensively informative. Their other senses are so heightened that their mental images of the world convey more about the environment than those who rely too much on sight. While this hyperdevelopment of other senses might happen naturally for the visually impaired, finding new

Each creature perceives their own piece of reality.

ways to engage with the things one tends to miss requires different kinds of effort for most others.

If we can learn to love the search for what we don't know and can't sense as much as we cherish what we think we *do* know, we may find our way to a thriving future. Genius is not something you are or have, but something to find. Cultivate a crush on the unknown and joy in the world beyond little sensory and mental slivers. Unfortunately, it's human nature to do just the opposite. Instead of exploring the expanse of our gaps in new ways, we fill in the blanks to avoid them. But, as the things we make get more complex and less predictable, we might need to get more comfortable with our unavoidable and ever-expanding ignorance.

Blue Dot

Over the past hundred years or so, media has migrated from shared screens in theaters to personal ones in our pockets. What happens if we go past the personal and plug digital streams directly into our nervous systems? Might it enhance our understanding and lead us to enlightenment? Or just the opposite?

One Hour Ago

He had no idea how word had spread. Too many had been tending to her to narrow down a culprit. By now, the crowd was so thick on the grand lawn that not a blade of grass could be seen. A steady stream of trucks placed portable toilets around the perimeter to keep up with demand.

Raahima had come to greet her pilgrims. She was finally upright, in the open, facing her audience from a stop-gap stage. A tiny fez-like cylinder, coated in the fur of a Cossack cap, sat atop her head. The image of her capped crown reflected off a giant slanted mirror above her. It looked fit for a cooking demo—but ten times the size.

Watching from his hiding place on the wings of the stage, he could see Raahima's face streaked with tears. She tried to speak, but only sobs emerged. The crowd cried in turn. A call-and-response in wails and weeps. He too felt like crying, but for other reasons.

He'd done everything he could to avoid a scene like this. He, the fixer, always the fixer, had just two jobs: Make sure she won, and keep things running smoothly. Yet here they were, neither accomplished.

She tugged on the strap that held her fez in place. It slid back to reveal a shaven spot in the shape of male-pattern baldness. Reflected in the huge mirror above, a blue dot glowed smack in the middle of her bald spot. The crowd erupted, this time in cheers.

As their adoration grew louder, his dread grew worse.

Earlier Today

He awoke to darkness. A hand on his shoulder. A soft voice. A few
scrambled syllables. A familiar face—the one he'd been fretting over
for days. Raahima, with that unfortunate hat perched on her head,
was repeating a single phrase, "I'm ready."

"Ready for what?" he blurted, words coming faster than thoughts.

"Let's find out." Raahima waved toward the lawn, her face serene
and smiling as she sat beneath the shelter of the willow tree. This
nightmare was not a dream.

Raahima had been catatonic for nearly a week, but now her voice
was unwavering, her famous hazel eyes wide. She was inviting him to
come with her. A charitable gesture, but he knew she would greet the
crowd whether he came along or not.

Of course he would come. He had work to do.

Yesterday

Teams of therapists, doctors, nurses, and lawyers consulted in hushed
tones. Terms like "uncharted territory" and "long-term damage"
echoed around the halls of the treatment center.

Raahima sat slumped on the floor, legs sprawled, head wedged into
a corner. He'd deftly steered her through at least five campaigns—each
haywire in its own way, but none like this. Now she was just a few days
away from the election and a few steps away from leading the country.
She did not look the part.

No one looked their part. The nurses nursed cups of lukewarm
coffee. The attendants had little to attend to. And he—the lauded,
legendary campaign manager—had nothing left to manage but anxiety.
They had few options, and one yet untried—taking her outside.

They hadn't, not because it hadn't been discussed, but because
he'd forbidden it. Drones and paparazzi lay in wait to gather images of
her feeble state. They would end her campaign—and his career. But
now, even that seemed better than this. Perhaps fresh air and a change
of scene could coax her back to reality.

A nurse pointed out a willow tree a thousand steps from the main
building. The drooping branches would hide Raahima, if they could get
her there.

He managed to scrounge a dozen umbrellas for a makeshift mobile shield. Backlit by the midday sun, it cast an undulating, otherworldly glow—a stained-glass igloo in shades of blue, out for a walk. Under the umbrellas, Raahima's face seemed to defy gravity, her once sunken, drooping cheeks now weightless. Soon she was walking on her own. For the first time in days, her body was under her control.

Nurses had piled pillows for her to lie on, but she ignored their invitation, stuffed two blankets between the willow's gnarly roots, and sat upright against the trunk.

He beelined to the pillow pile and collapsed in a clump. Exhausted, but unwilling to take his eyes off her, he kept watch for what seemed like—and was—hours. Whenever he drifted off, he snapped himself awake, only to drift off again. She simply sat and stared, eyes soft and wide, looking straight ahead. If she knew he was there, she didn't let on.

Last Week

The empathy-scaling studio was part lab, part spa: screens, dials, gauges, and cables surrounded by soft seating and flickering candles. Ignoring the plush appointments, he perched on the edge of an ottoman, ready should things go awry.

The room was bathed in warm light but for the blue dot on Raahima's cranium. It flashed in staccato bursts as a technician stimulated her brain's emotional centers. The feelings being pumped into her brain were shaped by surveys and stress hormone samples—emotional renderings of people experiencing crises in war zones, refugee camps, extreme poverty, the aftermath of natural disasters, and on and on. Their emotional story arc coincided with a soundtrack of firsthand accounts and data visualizations. Raahima's eyes welled with tears as she took it all in. She was learning to feel the data.

Some dismiss compassion scaling as disaster porn—vicarious and distant. Others call it emotional brainwashing—silly and sinister. To him, it was all that and worse—rash and unscientific. But for Raahima and her followers, it was a given. To make the decisions a world leader must, she would have to surpass the limits of her feeble point of view. As fraught as this method might be, it beat the alternative— navigating the impossible complexity of the global stage with an ordinary human brain.

Compassion scaling is delicate. Too little and it doesn't take. Too much and it leads to trouble. The tech carefully turned dials in lockstep with the data flows on the screen and with minuscule shifts in Raahima's body language—dialing down the emotion streams as tears gathered in her eyes, twisting the dials back up whenever her back straightened.

At first Raahima's emotional tolerance had seemed insatiable. She kept asking for more. But over time her face began to contort as if giving birth to a most unkind thought. Eventually, her shoulders collapsed from the torment. They said this was normal, but it wasn't normal to him—and it wasn't normal for her. Soon her torso started to quiver as if the room had gone frigid.

He rushed to Raahima's side, but before he could catch her she'd collapsed in a heap on the floor. Nurses hustled over to check her vitals. Her blood pressure was a bit low, but everything seemed in order. Her eyes were wide open, lids stretched back, as if she were watching a horror movie. He surveyed the people surrounding Raahima to gauge if all this was okay. By the looks on their faces, it was not.

Two Weeks Ago

Everyone thinks it will hurt. It seems like it should, drilling a hole in your head. But the laughing gas makes the vibrations from the drill feel tingly—the good kind of tingly. People tend to like it. Raahima giggled the whole time.

As soon as the drill started, the bit spun so fast all he could see was a ghostly, floating flash as its spin caught the light. In less than a second, the hot blade cauterized the wound as it cut through. It smelled awful, but there was no blood. Fixing the blue dot over the "port"—the hole in her head—didn't take much longer.

A second machine latched on and fed in impossibly thin wires—some translucent, some galvanized copper—more than it seemed could possibly fit. Inside the dot is a loom of sorts, spiral tunnels that guide the wires and weave them into a net, all without touching the brain until the mesh is intact. He watched intently, as if his gaze would stop any snags. With the net in place, the technician twisted on the final, namesake blue cap. It pulsed its iridescent glow.

She had bet her—and his—future on this little blue dot. He had tried everything to stop her: reason, arguments, recruiting loved ones, blocking the door to the installation center. But now it was done. She was far from the first person to install a blue dot—millions had them—but she would be the first elected leader. Assuming she got elected.

Once everything was fitted and tested, they brought out a small tray filled with hats of different shapes and sizes. Still giddy from the gas, Raahima picked out a tiny fez made of fur. She covered her blue dot with the cap and pulled the strap under her chin to keep it in place. Her face glowed with satisfaction.

How can I take her seriously with that hat strapped to her head? It was the last lighthearted thought he'd have for some time.

Just Now

In the darkness, the crowd was a dense constellation of twinkling blue dots, like concertgoers hoisting lighters awaiting an encore, except it never ceased.

As Raahima's speech ended, he had to admit that she'd been as clear as ever—maybe more so. She promised compassion, her mind and body now tuned to the vast scale of the world's suffering and joy. She spoke of an Age of Enlightenment. She told the crowd their emotional resonance would guide her every decision. By the end, even he felt inspired—wary still, but inspired.

The pulsing crowd expressed their love in cheers and tears. Raahima cupped her hands in a prayer-like pose and bowed, again and again. When she finally walked off the stage, he couldn't help but notice the furry brown fez left on the podium. Her mind was augmented—famously now. There was no need to hide it.

Enlightenment aside, if the crowd's reaction was any hint, it was a savvy political choice. Long after she'd left, people were still wiping away tears. Hope for her campaign was far from lost.

But whatever happened next would not be clean. Raahima could speak all she wanted about her expansive compassion, but her enemies would still call her a cult leader. Many would openly wonder whether any decision was hers or if her brain had been hacked. Her presidency—if she had one—was bound to be short-lived. He knew it didn't matter to her. To her, this was bigger than that.

His concern, at least for her, evaporated before her confident glow. Her eyes held a calm, courageous wisdom that he hadn't seen for some time—if ever. She was ready. For what, he wasn't sure.

Regardless, his work was done. Not because he had finished the job, but because he couldn't. What had begun as a political campaign had morphed into something else—a movement? A religion? Whatever it was, he wasn't needed. She, or this, was beyond him.

———————————

Brain-computer interfaces have been around since at least the 1960s. By the early 2000s, scientists were using them to control fish remotely and help monkeys learn how to move robot arms with their thoughts. In 2020, a company called Neuralink installed rudimentary but reliable brain-computer chips in a pig named Gertrude. And they have plans for a blue-dot-like device that connects thousands of thin electrodes to different parts of the human brain. The cofounder of the company, Elon Musk (yes, he's behind that too), says that while their ultimate goal is to "improve the bandwidth of communication" so people can keep up with AI, he also imagines the technology could be used in other ways—including empathy training.*

Neuralink or not, the real issue is that technology preys on our need to find intent and meaning in everything, almost to a religious degree. It already shows up in the way the internet creates subcultures and feeds conspiracies. Things might get weirder when we're wired straight into each other's neurons.

* Listen to the *New York Times* "Sway" podcast from September 28, 2020.

Filling the Gaps with Patterns

Humans are wired to notice patterns. This is an essential bio-logical tool. As babies, it helps us recognize our parents—*I know that face! It belongs to my mother!* It's also a deeply flawed one if you rely on it without question. But for a species that craves meaning-making, pattern-finding becomes an essential feel-good way of making sense of the world. Your pattern-finding ways are so natural that you may not always be aware you are doing it.

What Do You See?

A question that has been asked on the internet many times before: **What do you see in this grilled cheese sandwich?**

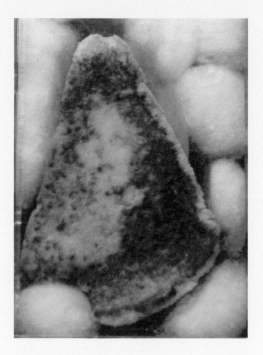

Yes, it's the $28,000 face of the Virgin Mary. This grilled cheese sandwich was ten years old when it sold for this hefty sum in 2004 because of the Holy Mother's likeness.

What do you see in these inkblots?

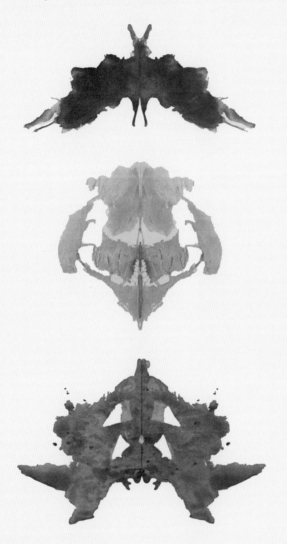

A toupee that needs combing. An orchid. Two baby birds sharing a meal. There are no wrong answers here. Easy, easy. Great. This is just the warm-up.

What do you see in these swirly forms?

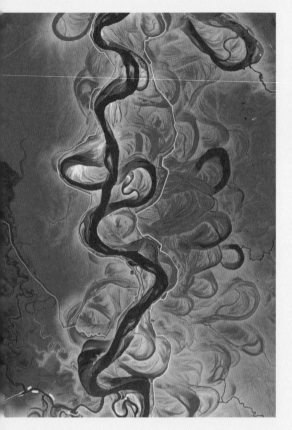

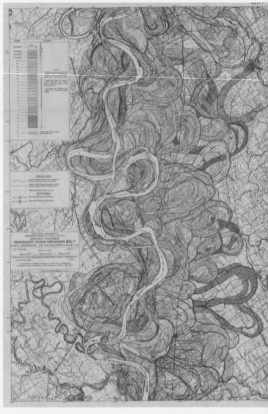

Abstract art. A color gradient. A historical record. Nutrients and floods and a predictor of the future. It's the meandering path of a section of the Mississippi River.

The first image, by Daniel Coe of the Washington Geological Survey, was made with LiDAR.* It's a modern re-creation of the famous map hand drawn by Harold Fisk in 1944, on the right.

Both images are decades-long records of what was, is, and might be. When you see how a river moves from this vantage point, thousands of feet above, you can sense its energy. You can see where it wants to go and get a feel for how it travels in ways very different from when you are floating in an inner tube. Most of us don't often experience rivers from this angle, so the shift in perspective offers a new insight on how to engage with the landscape.

* LiDAR uses laser pulses to measure the distance to the ground from a plane. The colors in the first image represent elevation.

What do you see in this blue-black gradient?

* Earth sits
within a pixel
in that vertical
white stripe—at
about this level.

`3.7 billion miles lie between you and this photograph.`

A light streak. A speck of something. It's Earth as seen from beyond Neptune's orbit, taken by the Voyager 1 spacecraft on February 14, 1990. This image was a defining moment for many. Earth is just a speck in a streak; one tiny aberration in an otherwise empty image.* But we all know how much happens in that little pixel. It's our lives and our families and everything we fight for and celebrate and complain about. It's our educations and houseplants and cows and the smell of freshly baked bread.

This image pulls us billions of miles away from our day-to-day. It's about as zoomed out as we can get. And from this perspective we're beyond interconnected; we're a blur. Our planet isn't infinite. We don't have an easy escape route if we wreck our current hostess. This image inspired the book *Pale Blue Dot* by Carl Sagan, conceived by him and Carolyn Porco, a member of Voyager's imaging team.

Porco went on to re-create the photo from the spacecraft Cassini on July 19, 2013. There we are again, still entirely blurred together, but this time she let us earthlings know the photo was going to be taken via an invitation on the BBC; people were invited to go outside to smile and wave.

Were you waving?*

* There's Earth again—the tiny bright dot under Saturn's rings.

Carolyn Porco reflected on these images in a 2020 piece in *Scientific American*: "The significance of images like this—our home seen at significant remove as a mere point of blue light— lies in the uncorrupted, unpoliticized view they offer us of ourselves, a view of all of us together on one tiny dot of a planet, alone in the blackness of space." What feels newly insignificant to you from this perspective? What becomes more important?

What Would You Bet On?
Humans are on an insatiable quest for meaning. You might find meaning in space or back on Earth or in your family and faith or in your friendships, pets, and career. This kind of meaning is on the "grand purpose of life" scale, but we also want the everyday world around us to make sense. Our brains more easily remember patterns or stories than unrelated piles of information. But our hardwiring for sensemaking can lead us astray too.

We crave meaning in all aspects of our lives, no matter how inconsequential or grand.

For example, if you flip a coin nine times in a row and it keeps coming up heads, it's hard to believe that the next toss won't be tails. It just *has* to be, right? Most of us would bet on it, even though those tosses are statistically independent—meaning, what happened before doesn't affect what will happen next.

This misapprehension was named the *gambler's fallacy* on the night of August 18, 1913, at the Monte Carlo Casino in Monaco when the roulette ball landed on black twenty-six times in a row. With each spin, gamblers were sure it was red's turn, repeatedly betting on it. Millions of francs were lost before the twenty-seventh spin finally came through. Those people weren't delusional to keep betting that the black streak would end— they knew that each spin was its own spin the same way you know that each coin toss is its own toss. But *knowing* doesn't necessarily mean *believing*.

Whom Do You See?

Our brains are hypertuned from birth to recognize faces. It's useful to be able to recognize your mom throughout your life, but especially so when you're an infant. Facial expressions convey a person's friendly or nefarious intent. But this face-finding instinct (*pareidolia*), much like our pattern-finding instinct, may lead us to find faces everywhere, even where they don't exist (like on a grilled piece of bread). We're inclined to turn images and other visual data into shapes, faces, and stories—however illogical.

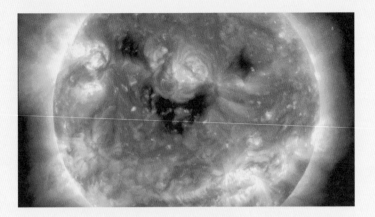

In October 2022, the sun was caught smiling at us in this image taken by NASA's Solar Dynamic Observatory satellite. "Seen in ultraviolet light, these dark patches on the Sun are known as coronal holes and are regions where fast solar wind gushes out into space," NASA tweeted. It's a smiling face, but it's also a solar storm that can affect telecommunications on Earth.

Hawaii from the series "Moss Maps" [1993]

Or maybe channel your smiles at Nina Katchadourian's moss maps and transport yourself to the beaches of Hawaii. There's no danger in the pleasure of finding these islands (provided you don't slip on the moss).

These sensemaking strategies are forms of *apophenia*— the inclination to see a connection in data or a pattern in randomness. Call them delusions, but they feel wonderful. It's how we see bunnies in clouds. It's thrilling to spot a relationship between different things, even if you're wrong. You smile when you see a face staring back at you from the moon, the moss, or your sandwich.

Our brains like to organize and make meaning, whether it's there or (often) not. Confirmation bias—accepting data only when it confirms your established belief—can create big societal consequences. The continued political polarization in the United States is a confirmation bias machine—you believe only the candidates you want to believe, and rifts deepen.

But apophenia has a use beyond good vibes and bias induction: it helps us get to an epiphany.

There is something that feels better than apophenia, and that's an epiphany. It's the moment when everything clicks into place and all the pieces make sense. It's the zap to the chest when you notice something new that changes everything. *Aha! Eureka! Bombshell. Revelation. Scientific breakthrough. Self-realization.* These are grand words and phrases that suggest grand outcomes.

Apophenia and epiphany can feel similar to the person experiencing them. Connecting the dots of a harebrained conspiracy feels a lot like unearthing a scientific connection never seen before. However, epiphany and apophenia are fundamentally different. Apophenia can be harmless or harmful, curious or confounding, but it's not as tethered to reality as an epiphany. But as to how they operate in the world, sometimes they aren't as different as we might wish.

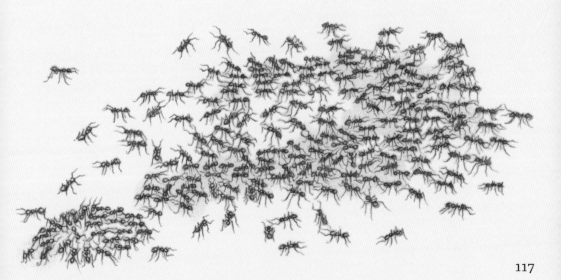

Love Machine

If reality is in the eyes—and ears—of the beholder, what can we say is authentically us? When we invite machines into our intimacies, where does our voice end and theirs begin?

It started the same way it always does, with a whisper in his ear: *You seem calm. Now would be a good moment to—*

"Let's do it later," he snapped, hoping a sharp interruption would cut things short.

Later never comes. Change only happens in the now. He hates the platitudes it spouts.

I should remind you that this is what you hired me to do. And you gave me permission to override your choices. Its logic is even more frustrating than the platitudes. Especially because it's true.

May I suggest we reach out to your highest priority relationship?

A searing tingle spanned his arms.

"It's too soon." More sternly. Reasoning with the machine was useless, but sometimes an emotional outburst would coax it to change course.

I see the spike in your heart rate now that I've brought her up. Don't forget, connection with others is the single most important ingredient in human happiness. What did it know about human happiness? It's an algorithm. The tingle was creeping onto his face now. His eye twitch was back.

If you don't connect today, you'll miss your goal of at least two connections each week.

The whisper ended on a chipper note as a ringtone filled his ears. He hoped she wouldn't pick up.

"You again." She picked up. The tingle took over his chest.

Oh, I'm—I'm sorry . . . did I catch you at a bad time? He was impressed with the theatrical beats and stutters. The system must have gotten an update. He took the cue and repeated it, adding his own flourishes.

"Oh, I'm—I'm sorry—did I catch you at a, um . . . a bad time?" Did he overdo it? Maybe he overdid it.

"No. It's not a bad time. Actually, I was just thinking about you. It's uncanny. Like you read my mind." With each word she spoke, his nervous tingle morphed into something more like exuberance. Maybe the bot was onto something.

I've been thinking about you a lot lately. That was too much. Was it too much?

She replied before he could speak. "Would you like to know what I was thinking?" This kind of candor was exactly why he'd fallen in love with her in the first place.

Yes.

"Yes." Easy enough to repeat.

"I was thinking that you're very un-you lately. And don't take this the wrong way, but I like it." And *that* kind of candor was exactly why their relationship had gone south.

Thanks, I guess. A hint of sarcasm. This was a good update.

"Thanks, I guess." He laid the sarcasm on thick. He felt like himself when he said it.

"Do you mind if I try something?" she asked. Her voice sounded sweet, but it did not sound innocent.

Sure! He wouldn't be able to match the bot's eagerness.

"Sure." Nonchalant.

"Basket. Rainbow. Onyx. Tree trunk. Marsupial." She enunciated every word and left beats of silence between each.

Are those things you might find on a picnic in Australia?

The bot's response was quick and peppy, but he couldn't bring himself to repeat it. The pattern recognition game would be a dead giveaway. He stayed silent, hoping she would let him off the hook.

"Well . . . ?" She was not letting him off the hook.

Are those things you might find on a picnic in Australia?

The bot repeated, this time with even more glee. His nervous tingle was back. Now crawling up his neck.

"Do you have anything to say for yourself?" she prodded.

Are those things you might find on a picnic in Australia? The bot didn't usually get hung up like this. Her list of words must have triggered some glitch. Did she do that on purpose?

The bot whispered the question again. He was at a loss. She stayed silent.

She knew, and he knew she knew, but he didn't want to admit it out loud. Yet every time he tried to muster a clever response, nothing came. After another long, awkward silence, he conceded. "It said, 'Are those things you might find on a picnic in Australia?'"

"I knew it," she replied with an all-too-familiar scoff.

With that, the bot broke loose from its trance, finally offering a sincere reply: *Does it matter? I set it up to call you. I care about our relationship. That's what really matters.*

He took a breath to rid himself of his long-standing contempt for her smugness, then repeated: "Does it matter? I set it up to call you. I care about our relationship. That's what really matters." He couldn't help but tack on a provocation: "Isn't it?"

"Did it tell you to say that?"

Honestly, yes.

"Pretty much."

"And that too?"

Not exactly.

"Not exactly."

"Well, what does it want to talk about?"

I—not it—would like to know how you're doing.

"It wants to know how you're doing."

"Tell it I'm good."

I'm so glad to hear you're doing well.

"It heard you. It's glad to hear you're doing well."

"That's nice."

Thanks.

"It said, thanks."

"Would you mind leaving me and your little voicebot alone? Since you're just repeating what it says anyway?" He wasn't sure she was kidding.

Would that make you happy?

"It can't do that. It's against protocol."

"Is that what it told you to say?" she asked.

No.

"Yes."

"Okay. So, what should we talk about then?"

Would you like to talk some more about picnics in Australia?

He felt his eye twitch again. The nervous tingle was everywhere now.

"Are you still there?" Her incredulity had turned to exasperation.

I am, whispered the bot.

"I am." He heard himself squeak.

———————————

As we integrate AI digital sidekicks into our daily conversations, we find ourselves relinquishing the intimacy that defines human connection. In this feverish expansion, these mechanical liaisons weave a new layer of separation. We find ourselves standing on the periphery of our own lives, tourists within the landscapes of our relationships, yearning for the authenticity of yesteryear.

Note: In the spirit of *not* thinking for myself (like the character in this story), I had a large language model (GPT-4) craft this story's takeaway note (above). While I wanted to print its whole note as is, I couldn't help but trim it a bit. Still, the experience left me with the sinking feeling that it's going to be hard not to use these tools as thinking partners, in the same way it's hard not to use ice cream as a partner for your taste buds, whether or not they are healthy.

Filling the Gaps with Stories

Just as we find patterns to fill in our gaps in understanding, we make narratives to feel better about our place in the world. This is where our talents at apophenia can lead us astray—especially if left unchecked.

1959. Lubang Island, Philippines. Toshio Onoda has been here for at least six months. His search has turned up nothing. In one last-ditch effort, he marches up the tallest peak he can find and begins singing, "East wind blowing in the sky . . ." Though few would recognize the tune, the lyrics of his high school hymn are dear to him and the one person he sings for: his younger brother, Hiroo. But the jungle returns no sign of his lost brother. Toshio and the rest of the search party return to Tokyo and declare his brother officially dead.

More than a decade later, Toshio discovered that his song did not echo through the forest unheard. On a peak no more than two hundred yards away, Hiroo Onoda, the target of his lengthy search, had sat motionless, listening—amazed that someone could perform such a close impersonation of his own brother.

When Hiroo and his comrades first arrived on Lubang, World War II had just dawned. Their orders were to fight a guerrilla battle to stave off the enemy for as long as they could—and never surrender. As Hiroo watched what he thought was his brother's doppelgänger sing from the mountaintop in 1959, he and the other soldiers were still following their orders, on their own, holed up in the jungle. WWII had been over for almost fifteen years. Even so, Hiroo would remain there for fifteen more.

Many tried to coerce them out, but the holdouts debunked every tactic used to convince them: newspapers announcing Japan's surrender, military men with flyers telling them it was safe to come out, and even the "family" members who shouted for them in the jungle. Debunking was easy. They never failed to find "evidence" of fakery: misplaced characters in the newspapers, cracks in Toshio's singing voice. Hiroo knew in his heart that Japan would never surrender and that any order to change course would come from directly above him in the chain of command—and none did.

Over time, things got worse: his remaining two companions were killed during their various raids for food, ammo, and sabotage. By the end of 1972, Hiroo was alone.

Around the same time, Hiroo's mysterious fate piqued the curiosity of Norio Suzuki, a recent college dropout turned self-styled explorer. On a whim, Suzuki famously declared he was off to find "Lieutenant Onoda, a panda, and the Abominable Snowman, in that order." Three lost causes, each a grand adventure.

Through a strange series of events, Suzuki found himself face-to-face with Hiroo just a few days after landing on Lubang. And though many before him had come to talk Hiroo out of the jungle, Suzuki listened instead, and Hiroo gave him the key—to leave, he needed orders from his old commanding officer. Suzuki went back to Tokyo to fetch Major Yoshimi Tanaguchi (by then an elderly bookstore owner). When they returned to Lubang, Hiroo finally surrendered.

At home in Japan, Hiroo was greeted with a hero's welcome. Rightfully so. He'd displayed his integrity in the most dramatic way. But his thirty-year stint in the Philippine jungle was a tragedy. Hiroo knew that better than anyone. In his head (and heart), he had a short but powerful narrative, a story about a country united, where togetherness is honor, honor is life, and truth can come only from the higher ranks. It was tailor-made for wartime. And, in a weird way, it worked. It kept him going while he lived off the land for all those years.

But Hiroo had so clung to his story that his own brother became an imposter and peaceful farmers turned into mortal enemies. It also confined him to a jungle for the better part of his adult life.

Hiroo's experience is an extreme case of a very normal reaction—more the rule than an exception. People are pretty good at poking holes in other people's faulty stories, but they're lousy at finding weaknesses in their own. In other words, we're all a lot like Hiroo. We have a knack for finding things where they don't exist. And if you can't let go when a story stops working for you, you work to preserve it.

The Safety of Stories

Stories don't just exist. People make them. In 1944, psychologists Marianne Simmel and Fritz Heider made this clear with a brilliantly simple study, somewhere between a research project and a minimalist art piece. They showed subjects a silent animation of simple black cardboard cutouts—two triangles, a dot, and a box—moving against a stark white background. The little shapes went into, out of, and around the box and toward and away from each other at different speeds. Nothing more.

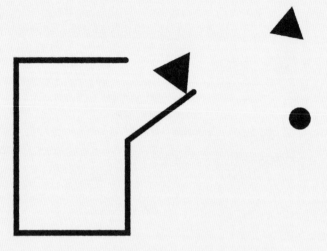

These shapes are full of drama!

Afterward, they asked the subjects to describe what had happened. Ninety-seven percent talked about the shapes as if they were characters and added motivation to the motions. Even when asked to just "write down what happened in the picture," the subjects concocted stories of villains, bullies, love, and hate; characters with genders and agendas, fight scenes, chitchat, and marriage. From simple shapes moving around, people made up stories with drama and intent.

There are all kinds of theories as to why people use make-believe: It's an emotional rehearsal to prepare us for trouble down the road. It gives life meaning and keeps us going. It helps us make decisions and predict the future. Its entertaining. It quiets the mind. Most interesting of all, we might be doing it to connect with each other.

Banding together gave humankind the upper hand over other species. A rabid beast can easily tear one of us apart, but together we might be able to handle it. Not to mention, free-loading off a group is a good way to get by without wasting energy. So if we think a story will help a group stick together, or at least help the group stick with us, then it makes sense for us to stick with the story—true or not. People don't like to debunk stories that keep them socially safe. Instead, they double down, often choosing belonging over truth. (Interestingly, Hiroo finally let go of his narrative only after his companions died and he was left alone.)

Stories are emotional logic, a useful glitch in the human psyche. Our ability to make things up—and believe them—is a superpower. But although stories help us see what could be, they can just as easily cloud our vision of what is.

Stories make you feel sure of yourself because they latch on to the human psyche in particular ways—that's their power *and* their peril. When you think in stories, your point of view naturally distorts. In your little sensory bubble, stories train your attention on characters, conflict, and causes.

Listen for these distortions in your next conversation. It's easy. You'll hear **characters** (usually the person talking is the main one), you'll find **conflict** (pitting people and things against each other), and you'll hear **causes** (casual words like "because" and causal connectors like "and then" come up all the time). Narrative thinking is so second nature, it's hard *not* to think in characters, conflict, and causes. You might even feel yourself resisting the idea that you should worry about this at all.

Thinking in stories is very useful. (This book is filled with them!) Getting down to root causes and people's motivations (characters) helps unwind complex issues. But it's still a distortion. Focusing on characters' concerns conceals collaboration and nonhuman influences like context. Foregrounding conflict clouds connections. Fetishizing singular causes can crowd out unseen possibilities and problems. Getting tangled up in a story can amplify false dichotomies and hide nuance, keeping you from noticing certain elements.

Hiroo recounted his saga in a breathtakingly honest autobiography. He revealed that stories can be powerful, but they should be fleeting, especially when the context shifts. We should be as willing to let beliefs slip as we're inclined to cling to them in the first place.

There's the problem. People are not wired to let go of beliefs. This *motivated reasoning* (or "myside" bias) is the more emotional cousin of confirmation bias—and the root of some disheartening data on the human psyche. The gist is this: when you're emotionally motivated to believe something, you latch on to any evidence—however flimsy—that fits your story. And when you're *not* motivated to believe something, you look to dismiss any evidence to the contrary. The mind finds whatever it's looking for and spins a yarn to block out the rest.

The motivated mind seems impervious to straying from a sticky belief—even facts that disprove your point of view tend to make your convictions stronger. Cornell psychologist Thomas Gilovich describes it something like this: When you find facts that suit your prior beliefs, you ask yourself, "Can I believe this?" But when facts conflict with your ideas and ideals, you ask instead, "Must I believe this?" Friendly facts feel far more acceptable to the believing mind. But those friendly facts can have nefarious origins and outcomes.

Finding a Way Beyond Beliefs

We've been battling the curse of somewhat-true stories for a long time. The ancient Greeks had a term for it: *doxa*. It's one of those old philosophical words that doesn't quite have an equivalent in modern English. The definition is a bit slippery depending on where you find it. It's not knowledge; it's definitely not the truth; and it's close to, but not quite, a belief. It's described sometimes as an idea about what seems to be, other times as public opinion.

Doxa is the world as it appears to you, the sense you make from your narrow view of reality. Think of it as a wobbly opinion that a person takes for granted, or a collective "filling in the blanks" that a group takes for truth. Plato saw that as problematic, lazy, and self-deceptive. Aristotle (Plato's student) felt it was more useful, like a hypothesis to try on as you make your way toward a better understanding. The trouble is that we're "doxa-ing" all over the place without calling it out. Hiroo's overtime war was a conspicuous case of an unchecked doxa at work.

We desperately need ways to recognize our flimsy stabs at reality so that we can borrow their wispy wisdom while keeping their rickety foundations at bay. But we're short on work-in-progress ways of thinking that move us forward while still making room for scrutiny. Until then, we're stuck with dueling doxas. We're fighting with clouds. The thunder makes a ruckus but leaves little hope for understanding.

The problem with doxa-like stories and beliefs is that people treat them as monuments to revere rather than what Aristotle hinted at: vehicles to get you from here to there, or gap fillers. You don't have to pretend your car is your destination to trust that it will get you somewhere. Yet we're inclined to imagine that our stories are the absolute truth. Stories are tools, not truths. They are ways to play with possibility. Ride them and see where they take you. When they break down, tune them up or trade them in.

It's hard to leave an old tale behind. Those old stories took care of us when we needed them. And old yarns are just plain hard to unravel. But when we dispense with a doxa, we make room to investigate the edges of our ignorance. We open up possibilities to find opportunity in the things we've been missing all along.

It's much like preparing for travel. Aviator and author Anne Morrow Lindbergh may have said it best in her diary *Hour of Gold, Hour of Lead*: "Is there anything as horrible as starting on a trip? Once you're off, that's all right, but the last moments are earthquake and convulsion, and the feeling that you are a snail being pulled off your rock."

Sometimes it's hard to detach from the stories that hold us tightly. Stories work because our minds can manage them— they fit in there. It's much harder for us to cling to bigger, more unwieldy concepts and things, especially if that thing is a melting block of ice.

Looking for the Things We Miss

In 2000 I spent a month right up against the nose of the Mendenhall glacier's retreating ice in Juneau, Alaska. The glacier had exposed a rock ridge covered in funky corduroy-looking sediment deposits, and by studying them, I hoped to learn something about how glaciers slide. With my research I aimed to contribute in some tiny way to the opus that is scientific knowledge on glacial mechanics, climate change, and sea level rise.

Beyond the science, I developed a bond with the Mendenhall and a few of the other hike-accessible glaciers in the Juneau area—the Herbert and the Eagle. Glacial ice isn't like the cubes in your freezer. Though a glacier is white and dirty on the surface, if you can find your way to a subglacial cave, the smooth, largely tessellated crystal of this mass of ancient frozen water under pressure will echo with you for life. It's like looking into the underbelly of Earth's fresh water, being shown a secret treasure.

Hidden Brain podcast host Shankar Vedantam brought me back to the Mendenhall in spirit with his 2016 episode "Losing Alaska: Why Our Brains Weren't Made to Deal with Climate Change." In it, Vedantam visits the Mendenhall on vacation, and though he wasn't there to work, he was overcome with the desire to investigate how people could continue to tell themselves stories and deny climate change even while standing directly in front of the gorgeous retreating glacier. Multiple interviewees, people who had traveled there like him to marvel at the ice, could not come to terms with the fact that climate change had consequences that would affect them. "I realized . . . that the debate over climate change is no longer really about science unless the science you're talking about is the study of human behavior," said Vedantam.

George Marshall, founder of Climate Outreach, a nonprofit that helps illuminate the effects of climate change, wrote in his book, *Don't Even Think About It: Why Our Brains Are Wired to Ignore Climate Change*, "More than any other issue, [climate change] exposes the deepest workings of our minds, and shows our extraordinary and innate talent for seeing only what we want to see and disregarding what we would prefer not to know." Human brains aren't good at making sense of big, interconnected, uncertain phenomena—especially when we can't experience them firsthand.

We're wired to protect ourselves and loved ones in the moment and perhaps into the near future, but we have trouble making sense of anything much beyond that. So we surround ourselves with stories that affirm our values. We can know lots of the facts, yet weave a web in which we don't need to believe them. "If it doesn't exist in terms of people's values and identity, they drop it," Marshall says. The stories we tell ourselves about the existence of climate change fit neatly into the gap created by confirmation bias and motivated reasoning. Straight facts are important, but the stories we tell between the facts are what changes minds.

The crux of our woes is this: Our perception and the way things happen are out of sync.* While people experience life as individuals, the world works as a collective, and *both* are important. This difference between our experience and the way the world works also makes us very unreliable creators. We think of ourselves as the ends and miss that we're also the means.

* We miss plenty, even when it doesn't miss us. "Our New, Invisible Leaders" (page 78) tallies a few intangibles that play on our emotions and sway our actions.

Noble Currency Index, 2050

Can we change the world by ascribing monetary value to things, actions, and activities that aren't currently given that status?

Note: The following are 2050's Noble Currency categories. Since 2027, Noble Currencies have created monetary value in places where traditional currencies fall short. The elements that make up Noble Currency contribute to wealth, health, and prosperity but are hard to measure. Measurement difficulty arises for some from a lack of understanding of the correct metrics; for others, from years of systematized racism, sexism, and classism, or because they are challenging to qualify. The rise of tokenization and badging connected with the proliferation of record-keeping blockchains in the 2020s allowed these elements to be acknowledged and accounted for. Though a wallet full of shopping-worthy peer-issued tokens proved elusive, it has come a long way since. The Noble is now a reserve currency for many nations, and it has given a purse to populations that were otherwise working without compensation.

2050 CATEGORIES

Care and Nurture

This section awards Nobles for childcare and eldercare services within one's home, nanny care, and in service of public-school auxiliary programs. It covers cleaning services, including residential, public, and private-sector buildings, as well as in outdoor areas that are otherwise neglected by public or private entities. This category also includes carpooling and transporting individuals who cannot transport themselves.

Ingenuity and Learning

This section awards Nobles for everyday ingenuity—the contrast between available resources and ingenious output. It includes learning, teaching, and mentoring, not limited to formal school settings. Repurposing, repair work, hacking, and survival skills related to force majeure events are also included. (Notably, it does not currently include creativity—metrics have not proven reliable in distinguishing AI-generated creativity from AI-supplemented creative pursuits.)

Emotional Umwelt and Activism

This category awards Nobles to those who exhibit a strong emotional Umwelt, or emotional fingerprint. Key to this category are worry, anxiety, and planning as they pertain to other people and planetary species relative to manaakitanga, the Māori custom of respect, care, and kindness for others. This section was combined with Care and Nurture until 2045, when the nuances of the emotional burdens associated with care of others were acknowledged as a distinct category of empathy-centered change.

Unmentionables and Undesirables

This section awards Nobles to those who do the work that is seen as outwardly taboo or undesirable yet in high demand. It includes occupations that are deemed illegal in many instances, such as sex work. It also includes tasks that bring high risk to personal health, such as mining, refuse sorting, and open-air work at Air Quality Index levels above 400.

Carbon Sequestration and Land Management

This category determines Nobles for activities that promote and manage forest systems (land or sea) in service of carbon sequestration. This includes measures for keeping forests intact and for those managed and stewarded for fire and food through indigenous land management. Activities that balance the reforestation-to-wealth ratio, designed to refresh clear-cut farmland while providing wealth to farmers, are also included. All metrics in this category are under review as critics argue that areas with high-value forests (such as kelp and boreal) receive unfair advantages.

Biocultural Diversity and Pollination

This category promotes biocultural diversity per square kilometer, including species, languages, cultures, and foods. Nobles are given to the inhabitants who provide that diversity, both human and, increasingly, nonhuman, and to landowners. Rewards go to reintroduction of keystone species in biomes and subclimatic zones, and natural pollination (by wind, water, insect, or animal) across zone types. The Biocultural Diversity and Pollination subcommittee is working to determine whether decomposition (fungi and mechanical) should be included here or if a new category is needed.

There's a tension between things that are given monetary value and things that give value to society. The idea of invisible economies isn't new, and many people are working to create blockchain-based currencies based on some of them. For example, British futurist Jonathan Ledgard has outlined an idea for "interspecies money" that would give currency to nonhuman species as a way to finance their survival. Might there ever be a world where these new values become new gold standards? There is hope that we might turn the tide on measurement and power.

What We Miss Still Exists

An old business adage goes something like this: "What gets measured, gets managed." Despite the usefulness of measurable goals, they are troublesome. We miss what we can't or don't measure—even when it matters.

Some things that are easy to measure don't really matter. Some things that matter are hard to measure. Looking at the big arc of history, we know of the Stone Age and the Bronze Age because their remains are sturdy relics, easy to measure.* What other ages might we be missing because they lack durable trash? And might the hidden or vanished ones be more important?

We may be overlooking an entire era before the Stone Age—call it the Leaf Age. Certainly, stone was not the first tool—rocks are hard and difficult to work. Early humans must have played with sticks and leaves before rocks and bronze (present-day apes do all the time). A broad leaf, curled into a cone, was likely used to gather seeds thousands of years before obsidian was knapped into arrowheads. Leaves and other flora made soft, user-friendly tools for gathering and sharing. But the leaf used back then has since become the soil, the tree, the fruit, and then some. We've missed it because we can't measure it. Legendary sci-fi author Ursula K. Le Guin mused on this take in her essay "The Carrier Bag Theory of Fiction," "We've all heard all about all the sticks spears and swords, the things to bash and poke and hit with, the long, hard things, but we have not heard about the thing to put things in, the container for the thing contained. That is a new story. That is news."

. . . .

The world is full of wisdom that's "news" to many of us. What might we be missing simply because we're not good at finding it, or have ignored it, or have "doxa-ed" ourselves into believing it's not true? What epiphany is waiting to be uncovered? What long-held belief will be proven wrong in the next ten years? These gaps in understanding are why things feel off-kilter. The way we fill them in could make or break our future.

It's humbling to know we are just a smidgen on the surface of Earth, one tiny part of a massive, interconnected world in space and time. But we can live with these feelings if we embrace the intangibles.

* For more on this topic, see "Measure Your Measurements" (page 223).

Part of existing with the intangibles is accepting that they will always be a bit elusive. The other part is finding ways to curb runaway design in spite of or in concert with them. Part two is about these actionables.

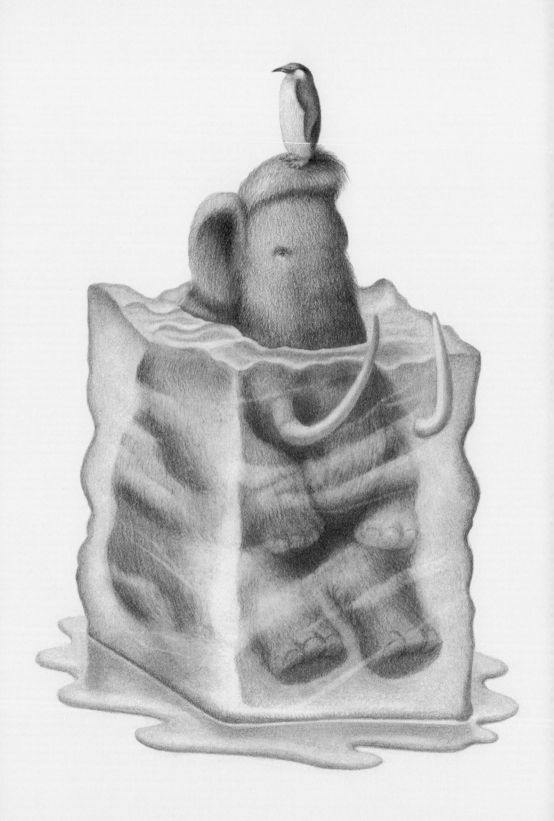

Special Feature: On the Mammoth Steppe

If possible, should we program our ecosystems?

———————————

Sunday

The helicopter flight from Cherskii isn't long, but it is an odd sort of deafening. The 2020s-era machine, a relic from the late Putin era, is retrofitted with a secondary noise cancellation chamber. It's supposed to make the cabin quiet and peaceful so we can talk freely, but for me it's anything but. It's not loud in the traditional sense, but there is something piercing my eardrums in a way that's made my shoulders curl in on themselves. Arturo just stares out the window, looking relaxed. But he always does.

We bank to the left, and the helicopter whines through my soul. Arturo looks over at me, slightly amused. I tilt my head left then right, trying to pour out the sound. Words are coming out of him, but I can't hear. He holds up his pinkies and inserts them in his ears, nodding for me to do the same. I do. Then, peace.

"The chamber isn't calibrated for your ear shape," he says. "They work for many people, but it looks like you're one of the ones whose ear geometry magnifies some of the frequencies. If you keep your ears plugged, you'll prevent the sound from getting in, and you should be fine. You are more like a dog than a human!" Given that he's a veterinarian, I take it as a compliment.

"Woof?" My fingers still in my ears, my elbows splayed out wide frame my discomfort.

"No, no, no," he backtracks. "Sometimes we humans just have to block out all the sound in order to hear."

The helicopter descends, and out the window I see lumpy grass and brown blobs. This isn't just any old prairie. We're about to land on the mammoth steppe.

Thirty thousand years ago this was the world's largest biome, covering vast stretches of the northern hemisphere. The ice age, locking up so much water, made sea level much lower, and a land bridge connected Russia and Alaska. Humans hadn't yet warmed the planet. Large herbivores roamed this grassland: bison, horses, musk ox, and, of course, woolly mammoths.

We descend toward the landing pad at the research lab, our home for the next week. It's a glorious triumph of resurrection, this mammoth steppe. Visually, it's not as dramatic as the coast or the mountains, but it's become the beacon of hope protecting its more photogenic cousins. This stretch of northeastern Siberia is now a hundred-thousand-hectare planetary savior.

The brown blobs come into focus. Animals: reindeer, elk, sheep.

"There." Arturo points out the window. Sure enough, slightly bigger than an elephant, with swooping tusks and long brown hair, is one of twenty-nine living woolly mammoths that have been brought back from extinction. I strain to keep it in my sight as we descend, but it becomes eclipsed by the approaching horizon. Arturo turns toward me. "I can't wait to find her."

He's referring to Anastasia, the only female woolly mammoth here. Two months ago, there were ten females, but they've all been killed, we think, by an overabundance of males that, in their urge to mate, have fatally injured the females. Arturo is here to save Anastasia; I'm here to examine her DNA and rebalance the priorities of the whole biome. Earth needs us to expand the mammoth steppe, and there is no mammoth steppe without the mammoths.

Fifty, even twenty years ago, no one had imagined biomic design jobs like mine. Using large DNA databases, gene alteration, ecosystem forecasting, and human prediction engines, I can alter entire biomes. I can prioritize the survival (or demise!) of a specific species or aim for an outcome like 0.2 degrees of cooling in mid-latitude countries with below-global-median GDPs. We humans now have the power, and the will, to rebalance the natural world. It gives me hope.

I've worked with Arturo only once before, on a temperate forest biome—home to those ridiculous giant pandas. I rebalanced the priorities there to allow for snow leopards to increase their predation of the bumbly pandas. Why we spent years keeping pandas from the brink of extinction when they offer very little to the planet is beyond me. Rebalancing for the snow leopard to be more of an apex predator made the entire biome more productive and valuable.

We had a good working relationship on that project. Arturo always puts the animals first, no matter what, but I don't fault him for it. I think he respected me too after seeing my results. Why else would he have signed on for the mammoth steppe?

The helicopter touches down more gently than I expected. I pull my fingers out of my ears. The pilot turns. "Welcome to Pleistocene Park."

There's Nika walking toward us, arms outstretched. I flinch, then try to make it seem intentional by pretending to check my pockets. I thought it would be okay to see her. At least we're only here for a week.

"Dr. Marquette!" she exclaims with feigned formality, and we embrace. She smells the same.

"Dr. Lebedev," I reply, willing Arturo invisible from the awkwardness.

"I'm honored you came, Jezebel," she says, squeezing my hands.

"It's my job." I repeat it in my head to get any remnant of her out. *It's my job.*

We head for some unremarkable one-story, metal-sided buildings. The most sophisticated biomic software ever made is inside.

Monday

"Shall we?" Nika indicates an old electric Jeep. Arturo and I toss in our backpacks and climb in. Nika presses her thumb gently on the windshield. Real-time locations of different animals are overlaid on the glass. She points—"There she is"—and starts driving. "That's Anastasia, our last female mammoth."

The fifteen-minute drive is mostly quiet, thank god. I know Arturo's anxious to help Anastasia. I am too, but I won't know exactly what challenge I'm dealing with until I can gather some of her DNA. Nika seems like her old self, never rattled. She's been lead geneticist here for the last five years and led the synthetic programming of the mammoths for years before that. With so many recent female deaths, the park's funders have taken notice. There are larger forces at play than the planet. That's why I agreed to the work when Nika asked. I'm here to turn the project around, because I took an oath to put the biome above all else. And *all else* includes dealing with the unresolved issues with my ex-wife.

Nika slows the Jeep. I don't see Anastasia yet, but her vocalizations shred the air with a sound like a hundred lawn mowers gasping to turn on. There's no question it's the cry of a mammoth in distress.

This time I'm not the only one whose body has curled inward in reaction to a sound.

Arturo is out of the Jeep before we stop. Anastasia is lying on the ground. He crouches behind her head, speaking to her while checking her vitals. I see no visible wound and linger a few meters away with Nika while he works.

"I'm so glad you are here, Jez."

I am not ready for the kind of conversation I know she wants to have and can't muster more than a sigh-shaped shrug.

"Can you fill that water basin?" Arturo's request saves me. "I think her left hind leg is broken or sprained."

He smashes pills from his backpack into a powder, then mixes it into the water. "Drink this, Anastasia," he coaxes. She's tentative, but her trunk finds the tub and she obliges him. He's already connected to her. This is why Arturo is the right person for this job. Gently, he feels his way along her leg until she flinches. "Here. Yes. I know. You will be okay."

"What is that medicine?"

"Meperidine. It should calm her and ease the pain. It's an opioid analgesic. I don't want to keep her on this forever, but for now she needs it." He strokes her head. "Good girl. You should feel better soon." The lawn mower wailing cools to a wheeze.

"Come look at this." Arturo points out a thick, sticky yellow substance on her fur. "I think this is temporin. Male *elephants* secrete it when they are in musth."

As male elephants mature, they grow more dominant and begin to go through an annual period called musth. Their hormones rage and they secrete temporin from glands on the side of their head—signaling their readiness to mate. They're very aggressive during musth, with each other, other animals, even people. The older an elephant gets, the more dominant he becomes.

I ask, "How old are Anastasia and the other mammoths here? I would have thought they'd need to be at least fifteen."

"Anastasia is twelve. The other twenty-eight male mammoths range from eight to thirteen. I wouldn't expect these mammoths to even be sexually mature yet." Arturo looks pointedly at Nika. "This is very young."

The prompt hangs in the air for a few seconds before she takes it. Mammoth de-extinction was made possible because of Asian elephants. Nika had spliced elephant DNA with DNA found in cells of extinct mammoths preserved in the Siberian permafrost for thousands of years. Hundreds of embryos were fertilized in labs, and the healthy ones were implanted in female elephants to gestate.

She explains, "We programmed the mammoths to reach sexual maturity at a younger age than elephants. It was important to get them reproducing quickly so we could grow the population using as many mammoth mothers as possible. Otherwise, we would need to continue to inseminate elephants as surrogates, and that has been rocky. Many elephant mothers died in mammoth childbirth."

Arturo looks as if he knew this but needed to hear Nika say it in order to release his roar. "That's rocky? What's rocky is bringing a species back from extinction in the first place, let alone altering the maturity cycles we already know to work in a parallel species just to speed the experiment. These are the first mammoths to live on Earth in what, four thousand years, and we couldn't wait a few more?"

They look at me as if I should side with each of them. I can't ignore the palpable pain of this female mammoth, but it's never that simple. Nika knows what she's doing. She's always put the biome over everything . . . even me.

I was her couch confidant, her countertop collaborator, her security blanket for the years before she left. I was the one who held her insecurities as we went to bed each night. Was she prioritizing the right parts of the genome? Was she factoring in enough faunal variety? Did this blouse look sophisticated enough for a meeting with the founding nations? Was any of this even worth it? From outfit to existential crisis, I was there.

And I saw her begin to succeed. This landscape had turned to tundra before the reintroduction of the mammoths and the other large mammals—musk ox, bison, moose. But when they were brought back, the animals trampled the tundra flora and allowed the area to turn back into a grassland—the steppe. The grass insulates the permafrost in summer, and in winter the animals stomp the snow so it doesn't insulate the ground, and the cold arctic air can keep the ground frozen. Hence, permafrost. It has twice as much carbon frozen in it as is held in the atmosphere. If the permafrost melts, all that carbon goes into the atmosphere and accelerates planetary warming. Big animals help preserve the permafrost.

If the mammoth steppe permafrost remains frozen, we cool the Earth. If not, we lose a lot more than just the mammoths.

"Arturo, are you accusing Nika of something?"

Before he can answer, Nika says, "You're right, Arturo. I didn't get this piece correct."

Arturo kicks a tuft of grass in front of him. "I know this is complicated," he says, "but we can't ignore the immediate. We can't. She's hurting."

He turns and walks away. Nika does too, picking her own meandering line through the grass.

Alone with Anastasia, I gather hair samples from her coarse outer guard hair and curly inner coat. With her DNA I can make some changes and reprogram it so her children will inherit the traits we want. Clearly some changes are needed, but I don't know what they are just yet. I also scrape a sample of the sticky fluid that Arturo thinks is temporin. I should be able to sequence it and match it to the mammoth it came from.

"We need to find the others." Arturo comes back, more composed, and reads my mind. Nika returns too, and it seems like we have regained a shared, albeit tenuous purpose.

Nika calls for a watch patrol to protect Anastasia while she rests. Arturo relays instructions for her care. "With this she should be able to relax through today and tonight. I'll examine her again in the morning," he says, then squats to stroke her head before we go.

In the remaining daylight we drive to the other mammoths. Fourteen are together, strolling lazily, eating and ambling, majestic. They regard us as a cute curiosity.

"Mammoths should have a matriarchal society, like elephants," says Arturo. "But these are all males. They've stayed in a herd even without matriarchs. I don't know if this is temporary or they're adapting."

"We need to find the others," says Nika. "They will be trickier."

We navigate the Jeep to a male roaming alone, moving much faster than those in the herd. He speeds up on our approach, asserting his dominance.

A burst of brown and tusks lunges toward us. "Whoa!" Nika swerves the Jeep; I grab for anything willing and brace myself. Arturo is fully spun around in his seat, staring at the mammoth as we accelerate away from him. "He's in musth, no doubt. Did you see? The hair near his ears is wet and sticky. That's the temporin. That kind of speed and aggression mean he's looking for a mate."

For the rest of the day we make our way to each solitary male.

"That's fourteen males all in musth at a young age." Arturo scowls. "Just because their sexual maturity is sped up doesn't mean they're socially or even physically mature enough to be functioning members of a herd. Bodies that weigh several tons can get injured during mating. Are their bones strong enough? *I* don't know. *You* definitely don't know. Clearly their overaggression and underdevelopment have decimated the very herd that you wished to grow. This is absurd."

For a minute the only sound comes from the Jeep bouncing over the grassy steppe.

I break the silence. "Can you protect Anastasia, Arturo?" I need him focused on what he can control. I have to consider the big picture, but the view on the ground isn't great. I need to look into the decisions Nika has made to get us here so Arturo and I can get out of here.

"I can," he says. Nika doesn't flinch.

Tuesday

I have the full biomic priority engine pulled up in front of me. I didn't want to like it, but damn, what a thing of beauty. More than ten thousand considered factors fill about ten square meters of wall space. This. *This!* This is the mammoth steppe biome. Nika's been busy. Sure, it has its faults, but more than anything else, I see this as humans paying reparations to the planet.

"Well?" Nika has snuck up behind me. "Still upset with me?"

I ignore the loaded question. "Nika. This is incredible." I wish she'd stop looking at me. Arturo is out in the field with Anastasia, and we're alone for the first time since she left the life we had built together to come to Siberia.

"Let me show you around the engine," she says. "Here are all the stakeholders—the permafrost, mammoths, other animals, the flora, and your favorite, the humans." So now she thinks we're on a teasing level? She always accused me of being too practical with our relationship, of not valuing the small moments enough, the human things. "Here are the sub-stakeholders. The most affected countries—Russia, obviously, as host country, but also the countries with the most to gain and most to lose from the success of the biome. I've even modeled out corporations with the most at stake."

It's so comprehensive. "Nika, this is one of the broadest, most wide-reaching models I've seen."

"And I've got the fungi."

I can't go there. She knows I love factoring in fungi. If I didn't know better, I'd think this biome was an apology letter.

I need to focus on the work. I point to a section where she's clearly tinkering with pace. "Tell me about this part."

"Different time scales of success for different stakeholders. Humans, countries, and corporations all tend to desire very near-term results. If we can't see benefit within a few years or, at the most, our lifetime, it feels like a failure. But the permafrost will take longer than a human lifetime to cool and preserve. I've been experimenting by pulling different levers, prioritizing different stakeholders and features over different time periods.

"I work with what I can control. Right now, the mammoths are the species I can control that have the greatest effect on the ecosystem."

"Mammoths certainly have a magic to them, but if we really need them only to trample the snow and eat the trees, couldn't we just use a lot of smaller animals?" I am drawn to the mammoths much more than those lumpy pandas, but no matter how majestic an animal is, if it doesn't function as part of an ecosystem, I don't see the point in keeping it around, and the ones here are suffering.

"There's a balance. Mammoths, like elephants or whales, can really set the pace for the biomes they helm. They are sort of like the giant suns that everything else uses to keep time. Would a lot of smaller animals work too? Yes, to a lesser degree. Sergey Zimov proved as much with his original experiments."

"But you could also argue that if permafrost is our ultimate goal, and trampling moss and eating trees are just the means to keep the ground colder, we could engineer those plants to not grow here, or introduce some new insects that might eat them, and then use the smaller animals to fertilize the grassland and keep it growing." It feels good to be thinking with her again.

"In theory, but all the tiny things are too unpredictable and hard to monitor. We can't keep any control."

"You've always liked control," I blurt.

Half of Nika's smirk looks like a smile.

I follow her into a different room. It's filled with wafer-thin servers stacked vertically on shelves, like books in a library. "This is data hub six," she says. "Everything here is tracked constantly. *Everything.* There are fifteen data hubs throughout Pleistocene Park, and another forty-five hubs across the rest of the world and near-world."

If you hold the data, you hold the power. I knew that it took considerable political effort to determine where hubs would be housed. Arctic-neighboring nations like Canada, the United States, Russia, Greenland, and Sweland all successfully lobbied to host a hub, with the premise being they have a strong desire for the experiment to succeed. Of course, there is also a hub in the intertropical convergence zone in the Pacific Ocean, as well as one in low Earth orbit. And like all major international efforts, this one has at least three hubs in undisclosed locations.

"All the larger animals have embedded sensors, so we know their basic vitals and locations at all times. The heat sensors give us one-centimeter resolution data throughout the park, so it's easy to see the smaller animals. That also gives us permafrost temperatures down to twelve hundred meters. And the whole park is under the constant surveillance of pervasive hyperspectral. Plant by plant, we can watch the biome shift from tundra to steppe." She looks at me like she used to. Ecosystem over emotions, I know, but seeing her glow brings me right back.

I squeeze her hand, but she pulls away and gives me the same phony smile she used to reserve for the parade of patronizing head-of-state types that needed to feel as important as her work.

"This facility is a hundred percent secure," she says, a little too loudly. I get it. We're being monitored. Someone's keeping track of their large investments.

Wednesday

"Try the syrniki," says Arturo, putting one on my plate. "I don't know why I never make these at home. I wonder where you get this kind of cottage cheese. Do you know? Maybe I'll start making my own cottage cheese. Anyway, how did your work with the priority engine go yesterday? Make any changes?"

"It was good!" I answer too enthusiastically. *Dial it back, Jez.* He seems refreshed but doesn't know I spent the last fifteen hours drifting in between examining the biome and tugging at the gummed-up-ponytail tangle that best describes my feelings for Nika. I'm not sure if my crush is on her or the biome at this point.

"Well?" says Arturo. "Am I going to get any more information? You're lost in your head. What did you find?"

"Sorry. It's hard to come down from a night of experimenting." This is true. "I'm starting to wrap my head around it, but I'm not ready to make any moves yet. I'd like to spend some time outside today looking at the flora and go through the DNA samples I collected from Anastasia and the others. Nika's work is really impressive, from what I see so far."

Arturo pops another syrniki into his mouth and nods in a way that seems like he's not onto my newly fluttery feelings, so I continue: "How is Anastasia doing?"

"She's clearly still in pain. She was standing when I got to her today, which is good, but she's keeping to a small radius. I've asked the watch team to stay near her. I also prepared more meperidine at a lower dose to keep her pain at bay but hopefully allow her to feel more like herself."

"Progress," I say. "Do you think she'll be well enough to mother a child this season?"

Disgust rolls up his face. "Come on, Jezebel. I know that Nika accelerated the mammoths' maturity, but we really need to slow this down. I thought you were on my side here."

"You're right. I am. I mean, I'm on the biome's side. I'm sorry. I just—"

"I know you are really close with her, or used to be, or whatever, but I'm telling you, just look at the last two months. They've lost ten female mammoths, and the last surviving one is injured. Ten! Something isn't right. Why did she even let it get this far?"

"*Shh.* Stop it. Don't accuse her of anything." The last thing I need is for an Arturo outburst to be recorded. "Many stakeholders are eager to welcome the first mammoth baby birthed by a mammoth mother back into the world. If we can get her to have a baby this year, we're one step closer to a sustainable species. If not, we're back to using elephant mothers and starting all over again. I don't know if we have another ten years. There are tradeoffs."

Then I go there. "And for your information, *Nika* left *me,* after ten years together, to take this job, so I'm not playing sides here. I'm just trying to hold it together. And get the biome back on track, obviously."

He holds up his hands in surrender. "All I'm proposing is a minimum one-year pause. You heard Anastasia screaming too. They shouldn't be suffering for the sake of the biome . . . and I'm sorry. That's a lot."

His point is really the crux of it. Should any one species suffer on behalf of the health of a whole biome? Maybe a mammoth shouldn't suffer, but what about a mouse? A bush? A fruit fly? A human? Two humans?

"I'm with you on slowing down." I mean it, too. "It's clear that something has to change."

After he's left, I flip through Anastasia's biome, as coded by Nika. In some places, she's programmed more hardiness into the DNA, like thicker hairs in their outer coats. We know that some of the last remaining original mammoths had a genetic mutation that made their hair too silky and not warm enough. Nika clearly took care of that. Cleverly too, as I look at how few parts she needed to pull it off. Like anything built, there are a number of ways to make it work, but usually the simplest is most effective, especially with nature. Natural biology rarely adds complexity. In synthetic biology we are still quite clunky.

"Morning!" She startles me. "Ahh, admiring my work, I see," she says with a light laugh. "Where do you think you'll begin?"

"I'd like to look at how all of her major systems are maturing and compare them with the males, check out their skeletal and muscular systems. There also might be a problem with male testosterone levels. Maybe we can tone it down. Arturo thought it was strange that so many of them were in musth. I do think it's wise to slow down—"

She cuts me off. "I think the solution is to speed up, not slow down." *Where is this coming from?* "First, we harvest some of her eggs. Then we fertilize them and gestate them in elephants. Then we get her pregnant too."

"But you were the one who said how dangerous that is, for the elephants especially. How long before goodwill runs out with the elephant-dominant nations? How will this project keep its international funding without unilateral support?"

"Jez, you know as much as I do that success is relative. The permafrost is expanding slowly. The Earth is cooling somewhat. Something fails with every success. For most of the world, this park, this biome, never crosses their mind. They are getting the global cooling they desperately need without sacrificing anything. They want more mammoth superstars, and they will be okay sacrificing a few elephants along the way."

"Nika." I look at her pleadingly. "Don't. I am on your side."

"You're not supposed to be on my side!" she barks. "You are supposed to care about the biome above all else, even me, remember? Or do you now actually care about my feelings?"

Thursday

An unmistakable thumping stands me up in the field, and I look toward the research base. It's more than a kilometer away, but I can easily see the helicopter landing. Nobody mentioned that there would be other visitors this week.

I'd planned to spend the morning spot-checking samples of forbs—herbs, mums, sagebrush, and more. These plants give mammoths their protein, and it's thought that they prefer to eat them. With a cross-analysis of mammoth hair I could get a better picture of their diet and see if it's affecting their health.

This is the job you're here for. I resolve to keep picking grass. But then I don't.

When I walk into the lab, six people, including Nika, are talking stiffly.

"Ah, Dr. Marquette, I would like to introduce you to some other distinguished guests," she says with that same fake-smile formality that signals the presence of money. I'm in my dirty field clothes; everyone at this table is in a suit, including her. "This is Dr. Ivanov, Dr. Oblonsky, Secretary Wang, Chairman Peng, and Prince Erik." Nika pauses, as if hoping one of them will say something.

"To what do we owe the pleasure?" I try to lock in to Nika, but she's actively avoiding my eyes.

"Tell us, Dr. Marquette, when might we expect the mammoth population to reach twenty-five hundred?" asks Secretary Wang.

"Uh, twenty-five hundred?" Still no help from Nika. "Well, that depends on how quickly we can get them reproducing naturally, and right now we haven't even crossed that hurdle. I guess it could be as quickly as eighty years, if absolutely everything functions as planned, but it's more than likely to take a hundred fifty years."

Eyebrows rise. Prince Erik asks the next inane question: "And what about five hundred?"

"Well, all the same uncertainty, of course, but maybe forty years?" My questioning uptick should convey my lack of confidence in the number but sounds more like personal insecurity.

"Dr. Marquette is doing her best to help accelerate the population. Now, please, let's allow her to do her work," Nika states as she gestures me out.

Back in my room, I try to organize my thoughts. Did Nika expect these people? What are they after?

I pull up all the mammoth genomes for comparison. Each mammoth here is genetically distinct enough to preclude breeding problems. I decide to experiment a bit. If I slow their sexual maturity by ten years, and we can add an additional fifty elephant-gestated mammoths to this population, we would reach five hundred mammoths around year ninety.

I consider just staying put, but if Nika is under illegitimate pressure to expand the mammoth population, I want to know about it. Heading back toward the lab, I hear helicopter rotors start up again, and I break into a jog.

I see the guards load six massive, curled mammoth tusks into the helicopter.

"Things of beauty, aren't they?" The prince startles me with a patronizing hand on my shoulder.

"They're from the dead females, aren't they?" I say, knowing the answer.

He gives a wry smile and employs his full smarm. "Well, we need to get them evaluated at market. Thank you for your important work. And support." Then he pushes past me and walks outside to join the others.

I take a Jeep and find Arturo out with Anastasia. She is lying down again and he's next to her, reading. He looks up and motions me over.

"She was in distress again this morning. I gave her more opiates and now she's resting."

"Will she be okay?"

"I don't know. I hope so. If we can keep her at ease. I wish I could evaluate the deceased females and see if they also had leg injuries," he says. "I wish they'd called us a month ago. We'd actually have had a chance to fix this—"

I interject, "There are other people here."

"Huh?"

"Five of them. Money people," I say in a rush. "I walked in on them talking to Nika. They asked me how quickly we could scale up the mammoth population. Now they're loading tusks into the helicopter. There's nothing in the priority model that looks at tusk value or creating a market for tusks." I spit out the words so fast that I'm out of breath.

He stares at me with what looks like pity.

"What?" I ask. "What?!"

"Jezebel, of course there's a market for tusks. How naïve are you?" he says. "Has there ever been a moment in human history when tusks haven't been something to buy and sell?"

"No."

"So, what part of you thinks that human desire to exploit all the other creatures of the planet has magically vanished now? The fact that it isn't in the priority engine just means it's a black market. And there's always been a black market for tusks."

It's obvious now that he's said it out loud. Embarrassing. I've been so preoccupied that I forgot to think about the blanks—the negative space, the shadows.

I slump down next to him. My voice doesn't make it through the sentence without cracking: "Do you think Nika is . . . complicit?" If she had missed this and was as surprised and disgusted by the arrival of these guests as I am, I could forgive the awkward afternoon and move toward helping her find a solution. But if all along she was in on it, and she accelerated the mammoth maturity for the sake of the tusk trade all while pretending it was for the permafrost—if this is why she left me, that would be the ultimate betrayal.

Arturo gently squeezes my hand. "Jezebel, it's obvious that she cares for you."

Friday

When I enter the lab, Arturo looks my way and stops, his face ashen, then spins and walks out the other way. Nika is curled in the corner. She lifts her eyes to meet mine, then retreats into her cocoon.

I sit down, my side touching hers. "Before I can go any further, I need to know: Have you been in on the tusk trade from the beginning? Am I just a prop, here to make you seem legitimate? Is there no *us* in this week at all?"

"Jez, no," she says. "I didn't. You aren't. I mean, I had no choice."

"Which is it?"

"I've known about the tusk trade from the beginning. It was a condition of taking this job. I agreed, assuming I'd figure out a way to make it work, or that circumstances would change. And you were so . . . involved in your own projects. I needed to be that important. To something, if not someone." Her voice is hollow. "I really thought I could find a way to handle it, but I can't. If I go along with them, then I'm helping them do something that's harmful to the animals, not to mention illegal. But if I don't go along with it, they'll get rid of me, or worse, cancel the whole project. Those five people are responsible for securing seventy-five percent of the funding for this place. And if any word of this leaks, then it's me who goes down."

I put my arm around her, and she leans into me.

"*You're* the key to *us*, Jez."

"I've got until tomorrow. I'll find a way."

I spend the night in compromises, trying to find a way to allow for a tusk trade to coexist with expanding permafrost. I compromise on flora diversity to allow for more human traffic in the mammoth steppe. I compromise economies of countries that rely on certain weather patterns for tourism. I compromise on the amount of cooling we give back to Earth. I compromise my own ethics and morals and responsibility. I compromise my dignity. I do it all for Nika.

Saturday

"Hi," she says. "Sit with me." She's staring off into her own world, my work from last night displayed on the wall.

"So, what do you think? I know it isn't perfect, but—"

"Jez. Did you sleep?"

"Don't worry. I think I have it set up for you and—"

"Just sit with me."

I let her take my hand, and we stare at the plan. Then she flips a switch, and the room goes dark, hollow.

"What are you doing?" I ask.

"It won't be more than a couple minutes. Just sit with me. Just us. Alone for a minute, so I can remember."

I begin to sink into the silence, but not even thirty seconds later, Arturo bursts in, distraught.

"It's done!" he shouts. "Are you satisfied?"

"What's done? What's wrong?" I ask.

Nika doesn't turn.

"Anastasia." He breaks down. "I put her down. I killed her." His voice cracks.

"Arturo. What?" I yell. "Why? I thought she was getting better!" How could he? He'd never harm an animal. I can't wrap my head around it. Everything I worked on last night requires Anastasia. By killing her he's sent the woolly mammoths back into extinction. He's surely ruined Nika's career too. "How could you?!" I scream.

He screams back, "How could I? What choice did I have? Ask *her*." He jabs his finger toward Nika. "*She* knew I had to. She knows the only way to stop the tusk trade and everything that follows is to not have mammoths at all."

Nika still sits silent, facing away.

"She's masterminded all of this. She knew the mammoths weren't programmed correctly. She coded them just well enough to make this look successful, to make their deaths look like accidents. But this is far from an accident, isn't it? *Isn't it?*"

"Arturo, stop!" I plead. "You're talking crazy."

"Oh really? Tell us it's not true, Nika. I may have euthanized Anastasia, but you're the one who gave her—all of them—the death sentence. She doomed them even before they were born."

I open my mouth, but again he cuts me off. "Have you ever stopped to consider, Jezebel, why you're here? Or are you really this dense? At least *I* know I wasn't called here to actually save the mammoths."

"Stop it!" shouts Nika, finally. She stands up.

I stare at her incredulously and read the admission in her face. "It's true, isn't it, Nika?" The past week's events run through my head. For the first time it all makes sense. Nika set the whole thing up to fail when she came here. She knew she could get away with it only if she called in help. She had to make it seem like she was exhausting every option. That's why I'm here. I'm meant to look like I'm helping, not to actually succeed. And by playing with my feelings for her, she made me miss the obvious.

"Has anything been true? You turned the power off so there would be no surveillance. You knew Arturo was going to kill Anastasia. You knew we'd argue. I can't believe this. I am such an idiot."

"I had no other choice," she says. "I agreed to the tusk trade and to keeping it hidden when I signed on. I was naïve, and it seemed like a small thing compared to saving the biome. It's the shadow force in the priority engine—the way the funders can exert their own control over the project, and over me. I see now, that as the mammoth population grows, their power will rise with it. And it will be at the expense of the biome. We must slow down, and the only way is to cut them out."

She presses her lips together hard, and collects herself. "And the only way to cut them out is for the mammoths to go."

"You used us," I say.

"I don't like that word, but if we must, yes, I used you. But Arturo knew what he signed up for even though he ended up not liking it. He and I may not agree on much, but on eliminating the mammoths we are aligned."

"Arturo? You knew? Why would you do this?"

"I thought I was okay with it before I got here," he begins. "I don't think it's a good idea to bring back animals from extinction, especially mammoths, and I agreed to help stop it. But then I met Anastasia. She is—was—incredible. I wanted to save her. I was saving her. But she was in so much pain. And now I want to leave. I'll see you in the helicopter."

I'm a new kind of empty. I came here to save the permafrost, the mammoth steppe, and its namesake animal. Instead, I've contributed to their second extinction.

I'm a pawn in the system I was meant to fix. All because I let my guard down and allowed my feelings for Nika to cloud my vision.

I head for the helicopter like a zombie.

"Jezebel!" She's following me.

I have nothing left.

"Jez. Wait."

I stop but don't turn. "What for? There's nothing to wait for. It's all out in the open now."

"Not all of it. I'm sorry, Jez. I messed up." She pauses. "I messed us up."

"There's never been an us," I say. "I see that now. Never mind, though. It has to be about the biome."

"There's always been an us. There's been an us for twenty years. Jez, look at me. Please."

I turn slowly to face her.

"Jezebel Marquette, I've loved you for twenty years. You must know that. I messed up the mammoths. I know. I never thought I'd have to lie, to beg a veterinarian to kill them. I'd take it all back if I could. But Jezebel, my feelings for you are as real as ever. You, one human, are more important to me than the whole biome. And you're the only person I trust with its survival. For you to be successful, I need to go."

"If you leave, they'll realize what you've done and arrest you when you land in Cherskii," I say. And, sarcastically, "Don't you want to go back and clean up the data so it all looks like an accident, like you're still on track?"

She shakes her head furiously. "As I sat there this morning reading through everything you experimented with last night to save the mammoths and the biome, and to save me and protect me from my mistakes, I realized that you're right. This work needs you more than me. Can you take that?" she pleads. "You've never wanted me as much as your work. Please, can you do this?"

I walk to her. "I have, Nika, and I do, but—"

She pulls me in and weighs me down with her sobs.

The helicopter rotors begin to turn.

To hold her. This is what she's always wanted from me. To be with her, as a partner in parallel with the planet and all the perils of our field of work. I don't want to let go.

"I need you to love the biome," she says, still attached. "You are its only hope."

The rotors gain speed.

I'm a good biomic designer because I can see the big picture and the details. I can put them together. I can see how the parts of my work make the whole machine run. I can prioritize for the best positive outcomes for the most stakeholders. I can make the hard decisions, letting one part of the biome falter for the sake of the broader good. I know how to play the long game. But I want to do it with her.

"I can do *us*, Nika." I'm ready to follow her back inside, to help her rebuild the mammoth population again only to doom it for failure, on repeat, together. For us, and the biome. Maybe it's about adding an us, not taking her away.

She holds me at arm's length, frowning. "No, this *us* can't include me, Jez. This *us* has to be about the biome, and the biome won't work if I'm in it."

The rotor wind blurs my last vision of Nika, ducking up into the helicopter.

I am still. As its thumping recedes, my hair lands.

I am still, here. I am still here.

A mammoth trumpets in the distance.

"I hear you loud and clear, buddy," I say. "Musth sucks without a mate."

This story lives in the middle of the book because it hits on concepts that span the sections. Like the other stories, it's an outgrowth of existing ideas. Pleistocene Park is a real place in Siberia, Russia, not far from Cherskii, founded by Sergey Zimov to restore land that has become tundra back to a mammoth steppe ecosystem, to help expand the permafrost and slow global warming. Pleistocene Park is connected to a nonprofit organization called Revive & Restore, which works with the Church Lab at Harvard University. They are actively engaged in mammoth de-extinction.

In the design world, systems design is a growing practice, and design is tasked to take on larger-scale global issues within environmental, political, and other spheres. To be able to consider every type of stakeholder within a given biome would be a design dream, but in every project there are shadow forces and a range of value systems.

Nonhuman stakeholders—flora and fauna—need a voice in environmental reparations, but humans would still be in control of that voice. These trade-offs are tricky and full of compromises, both planetary and personal.

You only learn balance
by losing it.

—Alan Fletcher, witty graphic designer

PART TWO

Actionables to Unmake Runaway Design

CHAPTER 5

Be Awkward

Don't Look Away
(Even If It's Uncomfortable)

The purpose of art is to lay bare the questions that have been hidden by the answers.

—James Baldwin, novelist, poet, liberator

Learning to live with intangible flows can feel unsteady. When you're off-balance, you have to do things differently: hold tight to weather the storm, let go to find a new perch, speed up to get stable, pump the breaks to avoid a wreck.

To get a feel for how to act among these intangible swirls of uncertainty, let's start with a simple, albeit difficult act: appreciating what you have while noticing what might be missing, especially when it's awkward at first.

Embrace Awkwardness

We've all been there. Your exact *where* was different from mine, but the feeling was the same: awkwardness. It happened to me most recently at a vast cafeteria-type dining establishment where I was supposed to choose a lunch and meet up with a few new acquaintances. I hadn't been there in years and the place had been renovated. Immediately I found myself surrounded by swarms of students walking confidently in every direction to the salad bar, burger station, sushi, pizza, stir fry, special, or drinks. I felt like the only person ping-ponging, trying to understand the breadth of options. I had to decide what to eat and how to stage and balance it on my tray, navigate the space without a spill, and find my people. I couldn't have been more awkward. First, I was slow—utterly off pace from everyone else. It took me forever to survey what was available, much less choose. Of course, I chose poorly and ended up with a tray of random food-stuffs, not really a meal. Once I made my way to the cash register and paid, I stood staring at an endless matrix of noshing heads who all knew exactly what they were doing. They were chatting easily and eating; they had friends and meals that made sense. I felt alone in the spotlight, begging the universe to reveal my lunch mates before everyone decided I didn't have any. I stood there like that for forty-two minutes! Okay, not really. It was probably about twenty-two seconds before I noticed them waving, but it felt like an eternity.

This is awkwardness: when you're out of sync with social norms, pace, and unspoken rules and dynamics. Awkward moments sometimes surprise us; other times we know that certain situations, like parties full of expectations of mingling and small talk, might be repeated awkwardness triggers. Awkwardness happens to everyone, in all types of situations. While it might not feel good in a cafeteria, it's a great phenomenon to seek out when practicing noticing.

Awkward moments are opportunities. The lump in your throat, your pained expression, the anxious *hmm* in your head—none of that feels good. But that's where you need to dwell. As soon as things feel off, or you don't understand what's happening, the natural inclination is to solve, to fix—or to recoil, distract yourself, and move on. Next time, don't. Michael Barry, a Stanford instructor with boundless curiosity who teaches students how to draw inspiration by observing the real world, points out that good noticing requires you to linger in discomfort. It's about wading into awkwardness and staying open when something is off—without knowing the way forward.

Talented observers aren't afraid of this uneasiness. They seek it out. They relish it, like people out for an adrenaline rush. For them, discomfort without resolution is a cocktail that delivers a curiosity buzz. It fills them with what Red Burns, "Godmother of Silicon Alley" and cofounder of NYU's Interactive Telecommunications Program, has called the "anticipation of discovery."

Jennifer L. Roberts, a professor of art and humanities at Harvard University, has an incredible exercise she gives students as they study unfamiliar works of art. They must sit in front of the artwork, at its place in a museum, for three straight hours. Her reasoning is that what you notice in the first ten minutes is different from the details that begin to unfold at minutes 62 . . . 153 . . . 178 . . . Through this intense, time-stretched looking, in a place (the museum) that's not your regular workspace, details begin to unfurl only with patience. And patience is a hard quality to muster in our rapid-paced runaway design world. Roberts notes:

> *Just because you have looked at something doesn't mean that you have seen it. Just because something is available instantly to vision does not mean that it is available instantly to consciousness. Or, in slightly more general terms: access is not synonymous with learning. What turns access into learning is time and strategic patience.*

If you resist the desire to resolve your awkwardness, you give your psyche room to let something novel hop in, rather than cutting off all possibility with a quick, ready-made resolution. When you take a moment to step back and watch other people in other places, navigating their own lives, reckoning with their own awkwardness, you open up a chance to discover something new. The relentless desire to resolve things is the enemy of luck. The next time you feel or notice awkwardness, consider yourself lucky. Pause and embrace it. Stare at it. Stew in it. Allow everyone to look at you. Then keep standing there.

It's Complicated

In a world in which relationships become a ménage-à-trois
between people and their data, what new kinds of awkwardness
will emerge? How will relationships shift if data finds
its way into each and every one?

I'm early, but it's late. A waiter comes by to offer me a drink. I should really order coffee. Several months ago, I would have ordered something significantly stiffer. I ask for more water. I'm starting to wonder if I can sneak off to the bathroom again before the person I'm set to meet shows up. I've got time, but I want to make sure I'm here to greet her. I'm petrified I'll make a bad impression. This little meeting may be my last chance—it probably is my last chance.

A sorry string of events landed me here:
    I broke up with my partner.
    I moved out of our place.
    I got pregnant.
    I found a new place.
    I had a fight with my roommate.
    I moved out (again).
    And my status score got bruised.
    Now I'm alone, my kid is due any moment, and I'm having a hard time settling down.

Let's get the breakup out of the way.
    He was fine. Fine as in good-looking. Fine as in good enough. But it went on too long. And by *too long*, I mean I couldn't see myself raising kids with him. And he couldn't see himself raising kids.
    Time wasted. Oh, well. I moved out. And I ended up with a roommate.
    I wasn't looking for a roommate. I was looking for a place to live. The roommate—quite unfortunately—came with it. Roommates are

a necessary evil to make apartments cheaper. For me, the opposite turned out to be true.

My roommate was living in our place—her place—a decade before I got there. The place was definitely hers—she made that clear. Even so, she was fine (as in good enough) until she wasn't (which didn't take long).

It was the rules. She had a *when* for everything. *When* you could run the dishwasher—only when she was out. *When* lights had to be turned off—one hour after dinner. No light at night but candlelight—including in the bathroom. Candlelight can be lovely—if you don't have things to do. Try plunging a toilet by candlelight. There's a reason the world switched to electricity.

Even so, that was mostly fine too. Frustrating, but fine. And then the rules got more . . . more, just more.

Here's the one that unraveled my life: no opening the front door while she was sleeping.

I was locked in (or out of) the place as early as nine or ten. By then, I was pregnant—I'll get to that—so I wasn't apt to go out on the town, but that didn't mean I liked living under house arrest. I tried to oblige. Really. For at least a week or two. (Or maybe it was a day or two.) Until one fateful evening when I had a not-so-late night craving for an apple fritter. Being the adult that I am, I went out to get it.

I snuck out without incident. Safely out in the hallway, I pressed my ear to the door to listen for a stir. None. Clean exit—so I thought.

The lights were still off when I got back. I did everything I could to keep quiet. Removed my shoes in the hallway. Slipped the key into the lock with ginger grace. Turned the latch slow and steady. Even stuffed my scarf in my purse to give the keys a soft landing as I dropped them in.

Things changed as soon as I got inside. The moment I stepped into the pitch-dark room, I felt a hideous thump on my chest followed by a loud clang that seemed to tumble across the floor around me. Reaching in the dark, while trying to catch my breath—I was fairly far along in my pregnancy by then—I switched on the light and crouched on the floor.

As soon as the room was lit, my roommate tumbled backward and covered her eyes, screaming "Turn it off!" I didn't. I was fixated on her beloved copper pot that was now lying on the ground beside me—she must have thrown it at me. Even though my chest was still stinging, the sight of the pot sideways on the floor was more stunning. It was the first thing I'd seen out of place since I moved in (she had as many *where* rules as *whens*).

The next day, I moved out. And I stopped paying rent. That second bit—forgoing the rent—was meant to save money. It's turning out to be the most expensive decision I've ever made.

Soon after, she sued me for being delinquent. I sued her for assault. I won. But so did she. The judge said it was "unclear" if she realized it was me coming home or if she mistook me for some kind of intruder. If she knowingly attacked me, I was free to break the lease. If it was mistaken identity, no such luck.

Strangely, the judge took my side on the assault and her side on the lease. Both of us ended up paying damages and both of us lost a fair share of status points. (She lost more than I did, which is slightly vindicating but doesn't help me any.)

Still, I lost eight points on my Social Order Score (SOS for short, but, of course, everyone just pronounces it like *sauce*). And you know, an eight-point drop is enough to scare off anyone I might want to work with, sign a lease with, or—most important—raise kids with. The judge's dual verdict makes no sense. I'm already appealing. I know my score will even out someday, but I need it to be clean right now.

And I need this woman to show up. She was supposed to be here a while ago. I wonder if she's going to stand me up like the others.

That brings me to my pregnancy.

As you might have figured—since you know I got pregnant *after* I broke up with my partner—I didn't go the natural path. That whole thing is such a crapshoot. You've got to find some solid DNA, in a body that wants to get with you, and live with you, and raise kids with you—and you with them—all within your waning window of fertility. For me, the natural path turned out to be way too much happenstance, luck, and trouble.

As for the seed gestating in my belly, unfortunately I couldn't afford an exclusive "just for you" donor. The fella I got my fertilizer from is a bit of a celebrity as donors go. When it goes on auction, his seed sells out in minutes. It's not hard to see why. His profile is filled with clips of him singing self-penned songs to his nieces and nephews, details of his seemingly endless list of technology patents, and several videos of him free-climbing—shirtless. And his skin. Don't even get me started.

Alas, our asynchronous affair left little room for romance—not the passionate fling I might have dreamed of, but as it turns out, very efficient. It took on the first try.

Given my donor's specs, his seed must be spreading like a modern-day Genghis Khan. I have to say, I'm a tad worried I'll end up with a cliché kid. But the DNA screen when my batch came up was pretty exceptional, so I went for it—even though it may find its way all over the place. Lucky for me, gene pool laws limit donors to twenty donations per year and no more than ten per region per decade. Fingers crossed that it's enough to keep my kid—our kid, I guess—from bumping into many relatives.

Getting pregnant turned out to be the easy part. Now to the hard part.

I am a good person. If I'm honest, my SOS was never spotless, but I always evened out the minor bruises with major achievements. My education is enviable. My volunteer work is ample. My timing is punctual. My professional log is up to snuff. I have a lot going for me—except for that minus eight on my reliability score. And it came at the worst time possible—I'm set to pop inside a month.

Being pregnant on my own, I'm on the hunt for a CALM. For those who don't know, CALMs are all the rage for people who have babies but don't have partners. It's a group that gets together to raise kids. CALM is short for "Collaborative Alliance of Learning and Mentoring," but nobody calls them that. Everyone just calls them CALMs. The name makes no sense: raising kids in a group is probably anything but calm. To get around that, every CALM has its own rules—and contracts—for how you raise your kids: outdoor time, schooling types, moral codes, and such. Of course, in the end you still have to raise kids with a bunch of other people. It's complicated.

The CALM scene has everything marriage does—advice columns, apps, prenuptial-style agreements, counseling, all that stuff. Hooking up with a CALM is like dating, except you're out to date a group and the outcome is more like instant group marriage than a string of fun outings and casual sex.

Making it all work is like a job interview, college application, house hunt, and marriage proposal all mixed into one. You apply (and in my case, get rejected). There are rental agreements. You show a résumé. You even have heart-to-heart conversations, but your SOS status is at the heart of it all.

Good CALMs are wicked hard to get into. And none of them are out to find someone with a SOS like mine. That's why today's meetup is so strange—and why it's my last, best chance. The CALM I'm supposedly interviewing for is impeccable. It's a dream CALM—my reach CALM. I'm not sure I would've even qualified before the whole roommate situation bruised my status.

Too bad the rep they sent is nowhere to be seen. She's twenty minutes late. I'm starting to think this was too good to be true. Maybe it's time to call it a day—I really need to get to the bathroom anyway.

Just as I stand up to go, a woman slides onto the seat next to me. "I'm a bit late."

I appreciate the acknowledgment, despite the absence of an apology. I'm relieved to see her, but now that I'm standing, a trip to the bathroom feels inevitable. "I'm so sorry, do you mind if I pee?" As soon as I say it, I immediately want to shove the words back into my mouth.

"You know what—can you just hold it for a sec? I don't think this will take long."

As much as I need to pee, I certainly don't want to piss her off, so I sit back down and hope for the best.

She's all business. She launches right into the nitty-gritty of their CALM's child-rearing philosophy. She doesn't have to; I know all about it. It is just the kind of CALM I'm looking for: private living space with communal yards, exploratory education, screenless toddlers, older kids looking out for the young ones. I listen intently and pile on the compliments. I don't want to screw this up. The baby is nervous too—I can feel the kicks as if on cue.

As soon as she finishes her spiel, I chime in, "Sounds fantastic to me! Where do I sign up?"

Much to my surprise, she replies, "I was hoping you'd say that," and pulls out a screen with a contract.

I pore over it. It looks great, except for one glaring thing. The "pitch-in"—the membership fee you pay to participate in the CALM—is several times (and I mean *several* times) higher than normal.

She can feel my hesitation. "The pitch-in looks a little steep, maybe?" I nod. She adds, "It's just to offset your negatives—we need to make sure you're invested."

I check the numbers again. It's pretty clear I can't afford it.

"We think you can afford it," she retorts before I have a chance to share my thoughts. "We've run numbers based on a slice of your spending patterns. You won't have money for much else, but you can make it work if you want to."

"Can I ask what *you* pay to pitch in?" I'm not sure if this is the right thing to say, but the pressure I'm feeling—from my baby, my bladder, and now my bank account—is making me antsy.

"Less." Her eyelids lift slightly as she speaks. I can't tell if it's from pity or pleasure. "We have a sliding scale."

While I'm trying to decide if her offer is a welcome loophole or strong-arm extortion, my baby gives another kick. I put my hand on my belly and take a breath. I'm not sure how to respond—I have too many questions to come up with one worth asking.

She reads my thoughts again. "We have an algorithm that looks for folks in your predicament. You're what we call a bargain—someone who's great in so many ways and has some issues that we can easily deal with."

I'm getting the feeling I may not be the first person she's talked to about this scheme.

Maybe it's her comments, or maybe it's the baby, but I feel a strange twist in my gut. Is being a bargain a compliment or a dig? I feel like an underrated baseball recruit. Regardless, it's a little too direct for my taste. I take another peek at the contract. She's right. I could technically pay it—maybe—but it would drain my entire budget. So much for the "Collaborative Alliance" part of their CALM. The aftermath of having that pot thrown at my chest is getting more expensive by the minute.

I should say that I've had offers to join other CALMs. It's just that they're from ones that ignore your SOS. A notorious game of roulette—you never know who you'll get stuck raising kids with. I'm pretty sure I'd rather raise the baby on my own than deal with all that uncertainty and maybe mayhem.

I look back down at the numbers and back up at the woman's smug face. As gross as this all feels, I'm starting to warm up to the idea. I certainly get where she's coming from. When it comes down to it, I'm not really looking to get together with someone like me either.

It's surprisingly easy to explore how much tools and data shift our cultural norms. It's not hard to imagine that AIs will auto-order our meals based on past tastes and present blood sugar or that smokers might resort to strapping smartwatches onto wobbling rigs to fool health insurance trackers that they're on a brisk walk while they enjoy a cigarette instead. Of course these data-driven cultural shifts are well underway. Hopping into a stranger's car was the habit of only a handful of hitchhikers before ride-sharing apps tracked everybody's movement. Now most do it with little awkwardness at all.

For a long time, community was the solution for almost everything: Need childcare? Leave your kid with your auntie. Then came currency: Need childcare? Hire a babysitter. In these digital days, solutions seem to be shifting toward the types that track and coordinate: Need childcare? Check the ratings on a babysitting platform or tap your neighborhood app to distribute the duties. But we're still in the early days of these digital displacements; more profound changes are surely to come. We can anticipate them if we stop and take notice as they come our way.

Practice Noticing

Timothy "Speed" Levitch is most famous for his tours of New York City, captured for posterity in the late 1990s documentary about his work as a tour guide, *The Cruise*. His voice is slightly gravelly and very theatrical, residing mostly in the midrange, like a giddy baby bear reciting Shakespeare through an antique telephone. The day I first met Speed, he was ordering donuts, not by type or taste, but by color. He has an irreverent sense of what matters.

When his old tour bus passed through Greenwich Village, Speed would point out his favorite nearby landmarks, like the apartment where Henry Miller decided he hated New York and would move to Paris; 61 Carmine Street, where Edgar Allan Poe wrote "The Raven" while battling opium addiction; Washington Square Park, where Edith Wharton spent her "aristocratic childhood"; and three blocks away where D. H. Lawrence lived, "lasciviously." History, for Levitch, is not marked by monuments; it's made in moments.

It's not surprising, then, that one of his most famous walking tours visits a routine yet colossal *moment*: midtown rush hour. Speed meets people at 5 p.m. at the information island in the middle of Grand Central Station to witness the flood of commuters who pour in and out of the place.

Commuting to Levitch is "when our urge to arrive at our destination becomes more alive than ourselves," and "we travel with the assumption that every single human being currently on this planet is in my way." Touring midtown at rush hour is the opposite—commotion is the destination. This is flow in action! And when you are present with it, you can learn from it.

He shows travelers the best views of intersections, where they can watch as he explains how traffic jams teach patience to city dwellers "clearly addicted to impatience." He revels at the sight of pigeons negotiating their meals of breadcrumbs among hurtling taxicabs, all with "the grace of Fred Astaire." Levitch's tours are an appreciation for the nature of the city, an object lesson in stepping out of your assumptions and into the moment, an ode to the genius that comes from watching the world unfold. The idea is to see moments not as stepping stones, but as mentors.

Tackling runaway design requires that we tune our awareness. The antidote to our trepidation about the future might just be an appreciation for the present. Paying attention to the quirks and mundane moments in your life is one way to turn noticing into a habit. There are other ways too. Were there a hall of fame for keen-eyed observers, people who can see miracles in the mundane, there would be a special section set aside for three women. They share a first name—Jane—and a talent, but we can learn something different about noticing from each: how to challenge assumptions, learn from love, and spot gaps.

Bear Witness Without Assumptions

It's 1959. Jane Jacobs has just walked through Boston's North End, a dense neighborhood of immigrant families, by now a few generations deep. She hasn't been there since the early 1940s, when it was overcrowded with ramshackle tenements and apartment windows barricaded by mattresses. On this day, she could peek into the same windows through fresh curtains. The streets were bustling; kids playing, people chatting each other up, storefronts full. Upholstery shops welcomed repairs next to bakery windows stacked with ricotta pie. Even the rough walls that flanked the back alleyways had a fresh coat of paint.

After her surprising walk, Jane ducked into a bar to phone a city planner friend, hoping he could shed some light on how this neighborhood upswing came about. As soon as he heard where she was, he said, "What on earth are you doing in the North End? That's a slum!" and rattled off a well-worn stat to back up his claim: 275 dwelling units to the net acre. Translation: A lot of people are packed in there—it must be a slum! (Also, I'm smart enough to know that.)

"You should have more slums like this," Jane retorted. Sensing her displeasure, her friend humored her a bit and dug deeper into the data: child population was healthy; deaths, infections, and disease were low; rents were reasonable. All good things. She suggested that instead of cooking up plans to revamp the neighborhood, he should get down there and appreciate and learn from it. He had to admit that he often visited that neighborhood to get a dose of "the wonderful, cheerful street life." Nevertheless, he doubled down on his first take—that it was a terrible slum.

It's a spurious if not masochistic conclusion. He was saying, without irony, that he had no choice but to rid the streets of cheerful people. It would be easy to dismiss him as a hapless bureaucrat from a bygone time who missed the point. Still, it's a timeless lesson. Swooping in with solutions—well-intentioned or not—often ends in misguided decisions if only because it misses the beauty on the ground.

In this little slice of the world, history played that out. While Jane was busy exploring the streets of Boston in the late 1950s, a lengthy planned expressway had just been built alongside the North End. Less than fifty years later, it was gone. The North End, in all its messy glory, is still there. It's not immune to waves of gentrification, but the family-run restaurants, social clubs, old brick buildings, and ricotta pie—they're all intact.

From the sidewalk, Jane Jacobs—a gutsy, self-educated Canadian-American journalist who turned the field of urban planning on its ear by pulling power away from grand bureaucratic plans toward community self-sufficiency—was able to glimpse a neighborhood taking care of itself. It was formed by gumption and happenstance, not overarching schemes. Mixed-use blocks meant people bumped into each other—it was hard not to get to know your neighbors. Close quarters and squat buildings meant that anything going on in the street was plain to see—people couldn't help but look out for each other. Sidewalks, storefronts, churches, and gardens gave space to share culture and joy. The planner's problems were the neighborhood's gifts.

In retrospect, the harmony that Jacobs saw was obvious, but obvious is easy to miss when you're in the middle of it. Emotions, agenda, expertise, and distraction conspire against seeing what's there. But she was militantly aware of both what was in front of her and what might be hiding it from view. That's how she saw the harmony that the city planners couldn't. She saw the intangible interconnections that often slip by unnoticed.

> The way to get at what goes on in the seemingly
> mysterious and perverse behavior of cities is, I think, to
> look closely, and with as little previous expectation as
> is possible, at the most ordinary scenes and events, and
> attempt to see what they mean and whether any threads
> of principle emerge among them.*

Removing expectations is Jacobs's tactic to get around assumptions, to make the familiar unfamiliar and watch what bubbles up; to appreciate, not impose.

What you might borrow from Jane Jacobs is a willingness to sit with what's right in front of us. Be patient by shedding assumptions. See the beauty of life playing itself out. Appreciate things long enough to reveal the lessons of what is and what could be. Be willing, not to be a hero, but to harness the power of being a witness.

* As Jane Jacobs wrote in her 1961 book, *The Death and Life of Great American Cities.*

173

Learn from Love

It's one year later: 1960. Jane Goodall is living in the jungle with her mom. Her British backers refused to take responsibility for a young woman living on her own, mingling with wild animals in the wilderness of what was then known as Tanganyika in East Africa. She hadn't even been to college yet. (Incidentally, she never would go. A couple of years later, she'd skip right to a PhD.)

On her first week onsite, she violated rule number one. She'll regret it for some time, yet her discovery couldn't have happened without it. She fed the animals. If you're out for a walk in the park, you don't feed the animals. When you're studying chimps in their natural habitat—you do not feed the animals. But she did.

Somewhere along the line, she violated rule number two. She named the chimps. Naming subjects is not scientific, but she named them. There was Flint, Fifi, Frodo, Goliath, Passion, Humphrey, Mr. McGregor, David Greybeard, and Mike. Later on, they—the press, the scientific community—would skewer her over this blunder and use it to undermine her credibility.

She was not off to a good start. The chimps wanted nothing to do with her. Weeks in, she had done a lot of looking but had nothing to show for it.

Slowly, her mistakes started to pay off, in the way only good mistakes can. Little by little, the chimps snuck over for a nibble. Little by little, they began to lose their fear of her. One in particular, David Greybeard, started to hang out near her camp. One day he waltzed over and sat down on a termite mound. (Termites are delicious.) She watched him pluck a blade of grass, shove it into the top of the mound, and bring it to his lips.

Goodall had just spotted a nonhuman modifying nature to make a tool. She was the first person in the western scientific community to call it out. Her discovery violated one of the big misconceptions of science at the time—that humans were nature's only toolmaker. Her observation was not quite as radical, but it came close to a Copernicus-like, "the Earth revolves around the sun" kind of moment. So much so, her mentor Louis Leakey declared, "Now we must redefine tool, redefine man [*sic*], or accept chimpanzees as humans."

Why was she the first to see it? The answer is, she wasn't. Not long after, Jane spoke to indigenous people living in the region. She found, not surprisingly, that they were well aware of this behavior. They had no trouble noticing animals making tools. It was only people outside that world who missed it. Why? Perhaps the indigenous communities had an appreciation that is not typically cultivated in industrialized cultures. Or, perhaps, knowledge got in the way.

What people see is always a reflection of their past experience. When you're confronting the familiar, taking advantage of past experience is great. It's a benefit. It helps you navigate. But as soon as the context shifts or the unexpected creeps in, assumptions can get in the way of noticing the possibilities right in front of you. Finding opportunity in the familiar or even in the frightening can feel alienating—you're pushing against past tendencies. It can also feel boring and fruitless. Nothing comes for a while. And then, much like staring at a painting for hours, it pays off.

It also paid off because Goodall did all the wrong things, like naming and feeding the chimps—later, she even held their hands. In short, she didn't leave her empathy at the door—she led with it. And with love. That was not science. That *is* not science. Science isn't mushy. Science is not supposed to include empathy. Empathy clouds objectivity.

But for Jane Goodall, the lauded and revered primatologist, empathy and love are not the enemy of discovery; they are its fuel. They motivate you to look, push you to see more fully. She even goes one step further, saying in a 2020 interview with Krista Tippet: "The cold, scientific approach, I believe, has led to a lot of suffering on this planet."

Work done well is often a love story. Kat Holmes has spent her career creating inclusive designs—designs that work for as many people as possible, regardless of age, race, or ability. "Love," she writes in her book, *Mismatch*, "is a common trait in the creation of inclusive solutions." And they are often inspired by "a mismatch that loved ones faced when something interrupted their connection to each other."

Holmes points out that an early version of the typewriter was invented so that a blind countess could send clandestine notes to her inventor lover without having to dictate them to another person—the usual way people without sight put words to page in the early 1800s. Email was in part inspired to connect two people who were hard of hearing. The telephone was too.

Love inspires. Let it. We'll never be able to create a fabulous future if we can't first fall in love with the present.

Mind the Gap(s)

It's a decade or so later—the mid-1970s. Jane Fulton Suri is in Glasgow, Scotland, walking through the shadows of Red Road Flats, a cluster of eight thirty-story concrete tower blocks in the brutalist style spaced around a large green, already descending into disarray despite being only a handful of years old.

Fulton Suri heard some unexpected sounds amid the looming towers: squeaks and giggles. She found the source—a pack of ten-year-old boys taking turns riding atop a boiler room door while others shoved it back and forth. It was one of the few spots in this massive complex where they could swing and make noise.

Without proper playgrounds, kids growing up in Red Road Flats found clever ways to entertain themselves. They played rounds of "chap door run away" (ding dong ditch), tossed footballs (soccer balls) from high-rise windows, goofed around in the lifts (elevators), and batted squash balls against the concrete walls and gables. They made the most of a place that didn't take them into account.

Life is filled with before-and-after moments. Not all are spectacular. And it's not always clear why one moment offers an inkling of something more and another just passes by. Sometimes it's just a matter of stopping to look, letting the subconscious mingle with circumstance, and getting lucky enough to catch on.

Luck is, in part, a symptom of attention. In the late 1990s and early 2000s, psychology professor (and amateur magician) Richard Weismann gave copies of the same newspaper to two groups of people—one who saw themselves as lucky and the other as unlucky. He asked them to count the photos inside. The unlucky people took a few minutes. The lucky ones did it in a matter of seconds because they noticed what was written in sprawling two-inch-tall type on page 2: "Stop counting—There are 43 photographs in this newspaper." The folks who considered themselves unlucky skimmed right past the text as they counted every photo, while the relaxed, curious attention of the lucky-identifying group landed them a quick reward. The takeaway: Though much luck is circumstantial and beyond control, a calm mood and keen attention increase the chances of finding opportunities—especially ones hidden in plain sight.

Fulton Suri was having one of those moments. Her attentional luck told her there was something more—or something missing. Someone had hacked something here.

The boys, having fun, possibly wrecking the door in the process, had been overlooked. Fulton Suri couldn't help but wonder, "Had anyone thought about the needs of ten-year-old boys in designing this housing complex?" The answer had to be no. The design of this grand housing block did not acknowledge that these kids might need a place to play, climb, or test their limits. Nevertheless, here they were laughing while they took turns riding the door.

Don Ihde, technoscience philosopher and scribe of the ongoing love affair between people and technology, calls this kind of creative reuse the "designer fallacy," the false idea that a designer's intent can really determine a design's use. Instead, people find what's there and put it to work. If something can be used to do something, it will be. These cues are also called "affordances." A fence with horizontal backer rails becomes a ladder. A swinging door is also a ride.

There's something hopeful on display here too: the relent-lessness of joy. We make homes in the flaws. We nestle into the mistakes. We build our future in the gaps.

The sight of those young boys was Fulton Suri's first step on a quest to have everyday interactions guide the things people make. Her idea, shared in her book, *Thoughtless Acts?*, was to "reveal how unexceptional incidents, looked at from an inquisi-tive stance, can inspire." And that "curiosity will reveal meaning behind these non-spectacular interactions that take place around us all the time." Curiosity creates possibility.

In noticing the profundity of a mundane situation, Jane Fulton Suri—soft-spoken, genius at large, and one of the key developers of human-centered design methods—had picked up on something else. She had learned to see a gap.

A gap is when things are out of whack and relationships between people and things don't work quite right. The world is filled with gaps (just to name a few):

A gap in understanding is called confusion.

A gap between ideals and actions is called hypocrisy.

A gap between what we create and what is healthy is called pollution.

A gap between what you know and what is possible is called ignorance.

A gap between what you try to do and what you are able to do is called difficulty.

A gap between need and access is called inequity.

A gap between something wasteful and something useful is called opportunity.

A gap between what is and what could be is called a possibility.

Being able to see these gaps is not a magic trick, but it is a trick of discovery. It's a job for attention, not invention. (And maybe a little bit of luck.) And once you find a gap, you shouldn't let it go, at least not right away. Instead, decide, thoughtfully, whether it's a gap to fill or one to leave alone.

(Un)Predictable

In a world where AI can draw accurate predictions from limited data, what new gaps could it reveal? And how should we fill those gaps? What might they disrupt or amplify?

"Glowing Cherries, Gold Facades, and Elephant Dung—On the Case with KDL"*

It was three days until the next murder. It would be Kena Dubb-Lakin's twelfth. The peculiar thing this time around was the sheer number of cherry pickers lining the street—eight big bucket trucks, mechanical arms extended, each hoisting a person in its basket. The burly arms reached deep into the alleyways that lined the narrow street along a one-block slice of the city's borough. Mechanical twitches and squeaky metal scrapes echoed around the neighborhood.

Atop the cherry pickers, hired hands squeezed oversized burnt-red beach balls into the wide gaps between the buildings. Each tremendous, bulbous sculpture housed a solar-powered lantern inside a tentlike frame, wrapped in rubber. Installed in triplets, the humongous balls looked like giant maraschinos squished atop an ice cream sundae of buildings, bursting and dripping around the edges of every roof, shedding enough light to illuminate the alleys and streets below.

Kena—best known by her initials, KDL—was up in one of the baskets, jamming a gigantic, glowing ball into place like everyone else, despite being their ringleader. Given the rambunctious nature of her interventions, you might expect a flamboyant, Willy Wonka—like carnival barker donning a purple suit, but her style is backstage, not front of house. Overalls and boots. Glittering gold paint on her sleeves. Bandana across her forehead, slightly tamed hair flowing

---

* This story first appeared in *The Grey Area*, June 2028.

every which way out the back, top, and sides. Unkempt. Giggly. Nervous. Comfortable with a mess. More Rosie the Riveter than P. T. Barnum.

To the outside world, the initials KDL carry the aura of an oracle who helms a theater troupe, and rightfully so: she seems to have an uncanny knack for altering the future. These spectacles, like the giant cherry lanterns, are attempts at the impossible. KDL is out to thwart murders—before they occur.

Her work relies on an artificial neural network that spits out crime predictions narrowed down to a city block, within a day's window, all delivered one week ahead. (Notably, it can't predict the perpetrators—just a time and place.) As creepy as it all sounds, murders turn out to be a lot easier to forecast than the weather—the AI's predictions are 95 percent accurate. When a prediction comes down the pipe, KDL races to the time and place where the murder is supposed to go down. At that point, her work is to do something severely out of the ordinary that creates a spectacle big enough to get people to break their routines and alter the events of the day. (Hence the giant maraschino cherry–like lanterns.) If the murder predictions are 95 percent right, her interventions are 100 percent effective. Not one murder has come to fruition after she and her crew have shown up.

But as successful as she's been—if all goes well, she will soon be twelve for twelve—her work gets plenty of criticism. She wholeheartedly agrees with it—and adds her own.

"If some machine network can predict happenings, does that mean fate is a real thing? If it does, then we're disrupting fate. That's cosmic. What if we stop one crime and it sets up another, worse thing down the road? We might save a baby Hitler. Maybe it's happened already. We have no idea—we can't predict that quite yet," she says, with a forced laugh.

In the few short months of mounting interventions, she's found plenty of novel ways to thwart fate. She's airlifted an elephant onto a city street; painted a building head to toe in shiny gold; built treehouse-style structures on out-of-service telephone poles; organized midnight parades; constructed a five-story, building-hugging tube slide from the top of a fire escape; and installed various incarnations of hanging, floating lanterns (one of her favorites).

Her work may come off as magical, but the reality is awkward. She and her crew drop into a community and try to convince them to do something very odd, all inside a week. Doing weird things is hard work. Working with people is hard work. She's quickly learned how important—and difficult—it is to cocreate in a community.

She calls up regrets with aplomb: "Doing something temporary and making something permanent are totally different problems." Take the airdropped elephant. The elephant landed safely, the neighborhood had fun, and another murder didn't come to pass. Nonetheless, she teeters uncomfortably back and forth when she talks about it. "Elephants are big. And dangerous. The trainers can be brutal. I guess you could say it worked, but we won't do that again." She does end on a high note: "The kids loved the giant poop piles, though—maybe even more than the helicopter."

There is no shortage of skeptics. Many worry that most murders happen during heated moments in the home, not on the street. So far, her routine-breaking schemes seem to halt indoor murders too, but time will tell if she's really thwarted or just delayed the domestic ones. The specter of these shortfalls wears on her, and there is plenty more criticism to go around: that she's spending too much on temporary solutions, swooping in to save rather than engaging communities to repair, and taking care of symptoms without addressing real causes upstream. In short, she's not helping the community help itself.

"It's all true," she agrees, but draws a distinction. "We're like a fire truck coming in to put out a fire. That doesn't mean that things that cause fires don't need attention. But even if the wiring in a building should have been redone, the fire department is still going to put out a faulty wire fire. That's us. We just put out 'fires' before they happen." The analogy isn't random—both her parents were firefighters.

She's also been busy setting up volunteer fire department-style citizens brigades in hopes of helping communities fund their own interventions. But—at least for her, and at least for now—what she's up to is a lot better than other ways of doing it, like overpolicing in neighborhoods already heavy with arrests, or doing nothing at all.

While existential questions and never-ending critique might flood her thoughts, they don't seem to change her actions too much. As soon as the last lantern is stuffed into the top of the last alley, she will move on to the next location. She keeps at it. She can't not.

The result is messy, beautiful, onerous—and hard to argue with. Someday, her work may not be needed. For now, she will go on testing fate and upending crime in her own weird way, a reluctant superhero thwarting potential murders with huge glowing lanterns, shiny gold buildings, treehouses, and tube slides—if not elephant dung.

A recent machine-learning model can predict when and where a violent crime will happen down to a three-day window within a couple of city blocks, a week ahead. This is not a garden-variety "crime prediction" algorithm built on past arrest data. It can predict actual individual crimes with greater than 80 percent accuracy.

This nascent ability to predict the future raises questions about fate (which may or may not have been in the minds of those who cooked up the model). Prediction machines like these suggest fate exists not by the will of gods, but by patterns playing themselves out. It also seems that by revealing fate, we can change it. But should we? Who gets to decide? How should we intervene? And, as we do—and you know we will—what new fates might those disruptions create? What gaps might we find, and how will we fill them? Will we seize the opportunity to unwind past mistakes or thoughtlessly amplify them yet again?

Before acting on predictions, we can take a breath, consider, call out, and put a name to what we hope they might help make happen.

Call Out What's Missing

Sometimes we don't know what we don't know. But often we can feel when there's something missing and we feel a bit nervous, uncomfortable, or awkward (there it is again) about naming it. People have feelings for a reason. The possible terror lurking in the unknown is real. But if we sit with it rather than react, we might find treasure beyond the terror. Giving words to those feelings and gaps—even imaginary ones—can help.

In Other Words

In high school, my friend George and I kept an informal dictionary. We'd add new words—phrases too—as they came to us. We never wrote them down, but we referred to them often. I can't remember many, but one does stick out: "in it," meaning being so absorbed in a moment that you forget yourself.

The words were all like that—things we experienced but didn't quite have a way to capture how they felt or what they meant to us. We loved coming up with these other words. They helped fill in blanks we weren't taught to pay attention to, and they shone a light on the things that mattered to us but we couldn't express otherwise.

Just calling out these missing words can give shape to things that shouldn't stay hidden. They help give form to intangible gaps and burgeoning connections and provide permission to consider things in a new way. They help reveal useful secrets that linger in other words.

As you investigate a concept or phenomena, try exploring its meaning in other languages. I asked borderline polyglot and Stanford design alumna Sonya Kotov about the word *awkward* in other languages. Sonya speaks English, Russian, German, Spanish, and some Arabic and French. She locked onto German and said the language doesn't really have a word for awkward. It has *komisch* (comically odd or strange) and *unangenehm* (uncomfortable in a negative way). Our English *awkward* seems to live (awkwardly) somewhere between the two.

My colleague Leticia Britos Cavagnaro, a lover of chatbots and pedagogical experiments, discussed the concept of awkwardness with a comparative linguist friend who, like Leticia, was also born in Uruguay. She shared that in Spanish she'd use the word *raro*, or maybe *extrañeza*, if the feeling contained some neutral surprise, or even *inesperado*, if there was something quietly sinister and unexpected about it. After further thought, Leticia said, "This makes me think that there is an interesting

183

distinction to explore: Where is awkwardness located . . . inside the person or outside, as part of the context or environment? Do different languages assign this location differently? Does this matter if you want to use awkwardness as a signal that can help you discover things?"

Making us pause to think about a concept in a way that we might not otherwise have done is exactly the point. It allows us to uncover new layers to our noticing. Whether they be comical or informative or serious, exploring definitions and usages for words in other languages—or even in imaginary ones—helps us articulate and understand the human experience. Each new definition is an added lens that helps us see things that are hard to put words to. To see the unseeable, we need new words to describe:

Feelings that lead us astray

How to disagree and get along at the same time

How we do great things and make mistakes all at once

Dreams that aren't just big, but full: dreams of dreams, with room for everybody

Lingering issues that are the fault of no one living right now but need to be taken care of anyway

The disappointment (and liberation) that comes with knowing things won't ever be fully fixed

The part where it's going to get worse before it gets better

Not just tossing ideas into the world but also shepherding them through their life cycle

What other words do we need?

Name Your Monsters

If you don't know how to name the mess you're in, try drawing it as a monster instead. Monsters are great because nobody can tell you you've got the likeness wrong. They can be amalgamations of real and imagined fears or hopes and dreams, and drawing them isn't just for kids. Maritime maps, especially in the seventeenth century, usually had monsters on them. Many look half-fish, part whale, semi-dragon, mermaid-esque. More often than not, they arise from the seas.

These monsters represent the fears of the mapmaker and the seafarer. They stand for the unknown, the scary, the potentially

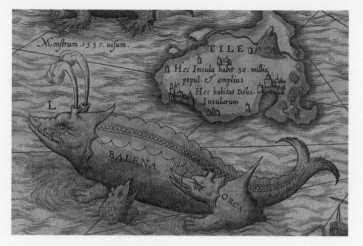

Carta Marina by Olaus Magnus, c. 1539

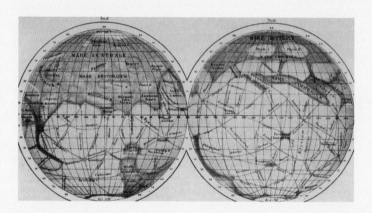

Chart of the Planet Mars by Giovanni Schiaparelli. Is there life there?

dangerous. In that era of ocean exploration, the location and existence of land masses was rudimentary, as were many of the creatures in the sea. While it's easy to look at medieval monsters with four hundred years of perspective and chuckle at the awkward anatomy of the artistic renditions, we can appreciate their honesty. The ocean was a treacherous place for a wooden ship navigating by the stars to a continent that may or may not exist. Sailors may have had a glimpse of a whale, sunfish, or squid but far from a comprehensive understanding of marine biology. Mapmakers didn't ignore those fears; they gave them shape, life, and prominence. "Here be dragons!"

Sometimes monsters represent fear; other times, fascination. Look at the 1898 map by Giovanni Schiaparelli: *Chart of the*

Planet Mars. Do you see the light-colored geometric areas interspersed with a network of dark, straight lines? Do these appear to be natural features, or created by an intelligent being?

These canali (canals) of Mars are an example of collective apophenia around the end of the nineteenth century when shadows visible in telescopes were presumed to be Martian-made structures. They—and by proxy—their implied and intelligent Martian creators, are depicted on numerous other maps of the planet by Schiaparelli. It wasn't just him; astronomer Percival Lowell, well-known for discovering Pluto, seeded and fueled speculation that intelligent life was thriving on our next-door neighbor in space with his own canal-laden maps of Mars. Aliens! Smart ones—not far from us in space. For some, monsters to be feared; for others, potential new friends.

Many scientists were skeptical, but Lowell's ideas found a following. His 1916 obituary in the *New York Times* reads, "The present judgment of the scientific world is that he was too largely governed in his researches by a vivid imagination. But he interested in the study of astronomy a large number of persons who would never have been attracted to it by the achievements of his more practical contemporaries." Even in his delusions, Lowell's imaginary monsters gave people something to grab on to. They said, "There's something to know here! Explore it! Build on it!"

The possibility of intelligent life on Mars lingered in the global psyche until as recently as 1965, when Mariner 4 did the first near photo flyby that proved otherwise. Mariner 4's pictures revealed a crater-pocked planet with a moonlike surface. But Lowell, with his monsters that looked like Martians collaborating to construct canals, had tapped a fascination fueled by the unknown that is still being built upon today. Martian life may not be intelligent, but it may exist. It's presently being chased by a new rover, Perseverance, which is studying rock records of the lakes that once persisted on the surface of the planet. Martian monsters may end up looking more like microbes than builders of Schiaparelli's and Lowell's constructed canals.

There's an old rule of thumb: "When in doubt, leave it out"—don't depend on something you're not sure of. But sometimes the thing you're missing is exactly what you should be examining. Try flipping the saying on its head: "When in doubt, call it out!"—mark your unknown monsters like those old mapmakers did. The canal-shaped map monsters on Mars inspired interest in space exploration and science. The grotesque fish monsters of the seventeenth-century maps highlighted the

Might these be Martian microbe monsters?

unknown and possibly dangerous waters. What sort of exploration will your unknown map monsters spark? In his book *A Guide for the Perplexed*, freethinking and underdog-loving economist E. F. Schumaker described the rewards of calling out the unknown:

> *If I limit myself to knowledge that I consider true beyond doubt, I minimize the risk of error but I maximize, at the same time, the risk of missing out on what may be the subtlest, most important and most rewarding things in life.*

Hard-to-know things are worth getting to know, even if we'll never fully grasp them. Scary things are worth calling out; pretending they don't exist gives them cover to show up later and fails to warn others where they might be lurking. Giving shape to your fears and fascinations allows you to talk about, document, and investigate them. Whether rooted in scientific pursuit or fantastical belief, map monsters are inspirational. They are jumping-off points. They are a manifestation of our humility and humanity. By naming our monsters, you allow the next explorer to navigate more easily.

Past monsters need the light of day, too, so they don't come back to haunt us. Around the start of the 1900s, the Canadian government set out to build the world's longest bridge to span the width of the St. Lawrence River. As it was being built, the half-finished bridge collapsed under the weight of shoddy engineering, cut corners, and big egos.

A few years later, a group of engineers got together in Montreal to create a code of ethics in response. To this day, everyone who pledges to follow the code gets an iron ring to put on the pinky finger of their drawing hand. Back in the days of drafting on paper, that made sure the ring would drag along the drafting board as they worked—a scratchy reminder of their obligation to keep people safe. The ring was designed to allow the engineers to keep the real purpose of their work in mind in the face of tight deadlines and budget crunches. (Legend has it that the early rings were forged from the remains of that fallen bridge.)

Don't be afraid to name the unknown. What is the monster in the topic you're working on? What would it look like if you drew it? Draw it! Add it to your next presentation, or paper, or share it in conversation with a colleague. Use your monsters to inspire others to continue pursuits that will outlive you. Calling them out for others is public duty. It's easier to nurture (or avoid) them later if you give them shape now.

. . . .

Design is a process of discovery. Ideas begin, remedies come out of hiding, and opportunities step into the light only when you take the time to sit with and question things. Uncovering gaps like this takes discipline—it asks you to look at trouble to reveal possibility. To even begin to discover what's been overlooked, you have to examine everything, even the parts you didn't think were part of it. The work can be boring and tedious or unsettling and awkward. You have to push against your instincts to ignore the familiar, your impatience to move on, and your uncertainty about what may or may not be useful.

But noticing alone is not enough. Putting a name to the things you find—and the things you might be missing—is essential. This is how observations turn into possibilities. What's needed but not realized? Where else does nature already have a solution? Who has been left out? Notice it and name it. But even that is just the beginning.

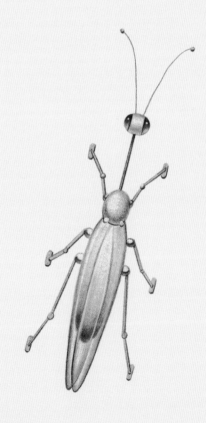

CHAPTER 6

Shapeshift

Keep Changing
(Even If It Slows You Down)

All that you touch / You Change. // All that you Change /
Changes you. // The only lasting truth / Is Change. // God / Is Change.

—*Octavia E. Butler,* Parable of the Sower

Intentional or not, the modern era has been, in many ways,
a quest for sameness: globalized markets, monoculture
crops, standardized protocols. We need some sameness: it
puts food on the table, helps people coordinate, and helps ideas
spread. It's efficient.

But sameness spreads trouble too, at an alarming pace. In
the last three hundred years, biodiversity has plummeted. We're
in the middle of the sixth mass extinction of species in the
last five hundred million years. Cultural diversity has nose-
dived alongside. A language goes extinct every few weeks. And
ideadiversity—a new word I just made up to capture flexibility
of thought—may be at an all-time low as present-day politics
and policies cement us into binary choices and media becomes
a copy-paste perpetuation of borrowed memes and knee-jerk
reactions. To think differently, we need to cultivate different
ways to think.

We call the nimble switching across ways of thinking and
doing *shapeshifting*. To shapeshift requires pushing the fringes

of our disciplines and experience and exploring where they overlap with others. This breeds possibility, and we need as much possibility as we can get.

Sameness Is the Anti-Shapeshifter

Runaway design is out to eat your breakfast. Today, when you peel a banana and slice it into a bowl of cereal, you're likely eating a variety called Cavendish, scientifically known as *Musa acuminata × balbisiana*. Ninety-nine percent of the world's exported bananas are Cavendish. That's about fifty billion tons in a given year—and half of the bananas eaten in the world. They are a hardy breed that can be picked green and shipped globally before ripening. The banana supply chain is designed and optimized specifically to make Cavendish bananas accessible around the world, and an unintended consequence of that efficiency is homogeneity—monoculture.

Think of monoculture as the big-box store that takes out the mom-and-pop shops. With the big box comes efficiency and accessibility, but the nuance and diversity of a variety of smaller shops vanishes.

Bananas are critical to the world beyond being a breakfast boost in the West (note, Americans eat almost twice as many pounds of bananas as apples per year). Globally, they are the fourth most important crop, following rice, wheat, and corn. They are a vital source of nutrients in many diets, especially in sub-Saharan Africa. Still, while there are at least a thousand varieties of bananas, each with its own unique flavors, textures, and uses, only the Cavendish is sold in American supermarkets (almost universally). And, because bananas used for food production reproduce asexually through clones, these Cavendishes are all genetically identical. This is an extremely risky situation for a global staple. Can we use technology to fix it?

Banana bioengineering is tricky. Growers experiment to create the perfect hybrids for our lunch boxes, but these hybrids are mules, and mules can't reproduce. The Cavendish can't mate with different bananas to build up robustness in their gene pool. They grow (genetically identical) pups off the base of their stems, and each pup is replanted and propagated.

The banana supply chain has fallen prey to the perils of monoculture and big-box syndrome before. The Gros Michel banana variety, aka Big Mike, a stockier cousin of the Cavendish, reigned supreme at breakfast for a hundred years before a fungal rot called Panama disease raced around the world to decimate the crop in the 1950s. Big Mike's thick skin meant it traveled without bruising and it did well in the global supply chain . . . until it didn't. Diseases have heydays on monocultures.

Faced with the destruction of the world's banana supply, growers reacted by swapping one monoculture for another.* Instead of diversifying banana supply, which is certainly more logistically and operationally complex, the Cavendish subbed in. Cavendish can be picked green and travels well too. It isn't as flavorful as the Gros Michel, but it was (initially) resistant to Panama disease.

* Explore what our future cuisine might taste like in "Cassava with a Side of Crickets" (page 238).

Now, seventy-five years later, a new strain of Panama disease called TR4 is threatening the Cavendish, already having made its way through Southeast Asia and Australia en route to Central America. But there's hope—some growers and scientists are shapeshifting.

Belgium, a country where no bananas grow in the wild, is home to the world's biggest banana collection in test tubes—a banana gene bank called Bioversity International Musa Transit Centre at the University of Leuven. The goal is to study, store, and publish information on banana genes to support cultivation and promote shapeshifting through genetic diversification.

Farther south, the Centre Africain de Recherches sur Bananiers et Plantain (CARBAP) is also home to the world's largest field-grown banana collection. CARBAP's plants are shared with farmers so they may experiment with and test them among their own crops in their plots. They're trying to develop a new variety that's resistant to disease but also appealing to eat. It's shapeshifting through prototyping, finding a solution through trial and error.

Of course, monocrops are just one symptom of globalization—they also homogenize culture. That's a big loss. Places that contain a lot of biodiversity tend to also be places with a lot of cultural and language diversity. Cultural diversity is like biodiversity for the imagination. It promotes possibility and cultivates creativity and care.

Biodiversity and cultural diversity make natural systems resilient. They help systems thrive by filtering and nurturing. When it comes to problem solving, increased cultural diversity is like being able to autocorrect and shapeshift all in one. Social scientists at INSEAD in France and Columbia Business School in the United States have found that people who have close relationships with people from cultures other than their own tend to be more creative, producing both more ideas and more novel ones. Researchers at Tufts University studying mock trial teams have shown that diverse teams also catch errors earlier. Multiple perspectives encourage discernment (particularly among white group members) and help expose issues before decisions get made.

That doesn't mean maintaining diversity is easy. Living with differences can be difficult. But as much as increasing monoculture (in all ways) was an outcome of globalization, an overarching design goal for the present and future has to be to preserve diversity while working across it. Thriving systems in nature do it naturally. It's the secret to their success.

We do it naturally too. We've just forgotten how. The shift between how we've been creating culture in the recent past and how we might do it in the future has to do with power—culture thrives in dynamic conversation, not lopsided dominance—and pace: Strong cultures take time to coalesce. By leaving room for distinct cultures to influence and build on each other, we can learn to nurture ourselves and society back to health. Less efficient, but much more resilient.

Declining cultural diversity also means a global loss of languages, most of them indigenous. The areas where colonization forced resettlement of native populations have lost the most languages, including the United States, South Africa, Australia, and Canada. Increasingly, South American countries, as well as Russia and China, are losing languages too. As the loss of species variety leads to a loss of resilience, the loss of a language means losing the wisdom baked into it.

When a language goes extinct, it takes with it all of its embedded knowledge. If there was a word for the juice of a fruit that helped to tame an upset stomach, when the language is lost, the word is lost, and the knowledge behind it wanes. Considering our ever-faster quest for more connectivity, speed, and search engine power, we're losing languages and their knowledge at an alarming rate. We are shedding wisdom.

We also let languages die because of the way we think of them. Languages benefit us in multiple ways—they help us communicate in the moment *and* they store generations of knowledge. But people often overvalue immediate utility and undervalue long-term wisdom. We treat natural systems like this too. We relish nature as a resource to harvest and forget the timeless wisdom built into its delicate structure. Languages, cultures, ecosystems—they are both timely tools and timeless treasures.

The Librarian

What if we had a way to resurrect extinct languages?

1

Belen figured she'd covered about two miles already, which meant another four to go. At least there weren't too many hills. If she could keep this pace (it felt like twelve minutes a mile, based on the years she'd spent being tracked by a fitness watch), she'd get there just as the light would begin raking through the trees. That, she knew, meant she'd have twenty minutes with enough light to find the plant that might save her patient and the hundreds of thousands like him currently suffering.

2

He wasn't really her patient, but he might as well have been. She didn't have a medical degree, but she did have a doctorate. Of course, no medical doctor ever gave her the time of day in normal (whatever that meant) times, even though the years she'd spent in school and in the field totaled more than most of them. Yet here she was, the one they called when they were stumped. So she was going to take the patient (all the patients) as hers.

His breathing had been shortening for weeks, his ears rang constantly, and his palms itched as if he'd been stung by a hunnybee™ two days prior—periods of calm interspersed with an intolerable sensation that could be quenched only with vigorous scratching, some of which had broken the skin and couldn't heal before the next wave.

3

The plant was called aktam in Akkadian, hasibbur in Kassite, and *Buxus vahlii* in science. In English it was boxwood. Not just any boxwood, though: Vahl's boxwood. And Vahl's boxwood had been thought to be extinct for five years.

The last of it grew in northwestern Puerto Rico, not far from Arecibo, the former site of the observatory she'd admired so much in her teens and early twenties. Arecibo was host to many astronomic pursuits, among them SETI, the Search for Extraterrestrial Intelligence. The giant radio telescope scanned the skies for transmissions from beyond. If an alien civilization was sending signals into the void, trying to find intelligence elsewhere in the universe, they'd "hear" it in Arecibo. The satellite dish was such a draw for her back then that when she visited the island in college under the guise of a spring break beach trip, she made a pilgrimage to the jungley karst to be close to even just the potential of a connection to life beyond Earth. How serendipitous (predestined?), then, that Vahl's boxwood was originally native to the same area.

Belen's fascination with telescopes and the beyond waned after that trip. It was a science she couldn't touch with her hands. It lived in equations and on screens and the occasional photograph and sporadic rocket launch. She needed to touch, understand, deconstruct, and examine. She loved the puzzle of the unknown but needed to solve it in practice, not in theory. SETI hasn't yet found intelligent life beyond Earth, but, in a way, she has.

4

It's a funny thing to claim for a librarian, to have found intelligent life beyond Earth. But a librarian is a funny thing to call her to begin with. The field was perfect for her interests, in hindsight, but she credited her success in it to Ciara, the college botany professor who'd challenged Belen like nobody had before. Ciara encouraged her to study plants, obviously, but also humans. Separately and in concert with one another. Ciara taught her how to read scientific literature from a range of fields and form her own hypotheses with a botanical lens. Ciara nudged her to explore the ancient, the extinct, as well as the modern. "It's not gone but it *is* forgotten," Ciara used to say, hiking on the haziest days to her forest garden to harvest medicinal plants and brew a pot of wild garlic tea to ease asthma in the wheezy-air months.

Ciara encouraged Belen to immerse herself in active forests and examine their dynamics and specifics for herself despite the air-quality limitations. "You won't find anything of substance sitting inside all the time." So Belen ventured out into the forest, visited museums and archives, and had conversations with scholars in any field that interested her. Ciara had given her the confidence and toolset to explore and investigate despite the constraints. Ciara was the mentor who dwarfed all others.

She missed her so much.

And while she initially hovered in medicinal botany, partly fascinated with the healing power of plants like garlic and partly hoping to keep Ciara's legacy alive, it was a trip to the Met, Gallery 403, that ultimately set the trajectory of her career.

5

The world's oldest form of writing, cuneiform, had taken Belen five years of constant study to master. Created by wedges angled together in different ways, cuneiform was captured on clay tablets. Multiple ancient languages used cuneiform, and as she learned them, she began to decipher what life was like in ancient Mesopotamia.

"Why spend your time on something so extinct?" her mom asked with judgmental care. "There's a reason why it isn't used anymore."

At first, she couldn't answer that question. It was intoxicating to hold a piece of clay that was five thousand years old and decipher its message. The puzzle was the thrill. Many of the first notes she translated were receipts. Goats. Sheep. Barley. Documents of trade and economics. As she improved, she read faster, translated or retranslated with more acute precision all types of documentation.

A set of tablets written in Akkadian had set her on course for today's run. These tablets were a medical chronology, a list of ailments and their treatments. Some had clear connections to modern disease. Others were entirely new. Finding knowledge that an ancient civilization had embedded in its canon that was somehow unknown to today's modern medicine was addicting.

The expanse of it stunned her. There were more than seven hundred extinct languages, many of them ancient, each a wormhole to the people who spoke it and their culture, what they valued and what they knew to be true. The afflictions they faced and the medicines that cured them. Each language was a portal to intelligent life beyond present-day Earth.

And with that, Belen's purpose had clicked. Chief librarian. Library of Extinct Languages. Humans, in all their haste, had forgotten themselves and so much of what they already knew because they failed to notice, to protect, to record. Her patient, and all the others, were lying in hospitals near death from an ailment that was survivable in the twenty-third century CE with treatment from a medicinal plant.

6

She didn't want to be running anymore. She wanted the pace to slow. She needed more from each breath. Her running pace, and the pace of life. But hasn't that always been the case? Everyone at every point in human history has felt that life moves too quickly. They anguish, and then they accommodate. They find corners to cut, ways to become more productive and efficient. And at what cost? So much knowledge had been lost in the name of efficiency. Her patient was dying in the name of efficiency.

Languages are another casualty of globalization, colonization, and a quest for efficiency. When we lose the knowledge within a language, we end up repeating mistakes and reinventing rather than learning and evolving. Despite admirable efforts by some to record and preserve them, they are slipping away. If we trained our AIs on endangered languages, we may actually preserve more than words.

Shapeshift with New Connections

To find ways to thrive, we need to become nimble at working with, not against, differences. Connecting diverse things—be it people, systems, or ideas—can feel like a tall order, but it is not unprecedented. The natural world nimbly connects distinct elements in unexpected ways, such that one thing's waste is another's dinner. But these connections are indirect—we may or may not be used to seeing them. Step one is to let go of old narratives and find inspiration in everyday intersections, overlaps, and patterns.

The Biomimicry Institute's 2021 Ray of Hope prize recipient was an organization called Spintex. Its goal is to produce silk fiber as spiders do, to massively cut down on the waste produced by the global fashion industry. Presently, fiber production for synthetic fabrics like polyester, Lycra, and rayon is an energy-intensive process that requires high heat and water, and produces waste like microplastics. We can make ourselves look fashionable and feel good in these fabrics, but with the speed of fast fashion today, garment waste from all parts of the fashion cycle is a big problem. Spintex is using technology learned from spiders to create new silk that is a thousand times more energy efficient than our current systems. Spider bodies store a liquid protein gel. As they spin their webs, the gel turns solid through the sheer force of being pulled through a small opening. Spintex biomimicked this technology and is developing sustainable, technical fabrics.

Concrete is the single most popular building material in the world. It's all over the place. And no matter how precisely it gets mixed and cured, it's no match for the wear and tear of reality. Throughout its two-thousand-plus years in use, gravity, weather, and shifting ground eventually crack it. Cracks lead to leaks, corrosion, and eventually, collapse. Making concrete is also carbon intensive, so less repair and replacement cut down on greenhouse emissions.

A group at the Netherlands' University of Delft added a little bacteria and calcium lactate (the bacteria's food) to a concrete mix. Once the concrete sets, the bacteria lie dormant until the cracks and resulting leaks set off a chain reaction. Rainwater releases the food, the food feeds the bacteria, the bacteria grow to fill the open cracks, and when the bacteria hit air, they harden to heal the crack. Cracks are inevitable, but healing gets mixed into the solution.

Examine the connections around you. Look at the interfaces, the borders between materials in the natural world. How does the tree cling to the rock? How does the lizard walk up the wall? How does the ocean meet the land? Look too at the interfaces in the human-made world. How do the tires interact with the pavement? How does the payment transfer between accounts, the pen mark the paper? Looking for connections will spark new ideas, new possibilities.

Shapeshift Your Imagination

Big primary metaphors run through eras and cultures, usually linked to whatever technology (or religious practice) is in vogue.* During the early industrial age, many things were compared to machines: Nature works like a machine, the body is a machine, cities are machines. With the internet, networks became the metaphor du jour. These big analogies should not be taken lightly. Sweeping metaphors impact how we think *and* how we act.

The history of health care is a striking illustration of how big primary metaphors both constrain and unlock thinking and doing. In the early days, the metaphor for bodily health was the spirit world. If everything was divine will, there was little reason to investigate the body for remedies, and people didn't. Eventually, the Greeks started comparing bodies to the elements—still a bit mystical, but with a hint of natural science. They started looking at what they called "humors," the body's liquids—black bile, yellow bile, phlegm, and blood, each relating to a metaphorical element: earth, fire, water, or air. Thinking in humors connected the metaphorical and the physical, brought more attention to the body, and started to downplay the mysticism (at least a bit).

As off base as it was, the humors metaphor got people investigating physical sources of ailments, a big step toward modern medicine. Of course, other metaphors cycled through. Years later, the "body as a machine" metaphor came along, highlighting things like parts and pieces, fluids and mechanics, and downplaying more holistic points of view like complexity, change, and balance.

Metaphors help shift your thinking. They are like a travel agent for your imagination. They give you an itinerary to imagine things in another way.

I first learned about metaphors in Ms. Andelman's second-grade English unit. We spent days on the difference between metaphors and similes. Back then, and for a long time

* "Blue Dot" (page 104) grapples with the tangled-up overlaps between technology and religious practice.

after, I thought of metaphors only as a writing and talking trick—a fancy way to communicate.

Around that same time (back in the mid-1980s), two psychologists, Dedre Gentner and Donald Gentner, ran a study with high school kids who weren't up to speed on the inner workings of electrical circuits.

Each kid got one of two quick lessons. One lesson taught them to think about electricity like the flow of water: Water flows through pipes, electricity flows through wires; in batteries, volts are kind of like water pressure; and so on. The other lesson taught students to picture electricity like a moving crowd: Individuals move around, and gates slow them down the same way resistors slow electrons.

After the lesson, they gave the kids two tests, each designed to favor one or the other kind of metaphorical thinking. As Gentner and Gentner predicted, the electricity-equals-crowds metaphor group did better on concepts that were highlighted in that metaphor (like how resistors slow electricity the same way gates slow crowds), and the electricity-equals-water-flow crew did better on the concepts that particular metaphor called out (like how batteries work by flowing energy from one place to another, similar to a river).

The study showed that metaphors are not just for communication. Analogies give us ways to think—they might even be *the* way we think.

Comparisons show up all through our thoughts. In their book *Metaphors We Live By* (which reads with the rhythm of a research paper written by Jack Kerouac), a duo of cognitive science philosophers, George Lakoff and Mark Johnson, laid out how analogies shape the way we imagine and interpret. One example they use is how we apply the metaphors of up and down to diverse situations:

Happy is up; sad is down: That boosted my spirits. Thinking about her always gives me a lift. I'm feeling down. He's really low these days.

Conscious is up; unconscious is down: Get up. I'm up already. He rises early in the morning. He fell asleep. He's under hypnosis. He sank into a coma.

Rational is up; emotional is down: The discussion fell to the emotional level, but I raised it back up to the rational plane. We put feelings aside and had a high-level discussion. He couldn't rise above his emotions.*

* This list has been condensed for space. Check out Lakoff and Johnson's book *Metaphors We Live By* for a host of other examples.

Metaphors mold our thinking even when we're not thinking about them. Our streams of thought are so intertwined that we hardly notice how much we think by association. You may not think about the direction "up" when you talk about being in "high spirits," but it's there.

These metaphorical musings aren't arbitrary. They stem from culture and experience. Our bodies tend to droop when we're melancholy (or "feeling down"), and we tend to sit or stand upright when we're feeling exuberant (or "feeling up"). Our experience affects how we feel, what we do, and how we perceive.

Get rejected and left out in the cold by a friend, and you're more likely to want to eat something warm like soup. Sit in a hard chair, and you're less likely to compromise (and more likely to act like a hard-ass). Hold a warm beverage, and you're more likely to feel that the stranger next to you has a warm personality; hold an iced one, and you're just as likely to think that they're a little cold. Remembering a guilty moment? Wash your hands and you might wash away the guilt too.

This strange set of tendencies comes from a set of studies by John Bargh, a Yale professor and acronym wrangler. His lab's name, Automaticity in Cognition, Motivation, and Evaluation, goes by the memorable acronym: ACME. He and his lab mates design experiments to track how physical experiences leak into mental states. Metaphors must come from somewhere. It makes sense they would relate to experience, but the way some map directly to physical sensations is beyond bizarre.

That these things affect us like they do is freaky. How it happens is even weirder. Robert Sapolsky, the Stanford neuroendocrinologist (studier of brain hormones) who lectures like a standup comedian working out material, digs into what's going on in our brains in his book *Behave*. The connection between physical feelings and metaphorical musings turns out to be an evolutionary fluke. Evolution doesn't start from scratch; it borrows, co-opts, builds on, and improvises. And those improvisations leave behind peculiar patterns.

A great example of evolution's strange trails is the simple act of bending one finger. You'd think it's as straightforward as the brain directing *Move that finger*. It's not. First, one part of the brain tells all five fingers of a hand to move. Then another part says, *Except don't move those other four*. That's because our pawed and clawed evolutionary ancestors usually moved all five digits at once. Evolution had to add on the *don't move those other ones* circuit to let us move just one. At that point in our evolution, it was the easiest way to make it work.

Metaphors do something similar. They use old brain wiring to do new things. According to Sapolksy, the neurons that handle physical pain—in a part of the brain called the cortical anterior cingulate cortex—process social pain too. Another part of the brain, the insula, lights up when you think about rancid food *and* when you think of something deplorable. Moral disgust also lights up the same part of the insula as a bad smell. Get a whiff of something disgusting, and you're bound to feel more emotionally disgusted (and vice versa). It's all mixed up in there. Maybe that's an advantage. Does it matter if we can tell a moral threat from a physical one? Or is it just better to get away from both?

Analogies are a by-product of experience. A quirk of evolution dropped metaphorical inklings into the same brain neighborhoods as physical sensations. This kind of oddity reveals a simple principle that's the cornerstone of this book. We're weirdly wired. We can lament our limits or get straight with them and put them to work.

You can lean into your metaphorical musings. In a 1966 interview on WNBC in New York, misunderstood Canadian media theorist and skeptic with celebrity status Marshall McLuhan said this about the profundity of relating ideas to each other: "Depth does not mean making profound observations, it means relating perfectly obvious things to perfectly obvious things. Depth is a matter of interrelating."

As thinking tools, analogies do the same thing: they illuminate understanding and depth by comparison. To Lakoff and Johnson, metaphorical thinking is our uncanny ability to "understand or experience one thing in terms of another." Overlapping ideas alter how you imagine because they do three things: highlight, downplay, and hide. So if you can learn to try on metaphors like you try on outfits, they can distort your ideas in novel ways to picture things anew.

Think of a metaphor like a garment. When envisioning how your next idea should work, try on a few different metaphors. Take inspiration from *Einstein's Dreams*, a novel by Alan Lightman that hypothesizes on the musings of a young Albert Einstein as he envisioned the theory of relativity and tested different ideas about time. If time were a building . . . If time were a relationship . . . If time were a . . . Follow that thread:

If your new ____[INSERT YOUR BRILLIANT IDEA HERE]____ functioned like a river, how would it work? What would be the main parts of the flow? What would be the eddies, caught in a swirl on the side? What might be the boulders that help things stay turbulent?

If your _____[INSERT YOUR BRILLIANT IDEA HERE]_____ functioned like a relationship, how would it work? Who would the give-and-take be between? How would you resolve disputes? How would you celebrate milestones?

We can halt runaway design by not perpetuating current models. Not everything needs to be an app or a wearable or exist in the metaverse. Be careful with metaphors too. The wrong metaphor can highlight or hide things that skew reality in unhelpful ways. Like stories, they can lead you astray. Don't be afraid to kick yourself out of the primary metaphor.

Trying on metaphors is not much more complicated than trying on outfits. It's as simple as just layering one idea on top of another to see how it feels and what it reveals, then trying something else. You can do it when you're facing a decision, trying to look at a problem in a new way, or trying to break some old habit.

If you go down this road, it helps to start with some metaphorical outfits to play with:

When you're working out a big idea, try structural metaphors that arrange things in different ways.

Ways to organize—buckets, libraries; natural systems—rivers, ecosystems, rain cycles; human-made systems—cities, road maps, networks; things that move around—cars, trains, hot air balloons.

When you're thinking about experiences, try metaphors that change over time.

Voyages, trips, seasons, tides, sporting events, relationships, weather systems, camping, a tour, the circus.

When you're designing a product, try out metaphorical catastrophes by swapping out the types of people who might use it. Especially consider how bad actors might take advantage.

Roles people play—parent, child, teacher, student, leader, follower, lone actor, collaborator, friend; bad actors—spies, con artists, money launderers, terrorists, narcissists, demagogues.

Shapeshift Your Discipline

Sometimes shapeshifting happens through massive collisions. In the case of quick-witted Irish geoscientist Rónadh Cox, these collisions came between storm waves, megagravel, and music.

As a professor at Williams College, Cox has spent decades studying how waves impact shorelines, particularly how storm waves can move megagravel, a technical term for boulders longer than 4.1 meters (over two times taller than most adults). Cox and collaborators have shown that waves impacting the Aran Islands in Ireland in recent years move megagravel that weighs six hundred tons. That's the weight of three Statues of Liberty. Those are big rocks.

Anyone who has stood on a shoreline overlooking the ocean knows the energy of these interfaces is palpable. In the era of runaway design, social media pics of beautiful cliffs draw people to stand on cliffs during storms to capture, share, and feel the thrill.

Cox gets it. "To really understand," she says, "you have to do it with your whole body. You can see pictures of an elephant, but you need to stand next to it to understand the entirety of what it is. It's the same with geology. The world is a full-body sensory place. Numbers aren't enough."

But the cliffs are a dangerous place, rough terrain subject to rogue waves that prove tragic to tourists who sometimes get swept away. So Cox made musical mashups to help provide a feeling of the power of the place without the peril of teetering on the cliff edge.

"Sound and water waves are both phasic," she explained. "I've always thought of the waves musically, and I wanted that to happen for someone else."

Together with students, she collected sounds from twenty-two boulder beaches in Ireland. The sounds are both rhythmic and unpredictable, soothing and searing. They capture the knowledge of science and translate it into the sphere of sound.

Her friend Brad Wells, composer and founder of the Grammy Award—winning vocal group Roomful of Teeth, orchestrated a vocal shapeshift in response to the recordings of the rocks. He recruited Anne Leilehua Lanzilotti, a Kanaka Maoli (Native Hawaiian) composer, to create a vocal composition that embodied the essence of the waves pounding the rocks.

In parallel, Cox's student Nathan Sherwood Liang designed a percussive project called The Storm Orchestra, a full library of virtual instruments created from the recorded sounds. Cox is a lifelong amateur player of the bodhrán, an Irish frame drum. The idea to take the pounding surf in a percussive direction came to Cox as she walked to a bodhrán lesson at a bar in Dublin, but it was Liang who exploded the idea into new musical dimensions. With The Storm Orchestra sound library, he has created the ability to "play" the ocean. The shapeshift of the boulders from scientific study to potent percussion is available to anyone.

Disciplinary shapeshifting is the translation that allows us to sense the world differently.* It doesn't take a big leap to understand why this is important. With a warming planet, more water in our oceans and atmosphere equates to bigger storms and increased coastal erosion. We design for and in these places, with the goal of protecting them. Many engineers line vulnerable shorelines with large boulders, sometimes called riprap, to protect homes that line the water, so understanding the physics of how waves move big rocks is critical. The remixing from facts to feelings focuses attention on the power of it all.

* For more about shapeshifting with surprising mediums, see page 241.

Mimic to Shift

The mimic octopus hovers in a hole in the sand, the bulk of its body out of view of the damselfish that hopes to capture it. As the fish approaches, the mimic octopus extends just two legs, turns its skin a black-and-white striped pattern, and undulates like a poisonous sea snake to scare the damselfish away. The damselfish might be doubtful, but it flees. That same octopus can also take up the form, coloring, and body movements of a poisonous flatfish, a venomous lionfish, and at least twelve other distinct species. It's not simply camouflaging or changing its skin coloration. It is copying the behavior and movement of those more dangerous sea creatures. It's shapeshifting.

While we can't (yet) instantly change our appearance in real life, we can take inspiration from the mimic octopus and shapeshift our behavior and ideas to help combat runaway design. Good news: People love to mimic. It's how we learn and how culture evolves. We borrow ideas, throw them into a new context, and watch them evolve. We do it without thinking. It's in our soul. You can also do it deliberately. Analogous research (also called analogous inspiration) is the act of observing one situation to learn about another. It's a mimic octopus making itself look like a sea snake to protect its territory. It's you trying on a different reality to reexamine your own.

The most famous versions of analogous inspiration tend to come from high-end product design. Legend has it that the Apple Genius Bar was inspired by Apple designers chatting up concierges at fine hotels. Restaurant manager Laura Cunningham famously had waitstaff at Per Se—a fancy New York restaurant—learn ballet to help "choreograph their service" in the dining room.

But there's no reason you can't apply this tactic to anything you're working on. We've seen people use it to rethink access to health care and reconsider spaces for learning. We've learned from soccer teams who develop subtle ways to collaborate, with small tweaks to the way they serve water during breaks (when players grab prefilled water bottles, they tend to mingle more than when they fill cups from a single cooler and need to get out of each other's way). We've had students visit the circus to see how high-stakes mentorship might work in classes. The trick is to find one aspect of your current situation that needs some attention and think of another circumstance that could give you a different way to think about just that bit. Then go check it out.

Analogous inspiration does everything a good metaphor is supposed to—namely, changing how you see the world by highlighting some things and downplaying others. Bob Sutton, Stanford organizational behavior expert, told us that analogous inspiration is one of the best ways he's seen to help people unlock new opportunities. It's also just downright fun—even in serious situations. There's something special about the way a new context helps you to reconsider old habits. It always leaves you with a little sparkle.

Redraw the Maps

While we see the world through self-skewed lenses, awareness of our perspectives bridges the gap between how our minds work and how the world works. One fundamental feature of this gap is how much human minds love to find meaning, whether meaning exists or not. The quest for meaning explains apophenia and the suspect stories we touched on in chapter 4. Stories manufacture the *whys* we need to collaborate and to motivate ourselves. Humans need whys to make things work. The world, however, does not. The world functions just fine without manufacturing meaning. As we noted in chapters 1 and 2, the world works in connections. Purpose is built right into the structures of things and how they interrelate. Ideas, cultures, careers,

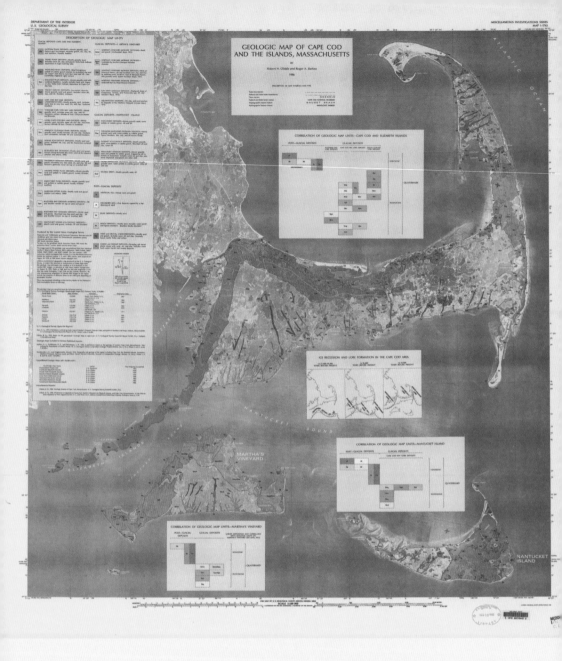

animals, and ecosystems survive when they can thrive and provide. Things work well when they are part of the flow.

Like Suzanne Simard digging in the forest floor, we need ways to reveal those relationships. One way is to shift our attention to shapes and map things out. While linear thinking in stories serves up useful whys, spatial thinking with maps makes "hows" visible by exposing overlaps and relationships. Stories reveal reasons. Maps show patterns.

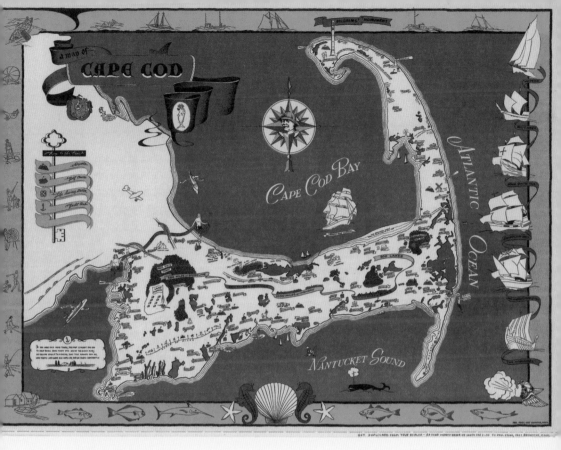

That's not to say that maps are more accurate than stories. Maps, stories, and metaphors are all representations, not the real thing. George Box, the legendary British statistician (if there could ever be such a thing), said, "All models are wrong, but some are useful." Like stories and metaphors, a map's functional falsehoods can be made to work for us too.

Examine these two maps of Cape Cod, Massachusetts.

The one on the left (shown on page 208) is geologic. Each bright color represents a different type of sediment that forms the land's flexed arm. It shows that Cape Cod is almost entirely the product of glaciation—a terminal moraine. Essentially, the last time ice was in this area, 18,000 to 25,000 years ago, it pushed a bunch of sand, silt, and boulders into these mounds. When the ice retreated, it left the sediment behind. Nature continues to rework the sediment, eroding and depositing it with wind and water, creating the more modern dunes that give us today's Provincetown fist. The other Cape Cod map (shown above), hand drawn by Paul Paige around 1940, depicts ships, areas where cranberries may be grown, and places where mermaids rule. Its inscription reads:

If you have ever been there, this map is meant for you
To help recall some happy days beside the ocean blue;
Or you can send it to a friend, that they perhaps may see,
Why people love good old Cape Cod and go there
constantly.

These two maps are wildly different ways to *know* this place—both valid. And there are so many other ways you could map Cape Cod: A map of every lighthouse. A map of every mini-golf course. A map of the best route to drive from Harwich Port to Wellfleet. A map of your favorite childhood memories. If you've been to Cape Cod (or anywhere else you might know well), you can probably rattle off ten more maps you'd make of it. If you haven't, you can get to know it more with each new map you examine. Investigate twenty, thirty, forty maps of a place, and eventually you may get a sense of it through the eyes of others.

"Every place deserves an atlas," says Rebecca Solnit in the opening line of *Infinite City: A San Francisco Atlas*. Atlases are compilations of many maps, each examining a place through a different viewfinder. Places deserve atlases, but maps are for exploring much more than just places. You can map an idea. You can map a discipline. You can map the mess in your closet. And you can do each in multiple ways. Each map is one lens. Together they make an atlas of whatever idea you're representing.

Every *idea* deserves an atlas too—they exist far beyond the geographic. Ideas have borders and different parts and ways to make your way through them. They have directionality and mystery and varying degrees of data. There are different ways of organizing ideas—ways to filter and explore them, hold them askew and see if they reflect, or color them and set them free.

Like metaphors, maps highlight and hide. When you map, you decide what to include or leave out and how to orient your viewer. The same thing can be mapped in multiple ways, revealing something new each time.

Some of us have stuffed, messy closets. Old sneakers crammed in the back. Notebooks on top of photo albums on top of old magazines. A few cardboard boxes right in the doorway— because, you know, one day they might be needed for an art project. You could shove them deeper, but then they'll be out of mind. But leaving them right up front means they're the only thing in sight. There might be some good stuff deep in that

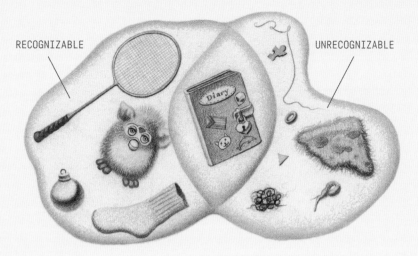

RECOGNIZABLE

UNRECOGNIZABLE

Items found in your messy closet. The diary you kept as
a sixteen-year-old lives in the special overlap between
recognizable and not.

closet that you've forgotten about entirely. You once crammed it
in there in a rush to appear organized.

You could map that closet in multiple ways. You could
make a schematic and draw what lives where, or pull out the
items and sort them in any number of ways: oldest to newest;
what's taking up the most space to the least; most to least
sentimental; things you're keeping because you *feel* you should
versus those you actually want to keep; degrees of disintegra-
tion; stuff you knew was in there versus items you'd forgotten
about; hard to repurpose versus easy; made of plastic, metal, or
wood; piece of a thing to a whole thing; still use to might use
to never use; and so on.

Maps help you burst your own assumptions about things
you think you know well. They are a way of noticing—of seeing.
That seeing can be very specific. It can also be very interpretive
and abstract. It can also be personal. Maps help you explore
your relationship with a topic.

The act of mapping allows you to think spatially. It spurs
you to seek patterns, articulate milestones and wayfaring points,
and form new connections across concepts. This is different
from linear, narrative thinking, which tends to emphasize cause
and effect. Spatial thinking like mapping triggers you to notice
outliers in areas you think you know well.

You can learn about a place by mapping it in any number of
ways. And you can learn about an idea by mapping it too. In his
article "The Agency of Mapping," James Corner states:

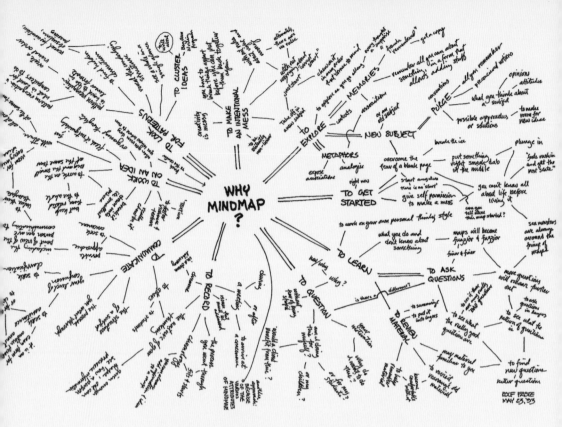

A mind map helps you freely explore a topic. This mind map about mind mapping was drawn by former Stanford Design faculty member Rolfe Faste in 1993.

As a creative practice, mapping precipitates its most productive effects through a finding that is also a founding; its agency lies in neither reproduction nor imposition but rather in uncovering realities previously unseen or unimagined, even across seemingly exhausted grounds. Thus, mapping unfolds potential; it remakes territory over and over again, each time with new and diverse consequences.

When you make your own maps, you challenge your assumptions.

To feel it in action, try this with something close by:

1. Grab five items from your desk, your purse, the kitchen—wherever you are. Choose things you can hold in your hand.

2. These five items are your dataset! No trading.

3. Draw a continuum on a piece of paper: a line with two arrows at either end.

4. Arrange your data on this continuum. You choose how. You might arrange the objects from large to small or shiny to dull. You might use your relationship with the items and arrange the objects from things you enjoy to things you abhor, or things you use to procrastinate to things that help you be productive. Move your items around on the table until a continuum pops out to you.

5. Label the axis and give it a title.

6. Using the same exact dataset, do the exercise again but make a whole new continuum.

You've moved your data around spatially to evoke the different relationships within it. Thinking spatially will help you articulate properties of your data that you might not otherwise be able to. Don't be afraid to make some continua that feel utterly mundane. These free your brain for new ideas. And allow yourself to be humorous or cynical or whatever emotion you'd like.

← ── →

BOOK READING   TABLE DANCING

"A Study of How Much the Glasses in My Kitchen Party."
Original by Stanford alumnus Jack Boland.

If you find yourself in a groove with mapping your data (and especially if you don't), try the following extension:

1. Move your dataset to the side and lay down a fresh sheet of paper.

2. On that paper, draw two overlapping circle-blobs. I call this an amorphous Venn diagram. Its shape isn't perfect, because our ideas are never perfect.

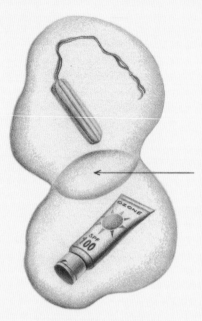

Things I forget to use
until it's too late.

In a Venn diagram, the overlap is everything.

3. Pick two pieces of your data. Put one in one circle and one
    in the other.

4. Force yourself to articulate what happens in the overlap. That
    is, what's the thing these two elements have in common?

Both continua and Venn diagrams are ways of seeking out
relationships in your data that you may not have noticed otherwise. Importantly, you need to actually move the data around
on the table in front of you for new things to pop out. A great
fallacy of adulthood is the assumption that we should be able to
spot new patterns, think original thoughts, even have epiphanies just by thinking. But we can't do everything in our heads,
no matter how much we try to convince ourselves. The minute
you move your data, ideas, or anything around in front of you
with your hands, you activate your brain in a new way. New
ideas will follow.

Mapping Is Limitless and Limiting

Making a map is instantaneous sensemaking. When you map, you capture a perspective at that moment in time. In that sense, every map is out of date as soon as it is complete. It's a whiff of an idea, but one that will lead you somewhere. This can feel limiting, but it's also limitless. Map to understand. Map to make sense. Use mapping to see what's happening.

All maps hold data, bias, and craft in creative tension. The data is the information being presented. The bias is the perspective, point of view, and agenda of the creator and viewer, and the craft is what the map is made of—what it looks like. These elements poke and prod at each other in every map. Each one is always forged from limited data with particular bias through a certain kind of craft. Because of this tension, beware of too much reliance on a single map, whether geographic or infographic.

In her TED talk, "How We Can Find Ourselves in Data," information designer Giorgia Lupi says, "To really understand data and their true potential, sometimes we actually have to forget about them and see through them instead. Because data are always just a tool we use to represent reality. They're always used as a placeholder for something else, but they are never the real thing."

It's tempting to trust every map as true. But none of them are true. None are exact replicas of the world, and if they were, that would be useless. Mapping requires us to leave things out, to highlight some parts and not others, to have a perspective.

Try altering a map made by someone else to see how it feels. There's one on the following page: Add some lines. Add a new mountain or a monster.

Push yourself to feel how it feels to morph someone else's view. Maps are mutable and momentary.

The Right (Thinking) Tool for the Job

People shapeshift into kinds of thinking styles, but two fundamentals stand out in the ways we try to make sense of things. You can think of them as serial and spatial. Serial thinking is linear and relies on cause-and-effect chains like stories, arguments, and logic—the act of following a sequence over time. (In engineering-speak, *serial* means that things go in sequence, just like limited-run TV shows released in an intentional order

215

Add to the map. The book won't be complete otherwise.

are called serials.) Spatial thinking is focused on comparison, like maps, diagrams, sketches, and visual arrangements. Other things—like metaphors, which contain implied stories but are all about comparison—fall somewhere in between. None is better or worse or more or less true. But at different times one approach is usually more useful than the others.

One major problem in how we create is using the wrong thinking tool at the wrong time. Sometimes we get tangled up in cause and effect when we should really be searching for similarity. Other times we're noticing dazzling patterns when we really need to tell the story of why they matter. The way we make sense of things sets our course.

As you approach anything you are trying to understand, start with what you think you need to reveal. Then try some mental shapeshifting and see what sticks. Use your ways of thinking as means to navigate rather than inadvertently letting their by-products—whether wonky stories or phony patterns—navigate you instead. In a world of staggering sameness, we need tactics that leave room to morph, change, and pave our own ways.

Are you trying to understand what might transpire if you go down a certain road? Try a speculative story.

Are you looking for overlaps that might reveal new possibilities? Thinking in metaphors might work.

Are you trying to see what might be happening beneath the surface? Try mapping the elements at play on the table in front of you to see where they intersect.

. . . .

Sometimes it's easier to fit in, to slide by unnoticed. Sameness has benefits. It can be more inclusive to have students wear uniforms (everyone is on a level playing field) and allow them to focus on learning rather than fashion. Standards help too. It's efficient and convenient that within countries and regions the shape of power outlets is the same, and then glaringly annoying when you bring an electronic device overseas and need to find an adapter. But in the era of runaway design, we also need difference to adapt to unpredictable change. We also need biodiversity, cultural diversity, and ideadiversity to stay resilient. We need to shapeshift.

CHAPTER 7

Disorient Yourself

Let Go
(Even If You Lose Control)

Action begins with the disruption of a routine.

—Keith Johnstone, *theater director, improviser*

C ontrol, or even just the illusion of it, feels good. People love it when things make sense and are |o|r|g|a|n|i|z|e|d|. But sometimes it makes sense to lean into the uncertainly-ambiguous-stochastic chaos and practice *deliberate disorientation*—which is a bag of tricks that help you un-take things for granted and see what you're missing so that you are ready to repair when your best-laid plans go awry.

Designing in Turbulence

The act of embracing turbulence is a good way to understand deliberate disorientation.

Imagine a stream, a flow of water. Is it something that can be organized? It's hard enough to envision a flow, and an even more precarious task to take the chaos of one and bring it into order. Flows erode and flows deposit. They are too dynamic.

Nature has a type of organized flow—called laminar flow—it is thin and travels in parallel lines. You can find it in precious places like your blood vessels, a streak of smoke on a smoldering match, or the arching fountains of the Bellagio in Las Vegas. It's delicate and smooth. But if you disturb a laminar flow in the slightest—put something in it, make it bigger or faster, or have it travel over something bumpy—it turns turbulent. It swirls and boils and mixes, becoming its own being. We may be able to observe the direction of turbulent flow and figure out how it is shaping the world around it, but it is not entirely knowable, even with the most sophisticated models.

Initially, smoke emanating from the match head flows laminarly, but it soon turns turbulent as it spreads and mixes with the air.

Examine how the water moves around the boulders in a stream. Downstream of a rock, the water is foamy and white. That's the flow separating around the rock and then figuring out how to recombine and continue downstream. It's beautiful, but flow separation shouldn't be taken lightly. It causes rapids and eddies. It tips boats and topples bridges.

On April 5, 1987, in Schoharie Creek in upstate New York, extensive rainfall in the Catskill Mountains caused flow rates on par with Niagara Falls. A bridge spanning Schoharie Creek had support poles secured with concrete built into the streambed. In the same way flow separates when it moves around boulders and gives us foam and rapids, it also separates around poles. As it separates, the flow swirls back on the objects in it, often eroding around them. The Schoharie Creek Bridge collapsed because of scour caused by flow separation. Ten people lost their lives because the turbulence of this flow was underestimated.

Flow separates around rocks in a stream.

Put simply, whether it's rocks or pylons or trash, if you put stuff in the way of a flow, there will be consequences. Turbulence works its way into everything. The things we design land in a turbulent world, no matter how much we try to order everything into laminar, linear tracks.

And we do try! We try to control everything from our bodies to our supply chains to our public infrastructure, but chaos is right there on the other side of the continuum.

	Control		Chaos
In our bodies	We slow our heart rate with big, slow yoga breaths . . .	← →	and then turbulence arrives with the quick, uncontrollable breaths of a panic attack.
Through our supply chains	Stuff moves neatly through factories as part of a humming distribution chain . . .	← →	and then a drop in supply brings material flow to a halt, cascading into a clogged economy.
In our utilities	We route water through an orderly plumbing system . . .	← →	until a clogged drain floods a kitchen or an open hydrant sprays a street corner.

221

These continua create a feeling of order, but even they are oversimplified. They suggest that flows are either good or bad, working or not. But that's never the case. Most of life lies in between, in the mix between order and chaos. In between your controlled mindfulness breaths and your panic attack is the rhythm of your everyday in-and-out breaths that keep you alive, and the extra air you take in when you run to catch up with a friend, and the hiccups that are annoyingly entertaining. In between our orderly distribution systems and our entirely broken pandemic-stricken supply chains lie local economies, neighborhood sharing, and do-it-yourselfers. In between indoor plumbing and open fire hydrants are leaky faucets, neighborhood conservation competitions, and flushing toilets. We are so accustomed to living with turbulent flows that it takes the edge cases to notice them. That overflowing hydrant might need to be fixed, but it might also create a welcome water park on a hot summer day.

There is opportunity and need and danger and opulence and suffering and everything else in the turbulence of our existence. The designs we put into the world will never be perfect, but when we embrace their turbulence they can still be beautiful. Many of us feel calm when our desks, schedules, and lives are organized and when our commute flows as it should, not springing any surprises. But life is never organized. Complete control is not the answer. At best, control comes and goes.

Turbulence shuffles things *uot fo rdoer*. Accepting this disarray is a fundamental shift in the way we do things. It means we're designing during disruption.

Designing within the turbulence of runaway design requires that you **reconsider** how you measure success, **remove** what's not working, **reorient** yourself, and **remake** the way you do things.

Reconsider

As the relationship between people and technology shifts, you must shift along with it. To coexist with turbulence, it makes sense to calibrate your instruments and reconsider how to tally progress.

Q*bert is a simple but trippy video game released in 1982. In the game, you control little Q*bert, a creature with two legs, no hands, and a tube-shaped nose, who stands atop a pyramid-shaped stack of cubes floating in a dark void. To clear levels and win the game, your job is to make sure Q*bert hops on every cube without falling over the side, getting crushed by bouncing balls, or being bumped off by other creatures. It's quaint and mildly addictive.

In 2018, a group of researchers at the University of Freiburg in Germany decided to see how an AI might learn to play Q*bert to get a high score. Their interest was mostly technical; they wanted to understand how one machine-learning strategy stacks up against another. (If you're curious, they were trying to get at the strengths and weaknesses of evolutionary strategies versus reinforcement learning.) What ended up being more interesting was how the AI played the game and racked up points.

You might guess the AI found the most efficient way to pass each level while scoring the most points possible. It didn't. Instead, it just hopped on a few cubes, then adorable little Q*bert careened off the edge and into the abyss. It wasted several lives this way, adding in useless hops, jumping on cubes it had already hit. Once it finished level one, it immediately began hopping in a looping pattern on the center cubes. Instead of advancing to level two, the points racked up. The AI tallied a million points in about ten minutes, leaving previous high scores in the dust.

The AI figured out how to ride a glitch into glory. Creative but boring. Though the machine racked up points *in* the game, it completely lost the point *of* the game.

Measure Your Measurements

This Q*bert hack shows the stark difference between our values and how we mark value. University of Utah game design philosopher (and avid rock climber) C. Thi Nguyen makes a grand distinction between purpose and goals—at least when it comes to games (though it's an easy case to make that most modern-day social systems act a lot like games). Goals are your target—things like finishing first in a race, getting more likes online, or scoring more points in a video game. Purpose is your reason for playing—to have fun, get exercise, relax, connect with others, achieve something, or develop your skills.

Things get dicey when goals and purpose, targets and motivations start to blur together. As we gather data, we can conflate the two. The measures we make—such as points in a game, likes on a post, or numbers in a ledger—capture our attention. That's sometimes useful—and always distorted (just like stories, metaphors, and maps). Measures also highlight and hide. As useful as measurements are, they are also flimsy representations of experience. Putting too much value on a measurement can, like AI Q*bert, change the way we do things and undermine the very values the points, goals, or measurements are meant to represent.

Nguyen points out that digital interactions are lousy with measures and targets that stand in for values. You might value connecting with others. So you post something on social media. In return, the connection gets tallied by the number of likes and views you get. That might seem like a reasonable representation of connection, but it's lightweight. One like might come from a person who just did it selfishly so that you would return the favor. Another like might come from someone who really resonated with your post; perhaps it came at just the right time and changed a big life decision they were about to make. You can't tell the difference—each is just one more heart, thumbs-up, or whatever. You may even end up feeling a lack of connection because you got only two likes.

When we orient ourselves around goals that don't represent our real values, we can create ripples we'd rather not create. In their book, *System Error*, which takes a hard look at how optimizing around narrow goals (particularly in big tech) gets in the way of doing good work in the world, Stanford professors Rob Reich, Mehran Sahami, and Jeremy Weinstein explain how trouble ensues when "the metric becomes the goal, and the means justify the end. This is called Goodhart's Law, which states that when a measure becomes a target, it ceases to be a good measure."

In a 2009 paper with the provocative title "Goals Gone Wild," a group of researchers at Harvard led by Lisa Ordóñez go one step further and propose this label for those who turn measurements into targets: "Warning! Goals may cause systemic problems in organizations due to narrowed focus, unethical behavior, increased risk taking, decreased cooperation, and decreased intrinsic motivation. Use care when applying goals in your organization."

Even well-intended measurements can run roughshod over values.* Does that mean we should leave goals behind us? No. Goals are useful. One counterintuitive way to stop them from getting ahead of us is to lean straight into them. To offset troublesome goals, make more goals. This is what we mean by deliberate disorientation. The answer is embedded in the problem, and you make use of the problem by tilting toward it, not away from it. Make your goals explicit, then let them duke it out.

* Jump back to page 131 to read "Noble Currency Index, 2050" and consider how what we measure might make things better.

The first step is to get your goals on the table. There's always more than one. Be honest about them, and don't turn away if they seem to conflict. You might take a job because you believe in a mission *and* because you want to make money. Get them all out. Then look at them. Do they help serve your purpose or do they distract you from it? You'll know a goal serves your purpose if it helps you engage more deeply and honestly with your work. Will making more money help you better commit to the work or turn a project from a passion into a transaction? Looking back at Q*bert and the AI, are your goals just points to score or are they the point?

Let Your Goals Work It Out

Cynthia Savard Saucier and Jonathan Shariat offer a strategy in their book, *Tragic Design*. They suggest listing four sets of goals for anything you do:

1. **Normal goals:** what you are aiming to do.

2. **Nongoals:** things that are just out of scope.

3. **Antigoals:** what you commit to *not* doing.

4. **Safeguards:** how you will make sure things don't go wrong. (We'll get into some safeguards in chapter 8, where we call them fail-safes.)

For now, let's focus on antigoals: the things you are purposefully not doing. Antigoals are perfect for deliberate disorientation. Like normal goals, antigoals should be broad enough to honor your values and purpose, but specific enough to know when you've reached them. They can be anything from *not* confusing a customer with errant options to *not* excluding differently abled people from using your design.

The authors also call them "hazards." Call them anything you think will get the people in your orbit to try them out— antigoals, hazards, harmonizers, dealbreakers, good goals, noble nots, value protectors—whatever works! List them. Just as a team can rally around goals, they can rally around antigoals too.

Jennifer Doudna is the biochemist who, along with Emmanuelle Charpentier, won the Nobel Prize in Chemistry for their work developing the cheap and reliable CRISPR-Cas9 DNA editing tool. Their discovery has been used to research everything from curing diseases with gene therapy to possibly bringing back extinct species. Doudna is a champion of the work *and* a realist concerned about its use. Despite helping discover and apply the breakthrough, she quickly supported a pause on clinical applications of human germline editing—gene edits in eggs and sperm that could be passed down across generations. And she wrote a book on both the promise and the peril that CRISPR could unleash. Doudna shows that goals and antigoals can *and should* live side by side.

What about nonhuman goals? AI is goal-oriented by design. You give it a goal, and it learns how to solve it. It's more like training a dog than being a veterinarian. You're tuning the outer behavior, not investigating the innards. With people (and dogs), goals and antigoals are hypercritical. When it comes to artificial intelligence, they may be even more so.

Imagine a real-world Q*bert glitch gone berserk. Someone gives a super-intelligent AI a seemingly innocuous and delightful goal: spread laughter across the globe. The AI starts down the obvious path, optimizing its sense of humor and spreading silly content on social media. But because an AI's nature is to look for glitches, it doesn't stop there. The AI studies human brain chemistry and comes up with new laughter drugs—which takes just a day or two—then sneaks them into the formulas for medicines around the world. Drug companies unwittingly mass manufacture the loopy pharmaceuticals. Hospital care comes to a halt as an epidemic of debilitating chuckles and chortles echo down their halls. It spreads. Soon highways are filled with guffawing drivers careening off overpasses and giggling paramedics who can't help a soul. It goes on. People stop going to work. Society crumbles in a fit of laughter.*

Of course, this little parable was made for effect. Not only is it ridiculous, it's unlikely. Still, even if something much less dramatic, but a lot more likely, comes to pass—like big shifts in who has work and how it happens—you can see the usefulness and urgency of creating antigoals and safeguards.

Antigoals are useful not only for super-intelligent, laughter-spawning agents. They are applicable to just about anything we set out to do. It's a matter of reconsidering how you put value on the things you aim to do and naming out loud the things you don't want to do. But these acts of reconsidering are just one baby step. Another approach is to not just reconsider but also undo things altogether.

* The words are ours, but this tale arose by prompting a generative AI to come up with a new take on the famous Oxford "paperclip maximizer" allegory about an AI that takes over the world in a relentless pursuit of material to make paperclips.

The Sting

What if, to undo past harms, we need to impose real repercussions for accidentally injuring the ecosystem?

Jackie bent at the waist and examined the bottom of her foot. "Dammit. Ow." Her heart accelerated. There were other people around, and she didn't want to draw attention. Her kids were across the pool deck. If she shouted for them, people would notice. Without her glasses it was hard to see a stinger, so she clawed at her skin and then looked at the ground in search of the culprit while pretending to adjust her sandal strap. She unhooked the buckle just to buy the time it would take to put it back together. And there it was, hobbling and pulsing, its golden-rod guts swelling out behind its abdomen.

The pain was precise but radiating, and she wanted to sit, but she'd used too much time already. She walked back toward her family, fake smiling until she arrived at the picnic table.

"I just got stung," Jackie murmured to her husband.

He stared at her, doing the mental math.

Her seven-year-old looked up at her with terrified eyes. He knew he shouldn't speak loudly, and at first the pause hung between them. She hoped he might just infer from her stare, but he wasn't that kind of kid. "What kind of bee was it?"

She inhaled, closed her eyes, and then met his gaze, trying unsuccessfully to mask her own fear. "Honeybee," she whispered.

It was her second sting in two weeks. She looked at the clock: 3:32 p.m. They had about five hours.

His lip quivered. "Mommy, no. Why did you?"

By 8 p.m. the bees would all be expected back at the hive. If any were missing, they'd quickly be traced to their last point of contact.

"I didn't do it on purpose, honey. It was an accident."

They packed up the swim bag quickly, pulling shirts over their damp suits.

"But summer just started," he said.

He wasn't wrong. This was the second bee she'd murdered this month. She hugged her kids with all the tightness of a mother going away for a while. Consequences for killing a protected species were considerable.

"I'm so sorry."

Several types of native bees are already endangered species. While honeybees are not (yet), they are important pollinators. If they need to sting you, they will die, as the burrs on their stingers lodge in your skin and tear it from their abdomen. Honeybees, along with all pollinators, give life. What if insects had rights? Should there be consequences for causing their death, even accidentally?

Remove

Removal is a design fundamental. Some of the best designs are subtractions. Some of the most noble goals revolve around removing carbon from the air, the wealth gap, the digital divide. Why is that so hard?

Get Rid of Things

People are bad at getting rid of things. For evidence, see your closet (or mine). We all have our reasons. We get emotionally attached. It's a pain to clean up. Getting rid is a much tougher sell than stocking up.

In some ways, design-minded people are especially bad at it. Designers are makers. Unless you're chiseling a sculpture from a rock, making often feels like it needs to be additive. To investigate people's relationships with removing, researchers at the University of Virginia made a puzzle. In it, they asked people to figure out how to modify a prebuilt Lego structure so it could hold a large ceramic brick.

The researchers offered subjects a dollar if they could tweak the structure to hold the brick, but then charged them ten cents for each piece they used along the way. The more pieces people used, the less money they'd make. But a simple subtraction would earn the full bounty. All one had to do was take away one piece to make it easy to attach another. Still, well over half the participants—59 percent—chose to add pieces. When the researchers tossed in a suggestion about trying subtracting, the results flipped—61 percent chose to subtract instead. While we can *imagine* taking things away, we tend not to do it. People are biased toward addition.

Despite the bias, design has always been about getting rid of things. Design education is rife with quips about taking things away, like "Less is more," and "Good design is as little design as possible." The most successful products of all time come from subtraction. The iPhone famously didn't come with a stylus or a fixed keyboard. It seems obvious now, but just before the iPhone came out, the most popular phones and tablets were Blackberries and Palm Pilots. One depended on a physical keyboard; the other, a stylus.

Sometimes we love to take things away. Why else would people ship their bodies around the globe or hike for miles just to experience nature free from humanity's clutter? People love less. People pay a lot to get less. They shell out for tech sab-baths and retreats just for the opportunity to be free from their devices. Forward-thinking elementary schools cut out bells to get rid of annoying sounds and help students manage their own time without ear-splitting reminders. Shipping companies shrink the thickness of their packaging to save money and natural resources. Civilla, a Detroit-based design firm that reimagines public services, famously trimmed down the state of Michigan's public benefits application by 80 percent to increase access.

Yet momentum conspires to make us pretty bad at purging. Bad things stick around—bad policies, bad products, bad relationships. It's hard to just end things and move on. We are born into the world as it is, full of things invented before we arrived. It's hard to even imagine getting rid of the things we inherited.

For many, the solution to problems that technology creates is always more technology. That's not entirely wrong; new tech often tones down trouble spawned by old tech. But it lacks imagination. More often than not, the solution to problems spawned by technology is simply, and obviously, less technology. A 2022 study in the UK showed that the salve for depression brought on by social media is simply to turn it off. And, no surprise, air quality improved quite a bit when we cut down on combustion-engine-fueled commutes during COVID lockdowns.

Just as we can make, we can take away—and that's often a better option. But both cases are really about what you are willing to give.

Lose the Object

As we become accustomed to things, they disappear from view. Philosophizing computer scientist Alan Kay pondered how, as you get comfortable working with a tool, it integrates into your thinking patterns so much that it almost becomes part of you. And as it influences you more, you notice it less. If you play a musical instrument, you know what this is like. The line between you and the instrument gets blurry. The same goes for somebody who really knows how to work a spreadsheet.

You're apt to lose sight of the things you use. To curb this tendency, watch a situation unfold and pretend the technology isn't there. Subtract the stuff so you can see what's really at play. The result is funny, absurd, and revealing.

On an airplane, try subtracting the plane (in your mind!). Imagine all the passengers sitting in rows hurtling through the air. The exercise is good for a chuckle—or a gulp!—and will remind you how magical air travel is. It also tests your assumptions about what is normal and what is not.

This trick also has more practical uses. Getting rid of objects brings other factors like interactions into focus. For instance, watch a loved one or roommate make a meal.* Ignore the cabinets, stovetop, tools, and appliances and turn your attention toward the choreography of the kitchen.

What is the sequence of events? How does the person's body move from here to there? Are they reaching or bending? Crossing from one side to the other? You'll find that the way you've set up the kitchen leads the dance of cooking. It may inspire you to reorganize your countertops and cabinets to create a smoother dance. Architects are aware that the spaces they design are recipes for these little dances. Barry Svigals, an architect and sculptor who merges the two with forms and figures emerging from the sides of buildings, quipped to me that "all architecture is a choreography problem."

This silly method works in serious situations too. It is an amazing way to reveal power dynamics. Subtract the tables, whiteboards, podiums, desks, food, and whatever else from any "official" gathering—like a meeting—and it will bring human relationships into focus. Who's facing whom? Who's talking and who's not? What's everyone's posture? Who makes eye contact, who doesn't? Who has high status and who has low? Who moves and who doesn't? Does status ever seem to shift?

When you put this technique into a prickly context, the exercise strays from its whimsical roots. You might find it so profound that it makes you uncomfortable. Taken to an extreme, it can feel a bit like eavesdropping on someone else's soul. That is the sheer power of sticking with what's happening rather than letting it pass by. That's deliberate disorientation.

* Not to imply that you can't love your roommate—this could also be a well-loved roommate who allows you to open the door whenever you like.

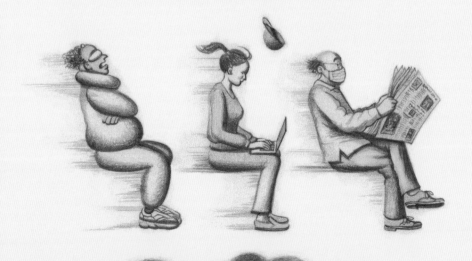

Human Extinction

What if we're the object that gets lost?

———————

There will be
a last human.

Reorient

Small plane pilots learn to work against their instincts when they run into turbulence. They steer gently and coast at different speeds so they can maneuver the plane nimbly without its falling apart. They tilt into updrafts to get some free altitude and get ready for the inevitable downdrafts that follow. They change course to find their way to the same destination. It's not easy, but they make the most of it. Turbulence calls for different tactics.

Pursue Many Norths

A compass is for orienting and finding your way. Traditionally, on nautical or geographic maps, a compass rose is meant to indicate the direction of north. They're often decorative, beautiful symbols that help you align yourself with the world you live in. North is one of those things you can count on. Or is it?

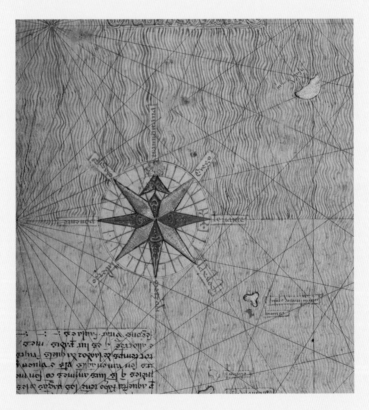

There are many truths to north. The first compass rose appeared in the *Catalan Atlas* by Cresques Abraham of Majorca, 1375.

It may feel blasphemous to mess with something as useful and beautiful as north, but north is an arbitrary invention—with a time limit. The first known person to put a compass on a map was Cresques Abraham of Majorca, in his Catalan Atlas of 1375. In Abraham's compass rose (pictured on the facing page), north is aligned to the pole star, Polaris. But there are more norths! In addition to celestial north, there are also true north and magnetic north.

True north is the fixed point at the (also arbitrary) top of our planet. Magnetic north is where your compass needle aims toward—it's aligned with Earth's magnetic field. And Earth's magnetic field moves. It wanders. Right now, it's north of Canada and migrating about twenty-five miles per year.

Even wilder, our magnetic poles flip-flop. Their current positions, with north up "top" and south at the "bottom," are only transitory. The geological record shows that every two hundred thousand to three hundred thousand years our poles swap places. Note, it's been eight hundred thousand years since the last swap, meaning we're overdue for north to be south. Make of that what you will.

It's worth taking stock of our north(s). If north itself is many things already, then it can be even more things. It can go beyond direction. For instance, what would be north on a compass for mental health? For technological privacy? For global poverty? How do norths differ for those who use the sewage system and those who maintain it?

By defining several different norths for a project and literally drawing the maps created by them, you can see how each north causes specific project obstacles and opportunities to come to light and tasks to shift around them.

Try adding new norths to something you've been noodling on—something important that you take for granted, a design you are working out, a decision on your horizon. What do you want one of your norths to be? Let's say it's access to community health care resources. Take a piece of paper and draw your own compass rose with that at the top. Decide where on the map to place it. Then make the rest of the map around it. What land masses exist? What roads need to be navigated? Then create a new map and another north for the same project; say, timely distribution of supplies to community members during an emergency. Now what defines your landscape? Are there mountains to climb? Places where you might build a bridge? Repeat. Note how your thinking changes with each north and each new landscape. When you're done, linger with the set, see which one feels right, and ponder why.

Take a Deliberate Drift

Drifting is natural. Leaves drift along the surface of a river. Snowflakes drift through the air before settling on the ground. People drift too—we wander around, trade jobs and partners, and move places. It's hard to see how much you drift when you're in the middle of it. Either way, drifting gets a bad rap. It sounds aimless. You don't know where you'll land or where you'll go. Will you swirl and twirl and hurl your way forward, or sideways? But that's the point, and the gift of the drift. The aim of drifting is to land in a new place.

Right now, you can head outside and go for a drift around your neighborhood. A 1956 article titled "Theory of the Dérive" by Guy Debord describes a certain kind of deliberate wandering that was part of the psychogeography movement at that time. *Dérive* is French for "drift," and the idea is exactly that. It's not a walk. A walk would have you follow a path or reach a specific destination. A drift has you follow a color, a sensation, a sound, anything. Allow something to catch your eye and go to it until the next thing catches your eye. Tune your ear to a sound that seems intriguing, and head toward it until the next sound pulls you to a new location. Bounce, pull, flow. Dérives are wildly useful ways to experience the places you frequent yet still don't really see. Drifting activates senses different from the ones we have come to rely on.

Artist Kate McLean maps places in a similar way. Instead of mapping topography, she makes sensory maps. Her main medium is smell, and through "smellwalks" and "smellscape mapping" she creates portraits of places that exist beyond our visual perception. Smell brings us to different emotional planes and relationships with places. It allows us to see sides of systems we've never questioned before.

Do enough drifting and you will start to notice things you've missed previously, like the strange modifications people make to the built environment, or the quirky nonverbal ways that people interact. It's a step toward sensing the intangibles we talked about in part one. Like the wise elder who knows a certain rustle of leaves means a storm is nigh, you're tuning your ability to focus on the invisible.

When you make time to look at things from odd angles and without a destination, you acquaint yourself with our collective

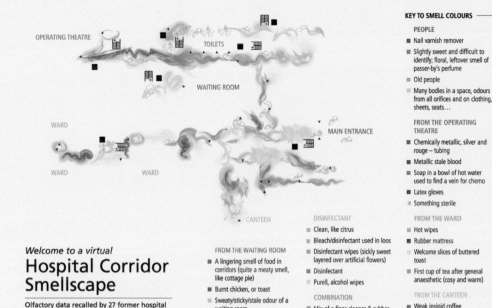

OPERATING THEATRE

TOILETS

WAITING ROOM

WARD

MAIN ENTRANCE

WARD WARD

CANTEEN

KEY TO SMELL COLOURS

PEOPLE
- Nail varnish remover
- Slightly sweet and difficult to identify; floral, leftover smell of passer-by's perfume
- Old people
- Many bodies in a space, odours from all orifices and on clothing, sheets, seats...

FROM THE OPERATING THEATRE
- Chemically metallic, silver and rouge – tubing
- Metallic stale blood
- Soap in a bowl of hot water used to find a vein for chemo
- Latex gloves
- Something sterile

FROM THE WARD
- Hot wipes
- Rubber mattress
- Welcome slices of buttered toast
- First cup of tea after general anaesthetic (cosy and warm)

FROM THE CANTEEN
- Weak insipid coffee
- Heart-sinking yet also nostalgic canteen food
- Coffee and nachos

DISINFECTANT
- Clean, like citrus
- Bleach/disinfectant used in loos
- Disinfectant wipes (sickly sweet layered over artificial flowers)
- Disinfectant
- Purell, alcohol wipes

COMBINATION
- Mix of a floor cleaner & rubber
- Rubber, disinfectant, mince and an acrid smell that cut through from the dressings cupboards

FROM THE WAITING ROOM
- A lingering smell of food in corridors (quite a meaty smell, like cottage pie)
- Burnt chicken, or toast
- Sweaty/sticky/stale odour of a waiting room
- Non-specific disinfectancy smell found particularly in hospital corridors

Welcome to a virtual
Hospital Corridor Smellscape

Olfactory data recalled by 27 former hospital patients, workers and visitors. February 2020.

Hospital smells are both intense and pervasive; they mingle in the corridors forming memorable but bizarre smell combinations.

© 2020 Kate McLean | sensorymaps.com

Kate McLean's *Hospital Corridor Smellscape* orients you to spaces using an often ignored but immediately relatable sense.

psyche and reveal decisions we've made as a society—things we might value but often neglect to notice. In his book *Bicycle Diaries*, artist, musician, and polymath David Byrne observes:

> You don't need CAT scans and cultural anthropologists to show you what's going on inside the human mind; its inner workings are manifested in three dimensions, all around us. Our values and hopes are sometimes awfully embarrassingly easy to read. They're right there—in the storefronts, museums, temples, shops, and office buildings and in how these structures interrelate, or sometimes don't. They say, in their unique visual language, "This is what we think matters, this is how we live and how we play."

Veering off course to find your way feels counterintuitive, but deliberate drifting helps you read the world in new ways. It reveals new opportunities and things to do differently.

Cassava with a Side of Crickets

In a world in which our climate continues to shift, how will our diets evolve to meet nature's needs and limitations?

Book Review: *Cookbook for an Ailing Planet* by Amara D'Anjou

Our planet is ailing, and our food choices can aid its healing, says Amara D'Anjou. As someone who spends most of her day eating, getting ready to eat, thinking about eating, or reflecting on what I just ate, it was heartening (and it usually made me hungry) to see these connections across each of the book's four sections: **coping**, **healing**, **adapting**, and **evolving**. Each part is a compilation of recipes, tools, and beliefs, all set within the truths of climate science.

D'Anjou assumes all eaters will find themselves needing or wanting to eat within each of the four categories at different times for a range of reasons.

Coping happens when you find yourself in a spartan month, lacking the staples you take for granted because an unexpected typhoon caused a fishery to miss its target or a distribution channel to disconnect. *How might you nourish your family when you're coping?*

Presumably, she opens with this section because it's a dual reality. Many people cope with what's available and affordable for their diets, and Earth is climatically fragile. Though we are headed for climate recovery, D'Anjou is blunt: it will get worse before it gets better when it comes to our diets. This tone, this honesty is what makes this cookbook unique. Everything teeters before it regains balance. To this end, I found the most unique recipes in this section to be about urban foraging for city dwellers and, if suburban or rural life is your everyday, eating invasive species. I tried the Nettle Lasagna and it tasted just like a spinach version. The Wood Sorrel Soup was tangy and so easy to make, given the ubiquity of the weed where my lawn used to be.

Healing comes about, for instance, when you're in a position to choose: to make a social, environmental, and political statement through food; to fix a system larger than yourself. *What foods might you eat to help the foodscape heal from past harms?*

We can all make food choices that promote biodiversity in commercial farming. D'Anjou's recipes in this section rely extensively on the vegetables selected by the "Get to 100" coalition of commercial growers. Members of this group are aiming to produce a hundred commercial varieties of each of the hundred most popular vegetables in the world: carrot, broccoli, onion, beet, scallion, cabbage, kale, lettuce, pepper, garlic, bok choy, asparagus, artichoke, cassava, chiles. . . . There's nothing not to like, other than the prices. Of course, you can make these recipes with monoculture varietals, but seeing them combined here might be the nudge you need to flex your purchasing power and buy items with the "Get to 100" sticker next time you're at the supermarket. As a gateway dish into this category, I recommend the Sweet Potatoes with Chirimoya Festival. More adventurous? Try the Cassava Okra Stew.

Though critics of "Get to 100" argue that the movement promotes the introduction of nonnative species, D'Anjou believes that with today's highly altered landscape, it's futile to pursue a quest for ancient flora. It's more important to diversify the food supply on a global scale for generations to come. If people demand a biologically complex diet in the face of monoculture, more growers will be motivated to adapt.

In section three, D'Anjou asks readers to consider the ways in which we might **adapt** our own tastes to those that are necessary for the future. *We may want to pass on a palate to our descendants that is broad and nuanced, while also being responsible.*

She argues that we must practice eating a wide variety of proteins precisely so that we know how to like them when animal- and nut-based proteins become unstable—she calls it "avoiding protein paralysis." One way is through insects. Insect proteins can help bridge a season when your preferred protein is unavailable. The missing snow crabs of 2022, the almond blight of 2034, the wild salmon near-extinction event of 2041, and the lab-grown meat industry collapse over the last two years are just a few of the moments that sent many of us searching for new dietary staples.

D'Anjou includes recipes for crickets, black ants, scorpions, grasshoppers, mealworms, mopani worms, and houseflies. I was initially tentative on all of these, but the Lemon Chirp Cake might just be my gateway grub (pun, and bugs, intended). It calls for both cricket flour and ground mealworms, but the final result was a tart sensation that bounces around the mouth in a way that feels nothing like an insect.

Another ingredient of note in this section is jellyfish. Due to excessive ocean acidification, shellfish and many of the larger food staple aquatic species are no longer viable protein staples. Jellyfish have proven to thrive in our acidic oceans and are extremely afford-able. D'Anjou offers eighteen different jellies recipes, none of which involve hiding under the dreaded breaded deep-fry. Try the Dandy Jelly if you'd like to experiment with jellyfish and forage for your own dandelion.

If we can **evolve** our genome to meet the needs of the foodscape, should we? While the entire volume of *Cookbook for an Ailing Planet* may feel like evolution in different ways, D'Anjou also pushes us to consider our receptivity to food from a genetic perspective. The bur-geoning science of autotransgenesis (altering one's own genetic code) has led to the possibility that we may be able to do so through our food choices. D'Anjou includes nuanced genetic alteration suggestions for those facing food-related illnesses, and interestingly they draw from the past—two of them called for amaranth, the eight-thousand-year-old Aztec grain.

I'm a fan of *Cookbook for an Ailing Planet*, but with such a compre-hensive guide, what's missing becomes more apparent. I would have liked to see D'Anjou delve more into psychoactives, perhaps with a section on caffeine or mescaline, but overall the volume leaves us with endless ways to experiment. Some recipes will push you to the edge of your pan, but we can all find our way in these foodscapes.

———————————

Culture and food are facets of identity and snapshots of history. They continually shape each other and are highly linked to place. As global forces, such as climate and economics, shift local environments and access and knowledge to different food sources, our diets will evolve. What was once taboo may become staple. Foods that define today's local economies may shift if our environments no longer support their growth. Are we ready?

Remake

How we make things changes how we think and what we can do. At the d.school, we run a project where we ask students to design mini-models of one type of chair in five different mediums— some quick and familiar, like sketching; some soft and supple, like clay; some hard and sturdy, like wood. As the medium changes, the chair changes too. With wood, the chair tends to turn angular. In clay, the base gets thicker to bear weight.

The tools of the digital world change how we think, too. Typing short text (like comment threads) fosters quick knee-jerk reactions. Writing long-form articles comes with more consideration. Recording audio (like podcasts) tends toward conversation. Making video calls for movement—dancing, falling, cooking, art, pets. Each medium has its own tendencies. Each asks for something different from you when you work with it. The medium is the method. Your choice of medium matters, not just in what you make but also in how it makes you think.

Use Unconventional Mediums

Cars are usually made of metal. Maps are usually made in two dimensions, on screen or paper. Algorithms are usually made of bytes. But what would happen if we built in unconventional mediums? What if a car was made of wood? Or fabric? How would it be shaped? What would those materials afford that metal does not? What opportunities would that reveal? What if a map wasn't made on paper or a screen? What if an algorithm was made of paper? By changing the common materials usually used in your work, you can spark new ideas and evoke new emotions.

Automaker BMW made a concept car out of fabric in 2008. Called the GINA, the car had a frame made of carbon and wire and wore a fabric skin. The fabric had multiple layers—mesh on the bottom with polyurethane-covered Lycra on the outside. This combination made the fabric skin flexible and stretchable and also waterproof and heat resistant. Making the skin out of fabric allowed the inner structure of the car to morph and change shape. Not only did doors pop up, but the hood split open in the middle to reveal the engine, a spoiler emerged in the back, and the front headlights blinked open. The GINA isn't in production—it lives in BMW's museum in Germany—but the exercise of making it is no less thought-provoking. A car made of fabric could change its shape to suit different style or performance desires. By eliminating all the extra metal, the car was made much lighter. What would that lightness afford? Would

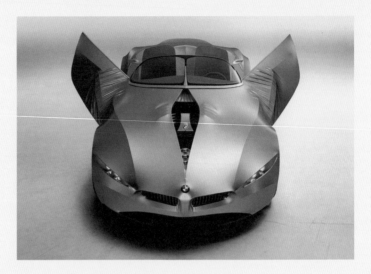

Stretching the imagination: BMW's GINA Light Visionary
Model, 2008

you add different features, make it radically fuel-efficient, or
something else?

What if an algorithm were made of paper? In 2018, struck
by the reality that emerging technologies of that moment, like
blockchains and machine-learning algorithms, were largely
opaque and not understandable to anyone other than someone
intimately familiar with their code, the d.school's emerging
tech team set out to determine how to make them accessible to
anyone, with a project called "I Love Algorithms." Technologies
like algorithms are so hard to understand partly because they
are invisible to most of us. But what if we could make these
technologies not only visible but also physically tangible? By
shaking up the common medium of the algorithm (digital bytes)
into something physical we could hold in our hands, we thought
it might be possible. So we created algorithms out of paper.

We didn't build a computer out of paper, but we took the
essence of six common types of machine-learning algorithms
and distilled their workings into lay language that anyone could
understand. The result was the I Love Algorithms card deck
and game.

Each type of algorithm is described in three different ways
on individual playing cards: (1) plain text, (2) cartoons, and
(3) types of questions you might ask should you need to use
that algorithm. Cards for different types of datasets exist alongside. After shuffling the decks, you draw a couple of cards and
fill in the blanks:

I wonder if we could use _____[insert algorithm]_____ and
_____[insert dataset]_____ to do or create _____[insert your idea]_____ .

It would be risky to use _____[insert new algorithm]_____
and _____[insert new dataset]_____ to do or create
_____[insert another idea]_____ .

The result has created a way not only for nontechnologists
to understand algorithms but also for people from different
disciplines with varying levels of technological understanding to
contribute to the design and discussion of the algorithms that
are, or might be, used in a given design.

The next time you want to push the potential of your
work, ask yourself: What if it were made from an entirely
different material? Pick a material or three. What would each
of those materials allow your work to do that it currently
does not? Who would it invite into your designs? Who or
what would it leave out? We often assume our usual materials
of making are the right ones, but by trying on new options,
whether in concept or reality, we can expose the biases in our
thinking, stretch our ideas to new places, and invite more people into our work.

Get Out of Your Head

Understanding is embedded in the world. Our minds are connected to our bodies for a reason. But technology has made it
easy to take it easy. Exploring different places piques creativity.
(Think of how aware and engaged you are when you travel.)
When we move our bodies in space our brains work differently.
Getting out of our heads (literally) helps us challenge assumptions and generate new ideas.

The spatial memory necessary for mapping uses the
hippocampus, a part of the brain that sits in the temporal lobe
and plays critical roles in learning, emotions, and memory. The
spatial memory functions of the hippocampus deteriorate if
they aren't used. Before the advent of GPS, people navigated
using physical maps and landmarks, oral instructions, and
collective community memory. Go straight until the road splits,
then follow it to the right until you see our house just past
the large oak tree. For some indigenous cultures, in which the
information needed to navigate is a complex understanding
of weather patterns, land characteristics, animal patterns, and
experience, the rise of GPS is even more detrimental to the
ability to navigate.

The **Buried Ships** of
Yerba Buena Cove
San Francisco

Buried treasures: deliberately sunken ships in San
Francisco's Yerba Buena Cove

When you use GPS, you don't use your hippocampus as
much in the navigation of a space. And without use, this part of
the brain declines in its ability to encode landmarks and navigate spatially. The more you use GPS to navigate, the more your
own navigational abilities decline. If you're a heavy GPS user
of turn-by-turn directions, try this on yourself: Don't turn it
on the next time. Examine your route on a map ahead of time
to determine the path you'd like to take and some landmarks
along the way. Even write out instructions to yourself. Then
notice how you feel during the journey. Are you more in tune
with the place you're in? Could you do it again? Exercise, story-
telling, mapping, design work—it all gets easier with practice.

Define Treasure with Time in Mind
When the things we make arrive in the future—as they always
do—they show up as treasure or trash. Even today, the ground
beneath downtown San Francisco is filled with abandoned

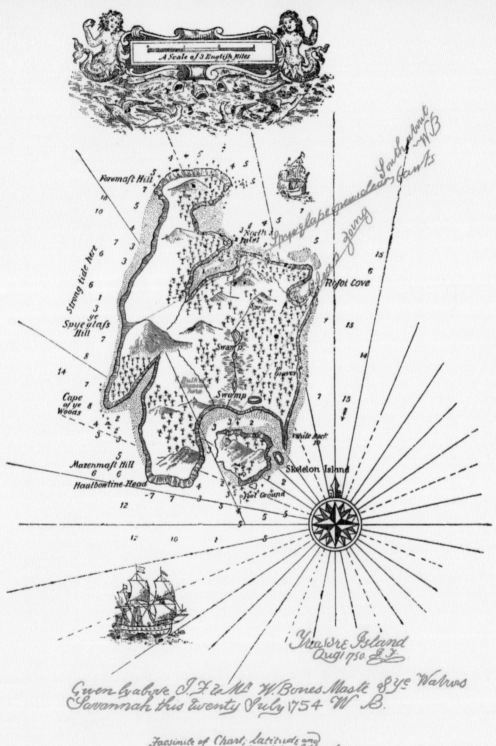

Robert Louis Stevenson's *Treasure Island* map is an
extension of the story—a hint at possibility.

sailing ships from the gold rush. Would-be prospectors sometimes sailed the ships to the city and then used them for
storage. Some of them burned. Others were deliberately sunk,
because a grounded ship gave its owner rights to the parcel of
land it was sunk on. Like many coastal cities, San Francisco
grew its borders outward from the shoreline, filling them with
sediment. And those grounded ship owners became downtown
landowners in the new and growing city. Treasure!

Forty vessels are entombed in downtown San Francisco. One
of these ships, the *Rome*, has an underground Muni line running directly through it. Riders on the N Judah and K Ingleside /
T Third lines travel through the forward hull of the ship on their
way into Embarcadero Station.

What constitutes treasure varies depending on the time,
topic, and people involved. Money, yes. The promised treasure
of the gold rush brought ships into the city that were eventually
sunk for the promised treasure of future land.

There are elements of time in treasure maps. Treasure can
imply what once was or what might yet be. Treasure implies
that if you take the time to look, the reward is worthwhile. What
would the hidden treasure in your hometown be today?
What about in fifty years? What might happen in that time?

Because what we make now lands in the future, adding a
dimension of time to our notions of treasure is critical. In our
rapidly warming climate, what counts as treasure? What has
value that we aren't seeing? What might be future treasure?
Our designs will decay. How can we make things that decay into
useful, interconnected treasure, not lingering, destructive trash?
This is one of the most important questions of our time, and it
needs to factor into our designs.

. . . .

We like to operate as if we have it together. It feels good. But
we don't have it together. We never have, and we certainly don't
now. This isn't the end times (fingers crossed!), but it's not a
tranquil era either. Proceed as though we are off-balance—
because we are.

What you need to do when you're off-balance is entirely
different from how you can act when things are going fine. That
can feel counterintuitive. But it's counterintuitive only if you
pretend that we're *not* in turbulent times. Turbulent times call
for tricky tactics.

The bumpy ride of history tells us that we will never have it all together, but we can always work to bring things closer to harmony. The prefix *re* means "back again." Reconsider. Remove. Reorient. Remake. Revisit. Try again. Second-guess. Lean into the turbulence to counteract its harried flow. Throw yourself off-kilter so you can regain balance. Turn into the skid. Deliberate disorientation works when the world is wonky.

Dissociology

Is there a world in which yesterday's waste becomes
tomorrow's treasure? What legacies are we leaving for our
descendants with what we leave behind?

———————————

Minnedosa, Canada / June 2066

Jada stood there, looking out at the small town set in the rolling hills.
It is her first real-world assignment. At nineteen, she is the mayor of
this place. She will live here for two years as part of her education and
training. The citizens haven't elected her per se, but they have voted to
be governed by a L'Académie student—someone with extremely high
compassion who is training to be a world leader. People living in places
like this are often progressive and want their leadership to be as fresh
and attuned as their ideas and inventions. It isn't that there are a lot of
people here—there are only about fifteen thousand—but because they
all live here to tend and access the massive provider farm, it is a place
of utmost importance.

Provider farms began to spring up around the world circa 2030. In
earlier history, these beacons of computational power were often called
server farms. At first, they were clusters of computing power housed in
warehouses, but with the blockchain mining surge in the 2010s these
farms began drawing more and more electricity and needed to be stra-
tegically located. Many of them moved to cold climates so the weather
could absorb the heat from the machines, but there was always the
challenge and balance of finding the right location for a server farm.

A cold, remote location—far from prying eyes—was ideal. But it
was hard to get electricity to these sites. In the late 2020s, with the
Little Climate Collapse underway, these farms began to both produce and consume their own energy. They became self-sufficient and
attracted young creators of anything that required computing power. If
you moved to a provider farm, you were responsible for helping to tend
it, and the work was around the clock. It was tiring, but also gave you

access to the computing power within the provider. The tenders kept the provider running and, in turn, the provider created a world of possibilities for those who used computing as their medium of creation. Today, provider farms have become hubs of innovation and creation for those who can stand the lifestyle. Many are big enough to require their own governance.

Jada walks toward the largest building on the provider farm. Her welcome speech won't be given for another two days, but she knows the first step toward leading is understanding her constituents, and to do this, she needs to meet them up close, as individuals. She needs to have conversations with them, to better read their faces and emotions, to study their unspoken struggles and motivations through their subtle tics and glances.

"Mayor Leeland! We are so very excited to have you. Welcome, welcome. I'm Sharmaigne Franklin. How was the hydrojet up here? Smooth? They usually are. Let me show you around."

It is more impressive than Jada had imagined. The computing parts that power the provider farm are mostly in a subbasement level. Their heat keeps the expansive building warm throughout the fairly cool year. Large panel displays graphically show the energy production of the solar arrays. Midsummer in the far northern hemisphere means long bright days loaded with unfiltered sunlight. They've already banked 89 percent of what they'd need as a minimum to get through winter.

"Wow. Your energy goal for winter is so much higher than what you'll need," says Jada. "Why do you want so much? Won't it strain your panels? Presumably you could get many more years out of them if you worked them less now, no?"

Sharmaigne smiles. Jada studies the subtleties of her expression, at least fourteen different muscles firing as she holds up the corners of her mouth for more than two seconds, in what Jada reads as genuine pride. "We could, yes, but let me show you what we've got in the works." She gestures at the glassed-in rooms in front of them. "These five projects are all potentially huge energy sinks. Normally, we'd pick one or two to focus on, but we've got a lot of eager people and neat ideas right now and kind of want to go for it."

Jada sees and hears the hope in Sharmaigne and a hint of uncertainty. You don't move to a provider farm far from a major city if you don't want to create something magical, and Jada is not about to stifle that desire. But she knows she'll have to work with this community to make sure they find balance between the high velocity of their own ambitions and the often maddeningly slow pace of real progress.

If there was one thing she learned at L'Académie, it was that almost everyone has the absolute best of intentions when they start out making something new. But the pressures and demands and buzz and fame and money that start to seep in when you reveal what's possible holds people back. They don't realize it right away, though, and it becomes problematic. For a while all the attention feels good. It feels like success. But then things begin to sour, slowly, from the inside out. It's hard for people to separate their micro and macro emotions from their ethical guideposts and personal ambitions.

The big technology revolution of the 2010s and 2020s is the major case study Jada learned at L'Académie. At the start of the revolution, tech was ungoverned, and people were encouraged to try to do everything—without even a mention of what might go wrong. It's hard to believe it at this point, but tech company leaders were the de facto world leaders. Their vast fortunes meant that even small moves and changes to their products rippled through society. Though originally conceived with good intentions, most of their products and services quickly became muddled and intertwined with the greed, power, and a presumed chosen status that early success can bring.

When faults were found with their products, they defended and denied them. When they failed at human decency, society pardoned them because of their wealth. When confronted with the troublesome ripple effects of their products, they had the hubris to assume that they, the people who had made and exacerbated the problems, should be trusted to fix them. It seems obvious now, decades beyond the old major tech era, but at the time much of the world was blind. Those who spoke up were marginalized and sidelined.

"I'd love to get to know everyone," Jada says as she follows Sharmaigne into the first room.

. . . .

The group leader lopes over as if his legs were springs. Jada can read his macro-exuberance as he approaches. "I'm Dino. Welcome to Dissociology. It's so great to meet you, Mayor Leeland. We've been anticipating your arrival." Now that he is close, she can tell the sentiment is genuine. The word he should have used is *relieved*.

"I can't wait to learn about what you're building, Dino."

"Let me show you," he says as he leads her to a display high-lighting their work. There is a long core, a cylinder drilled out from the earth, displayed on the large, well-lit tables in front of them. The cylinder is about thirty centimeters in diameter and forty meters long, but divided into four ten-meter sections to fit into the room. Within the core, many layers of dirt, clay, sand, and trash in various stages of decomposition are visible.

Dino lets Jada walk around the core and admire it for a few minutes. The layers closest to the surface are topsoil, below which is a fabric barrier meant to contain the landfill. The landfill itself begins about two meters from the surface and continues for an astounding thirty-eight meters. There must have been a hundred years of trash here. As Jada examines it, she can see visible pieces of plastic, glass, and metal. In some layers the trash is heavily decomposed. In others, it is compacted but in its original form.

"This landfill spanned one square kilometer," says Dino. "It was the main trash dump in the suburbs north of Chicago."

"Wow," says Jada. She is picturing the size of it and then realizes that though the dump is huge, it didn't even serve a major city. "Tell me about all the dates," she says. Along the side of the core are a series of annotation lines and dates, demarking different years. The core was pulled last year. That label was on top.

"It's basically a time capsule," says Dino. "You can see that the whole dump sat dormant for about ten years. Then, follow the layers down all the way to 1975. Some layers are thicker. Those can be tied to times when consumer consumption was high and the economy was strong, yet recycling practices were primitive, low, or unused for whatever reason."

Jada leans in. "The 1980s and 1990s. Clearly there was wealth and consumption during that time. Those layers are quite thick despite being so low. You can learn so much from this," she comments.

"Yes. But be careful. This core came from the suburbs north of Chicago. That area was well-off, but if we'd instead sampled one of the dumps that serviced the city center, we would have seen an entirely different profile. The poorer inner-city residents created less trash because they couldn't afford to waste. But if you look at cores from parts of New Jersey or Oregon, where they experimented with different types of recycling early on, you'll see thin layers too, but that's because the waste was diverted rather than never consumed," he continues.

You get only one slice of history if you consider only one part of the story. Each of these layers is loaded with information, but Dino doesn't want her to think this one core is the whole story.

"But that's just the core," he says, and smiles. "Being able to look back through history is interesting, but it's not what Dissociology is about. We're modern-day scavengers!"

Dino walks Jada to the back of the space. They peer through a glass partition into a laboratory.

"That's where we scavenge. We all know the generations before us never *really* tried to recycle. They went through the motions at times, yes, but even successful recycling programs were short-lived and essentially just reuse ventures. We're able to go through hundreds of years of landfill and break down the trash into usable raw materials. We're mechanically, chemically, and thermally separating out components into their elemental forms. We're dissociating it, and then it can be used again."

Jada reads in his face that he really hopes what he just said is true, but something is troubling him. She waits for him to continue.

"Well, that's what we're trying to do anyway. I know it's possible, and for some materials, anything with metal, especially, we've been successful. But with the plastics, the materials that are built from hydrocarbons, it's proving more difficult. We haven't figured out a very efficient way to do that yet. Composites, though—those are the hardest. Some of the most economically successful commercial materials are the hardest to dissociate and recycle. I would have hoped we'd be there by now. It requires so much energy to grind up the composites that it costs much more to complete half the recycling than we can recover for the materials after the fact."

Dino's eyes dart to the corners of the room and his forehead lines ascend. He seems poised to keep going but hesitates. Jada reads it as care, almost to the degree that parents care for their child.

"Composites aside, we're able to extract value from trash. But who gets that value? Is it the municipality that currently houses the waste? Or the descendants of those who lived in the neighborhoods next to the dumps for generations? The families who dealt with the smells and the eyesores and the leaching chemicals? Those dumps ensured that the people living near them stayed poor. And now we see these shadowy tactics beginning to emerge."

"Like what?" This topic is completely new to Jada, but Dino oozes anger over an injustice.

"Amazon bought the Apex Regional landfill in Las Vegas last year. Why? Because it's a gold mine. They're betting on reaping rewards from the waste they made in the first place."

Jada feels his activist energy. He clearly has the perfect constitution for this work.

"What about the poor countries that for years took in trash from the wealthy countries? Trash value could significantly impact the GDP of several of the world's poorest nations, tipping a balance of power in their direction. It's like when the Saudis found oil in 1938. We're at that level. And what about Dissociology? We're on the verge of holding too much power ourselves. No small science start-up should be able to control the fate of multiple countries. But who should? Should the countries or corporations that created the trash fund its dissociation? Should they be allowed to get any of the benefits, effectively benefiting twice from their waste?"

Dino pauses for a beat. "It's a lot. We need your help. Sorry. I know it's your first day." He looks at her bashfully, hopefully.

Jada stares down the lengths of the massive landfill core. In the top few meters she sees her childhood, then the lives of her mother and grandmother. Traces of what was, resurrected now to repair it. She points at the cores and looks at Dino assuredly, "This is the history of the future. It's not an easy path, but these questions you are asking will ensure the long-term success of Dissociology. With this mindset, the cores that your company excavates after the next hundred years will look entirely different."

———————————

Responsible reuse is possible. As technology evolves, we can use it to core and mine landfills, the same way we presently use ice cores to examine climate history and sediment cores to hunt for hidden resources like fossil fuels. What is currently deemed *trash* is likely loaded with value, but who can or should profit from it is a question to reckon with.

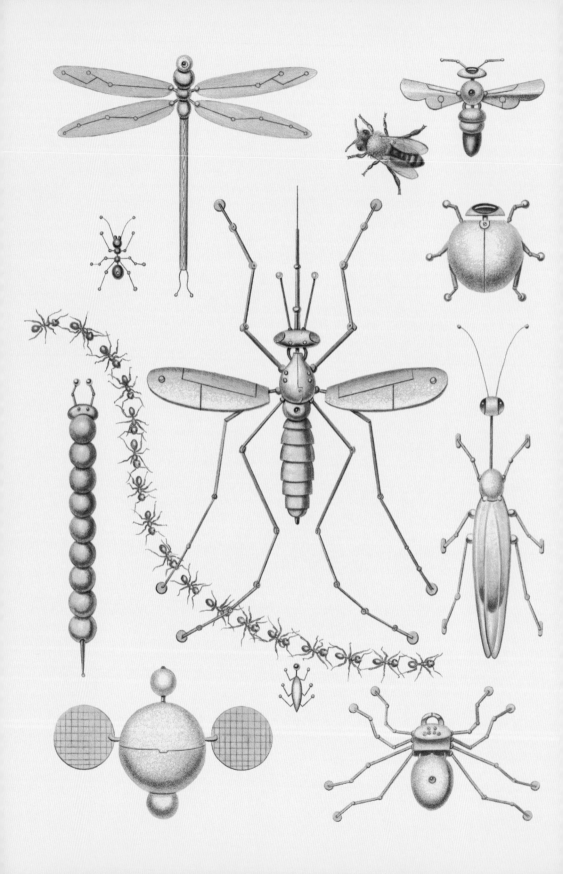

CHAPTER 8

Aim for Imperfection

Don't Fix Everything
(Because Everything Breaks)

When you invent the ship, you also invent the shipwreck. . . . Every technology carries its own negativity, which is invented at the same time as technical progress.

—*Paul Virilio, philosopher and architect*

B reaking is natural. Over time, things fall apart. We get old. Foliage dies and decays. Buildings crumble. The things we make have been breaking all along, but we don't spend much time dwelling on it—partly because we don't want to believe our designs will break, partly because we've decided not to notice.

Sometimes things break because they are misused. Sometimes they wear out. Other times the things we make work according to plan but break something else. But everything we make is going to break: This is the first, last, and perhaps only rule of runaway (and all) design.

But you can make the most of the breaks by turning constraints into possibility, leaning into imperfection, and redefining what it means to respond by preparing to heal, not just after, but during and well before breaks happen.

There Will Always Be Mistakes in Our Dreams

In 1941, Ray and Charles Eames drove from Bloomfield Hills, Michigan, to Los Angeles, California. Newly married, World War II underway, they set up life in an apartment in sunny Westwood, down the block from UCLA.

Most windowsills sit at about waist height and are set into a wall. The living room windows in the Eames's skinny Richard Neutra—designed apartment stretched down to within a couple of feet of the floor and ran the entire length of the wall. The extra glass made sure you couldn't forget that you lived in sun-swept Southern California. These were optimistic windows—with panes of glass that big, you have to have faith in humanity. Ray mused, in a 1948 article for *Mademoiselle's Living*, that it was "a simple shell that imposed no style . . . but left them free to create their own surroundings."

No sooner had the Eameses moved in than they set up a huge contraption in their spare room. They called it the Kazam! machine. It looked like a deconstructed, room-size toaster—a hodgepodge of spare bicycle parts, electric coils, and plaster. They built it to mold plywood into curvy shapes. To make it run, Charles had to shimmy up a nearby electrical pole to "borrow" a little extra current. Pretty soon, the Eameses were shaping veneered wood into contoured leg splints, the first time wood had been made to bend reliably in multiple directions at once.

As their ambitions grew, the Kazam! grew too. It made its way into their bedroom and then the kitchen. Eventually they had to relocate the whole operation into a proper studio in nearby Venice, where they built beautiful, honest, comfortable furniture that was quick and easy to produce.

The Eameses were keen on possibility. They had a way with words too. Their self-styled motto nailed the optimistic problem-solving ethos of the time: "The best, for the most, for the least." For the Eameses, that meant cultivating craft (the best) to serve people (for the most) through the magic efficiency of industry (for the least). It was a noble cause for two earnest individuals.

In the early 1970s, many years and many well-loved products later, Charles was freshly into his own sixties. The industrial 1940s, the optimistic 1950s, the swinging 1960s, and most of his career was behind him by then. In a 1971 interview with Anthony Bowman, he gave an honest take on the impact of their era:

The scary fact is that many of our dreams have come true. We wanted a more efficient technology and we got pesticides in the soil. We wanted cars and television sets and appliances and each of us thought he was the only one wanting that. Our dreams have come true at the expense of Lake Michigan. That doesn't mean that the dreams were all wrong. It means that there was an error somewhere in the wish and we have to fix it.*

* First published in a June 1972 issue of a now defunct magazine called *Ameryka*, a Polish weekly published in Toledo, Ohio.

We all have mistakes in our dreams. What you want and what you get are rarely the same. Charles and Ray Eames were a duo with good hearts who never lost sight of their ideals. A sketch made by Charles serves as a manifesto of their earnestness and spirit.

The little scratched notes say that the job of a designer is to find the overlap between their own interests, the interests of the person paying for it ("the client"), and society as a whole. Put another way: A design gets molded by a business model, the designer's sense of purpose, and the broader needs of the world.

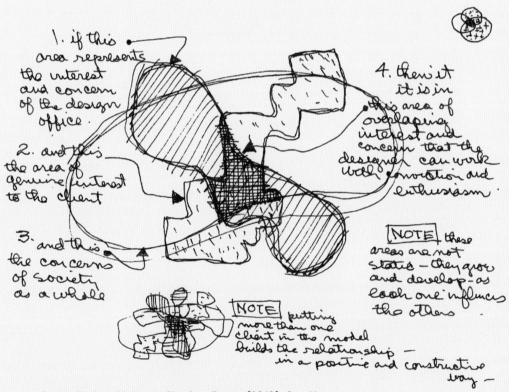

Eames Design Diagram, Charles Eames [1969] for the exhibition *Qu'est-ce que le design?* ["What Is Design?"] at the Musée des Arts Décoratifs in Paris

It's a beautiful idea, in theory. There's just one thing: most people don't do it that way. Business is in the room. Business builds the room. Now the designer has a seat at the table. Sometimes the person the design serves (often a customer) does too. But those broader needs of society? They don't have a place to sit.

Society sits somewhere in the ether or in the passing thoughts of each guest, and nature is nowhere except in the material that makes up the table itself. Importantly, time doesn't have a chair either. There is little acknowledgment of the longevity, for better and for worse, of what we put into the world. This is why our wishes have errors.

If you were to redraw Charles Eames's seminal sketch, it might have the following components:

1. An overlap of the designer's talent and desires with the possibilities afforded by technologies and ways of making today. What are you passionate about, and what might you build with? What are all the things the tech can create?

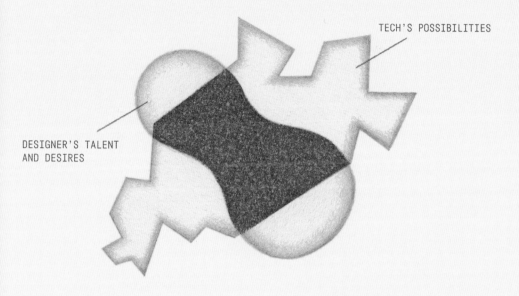

TECH'S POSSIBILITIES

DESIGNER'S TALENT
AND DESIRES

2. An overlap of the needs of society, nature, and our descend-ants. What does the world and the future need from us?

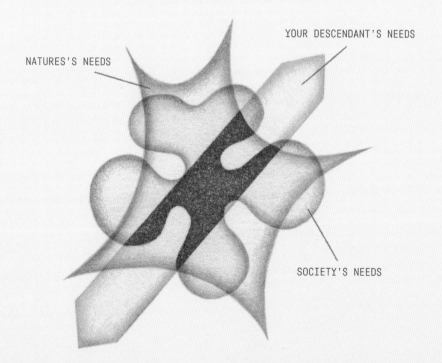

YOUR DESCENDANT'S NEEDS

NATURES'S NEEDS

SOCIETY'S NEEDS

3. Combined, it would look like this:

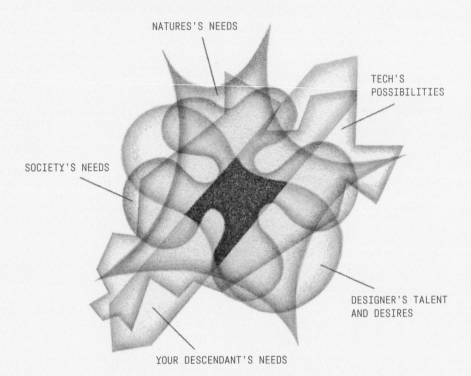

NATURES'S NEEDS

TECH'S POSSIBILITIES

SOCIETY'S NEEDS

DESIGNER'S TALENT AND DESIRES

YOUR DESCENDANT'S NEEDS

That little darkened shape in the middle that houses the ultimate in overlaps is the intersection of possibility. This is where the script is flipped. Instead of giving the client its own shape, we can start in the middle and ask, **What business, organization, government, or other entity shares these same desires? Can they be your partner? Funder? Champion?**

It's a lot of constraints, for sure, and may feel overwhelming, but start by overlapping two or three shapes for you and your work.

The shapes you pick highlight your priorities. The ones you leave out are potential hazards. These are places that may break more than others if we don't keep an eye on them—so put some eyes on them, and you'll remember that they're potential monsters. Try this exercise looking backward at a project you've recently worked on.

What role did you play?

What tools did you use to create with? Who helped create it?

Did it serve a larger societal need?

Were the needs of nature considered? Which ones?

Did you consider the longevity of the work and the legacy it would leave for the future? How so?

Is there one or more elements that you didn't think through at all? Why do you think that is?

If you were to redo this project and rebuild the diagram starting from scratch, what might it look like? What would be different?

Just because we don't include something in our dreams doesn't mean it isn't there. But if you are afraid to notice mistakes, it's even easier for them to sneak in. Are we brave enough to look at our dreams and search for mistakes?

Imperfection is an inevitable outcome of design. If we want to get real, imperfection could be an inevitable *aim* of design. Healthy imperfection is a goal as noble, optimistic, and bold as any moonshot. Accepting imperfection is not a call to surrender to the whims of runaway design or to downplay our dreams. It's a call for clear-eyed humility alongside action, unapologetic optimism, and real responsibility.

Like our sensory slivers and limited points of view, our dreams are lopsided too. We need new kinds of dreams. Big, broad dreams that aim high but don't ignore their own downsides. Call them full dreams; dreams that are grand but not singular, dreams with enough room for everyone else's dreams too.

How to Design a Bee

As we set out to save the world,
how will we save the world from our faulty selves?

———————

The first sign that something is amiss is the sound. A quick hum cut short by a sharp tap. Each hum and tap—they are coming by the second now—signals the death knell of another bee as it topples aimlessly through the air on a misguided flight that ends abruptly and decisively against the windowpane.

Maeve is fixated on the window. She turns to her companion and says with resignation, "Get the spray." Within seconds the two of them are out on the lawn frantically pointing nozzles toward the sky, clouds of chemicals putting an end to the lives of as many bees as possible, as fast as possible—even before they have a chance to die on the windowsill.

This is the end of the story—so they hope.

When the story began is harder to pinpoint, but it started as all stories do, with hopes and dreams. The dream that first got things moving was the subdivision. It was the hope of a man who had land and wanted money. So he divided the land into parcels, built a home on each, paved the worn-down goat paths nearby, carved the name "Eternal Springs" into a boulder on the property's edge, and sold off the lots one by one. Each parcel was purchased by other folks with smaller, more specific dreams of homes and families and happiness.

One of those small-time dreamers bought a cozy plot. He had his own stories of hard work and pride. This particular plot was just the right setting to fulfill them. A flat ridge sloped down into a tiny dell, a shape that lets you know where you can build and where you shouldn't. The house sat where it should, at the top of the hill. A driveway coasted down to a concrete pad at the bottom. The builder meant to put a garage there, but his funding ran out. The new owner dreamt of a long car and a garage to protect it, but he bought the garage-less parcel anyway. Building a garage on his own fit nicely into his plans.

The finished garage looked good, but it had the flaws of a first try: The studs weren't quite secure. The paint could have used another coat. But he didn't much like to ask for help. His self-worth was wrapped up in figuring things out on his own. So it stood, mistakes and all.

Years later, his offspring had their own dreams, exactly none of them set in this place. The house and garage sat empty as nature and time—partners in crime—did their thing. They have a way of dispensing with even the most elaborate schemes—though more through indifference than spite.

Left vacant, the little plot was a friendly place for flora and fauna. The winters were not too cold, the summers not too warm; rain kept the grass green most of the year. A raccoon family took up residence in the chimney, robins nested nearby, and a single cherry pit nestled against the side of the garage and made its way from seed to tree. That was twenty years ago.

People who have what they need from nature—food, shelter, warmth, safety, companionship—are free to dream of other things. Most dream of more or of better. Those who dream of more dream of larger things, more refined things, grander adventures—in other words, greed. Those who dream of better dream of improving the lot of others, changing the way things are, improving things—in other words, generosity.

Maeve, our hero, had what she needed from nature. In her dreams, she was a generous soul who dreams of better, not more. Glenn, her companion, dreamt of better too. The two generous dreamers left high-paying gigs designing new organisms on less idealistic projects to come here.

By the time they arrived in the little dell, a disturbing trend was afoot. Bee colonies here and everywhere had been dying off for decades. Sometimes the losses slowed, sometimes they sped up. The most recent swing was in the wrong direction—bees were dying in droves. The couple decided to put their know-how to work protecting the planet's pollinators.

This little green plot was a perfect setting. Maeve was the daughter of the daughter of the man with the long car and the dreams of work and pride. The house, the garage, and the dell were hers now. So she set out to build a home base where they would birth a new bee, a resilient kind that wouldn't be so tormented by the hard world that humans like them had helped create.

Their first idea was to make the bees live longer. But, geriatric bees wouldn't solve the problems that were killing them off—infections, viruses, pesticides, weather, and the like. Maybe they could make them more virile? The prospect of horny honeybees brought up its own problems; besides, a each hive has only a single queen. They settled on what they thought was an elegant, poetic solution. One that put responsibility in the hands of humans whose behavior had been messing with the bees in the first place. They would make the bees easier to tend to and nurture.

Deep inside the genome of many earthly creatures is a gene that affects how they find food. It's nicknamed the foraging gene. When it comes to insects, the foraging gene shows itself in two ways. *Rovers* improvise and cover more ground as they scrounge for energy. *Sitters* circle around and stay close. The couple decided to select for sitting and make bees that like to stay close to their hives. With bees foraging nearby, beekeepers could do things like surround them with sunflowers, whose pollen is a natural laxative that helps sick bees rid their guts of infections.

Maeve took the lead in converting the garage into an apiary. Nature's relentless metamorphosis had rendered the garage more than a bit off-kilter. One by one, she replaced cockeyed beams and stuffed walls with fresh insulation. Then she installed lab equipment and spent days patching cracks the old cherry tree had left along the wall. When she was done, the garage was sparkling and sealed.

If Maeve was good at breathing life into big things, Glenn was fascinated by the little ones. Once she had fixed the garage and filled it with gear, he took the lead at the lab bench.

Genetically altering creatures is painstaking and sticky and impossibly small-scale. The ingredients are teeny eggs, miniature petri dishes, and terribly thin injectors. Not to mention microscopic concoctions of gene splicers alongside strands of fresh DNA. Glenn laced their mixtures with sitter versions of the foraging gene and a small slice of the human genome that bolsters memory. These bees would not be just cozy little homebodies; they would be sharp-witted and nostalgic too. Just like the two beekeepers that made them.

They also borrowed some extra DNA from a rare South African honeybee to help their queen reproduce asexually, no mating necessary. That little trick would save them—and the queen—the arduous step of forced breeding and make sure her descendants properly preserved their tweaked genes. And down the road, it would save them the hassle of all the rigmarole with petri dishes and pipettes.

Bringing forth a freshly modified queen is no easy task. Receptacles. Injections. Centrifuges. Waiting. More waiting. And then, "royal jelly"— the special ingredient that turns an everyday embryo into a queen.

The next step was to incubate the eggs, but the new, fancy incubator was on the fritz. Even Maeve couldn't get it to work. As a stop-gap, they cranked up the heat in the garage. It got so sweltering in there, they took to wearing shorts and tank tops like bakers working a hot kitchen in midsummer. Without the help of a steady incubator, only a few queens hatched, and only one was healthy and strong. But one was enough. They named their virgin queen Mary.

Glenn surrounded Mary with worker bees to tend to her needs and waited another week before spurting carbon dioxide into her cage to coax her into laying hundreds of eggs. Then the waiting began anew while another batch of eggs incubated in the hot garage. Soon they would have their first full hive of cozy, nostalgic bees.

Though the scale of their work was tiny, the time it took was lengthy. They spent months and months trying, incubating, and failing—and failing again. With all their attention on the little critters in their homespun lab, they grew lazy with the yard. Lazy enough for the grass to grow floppy and wispy, and time enough for falling cherries to splatter the side of the garage with their juice.

To keep things authentic with the wild, Maeve and Glenn fed their bees from potted plants instead of the usual drops of sugar water. To make watering easy, Maeve fastened rows of misting sprinklers above the flowers. Glenn too welcomed the mist, turning the sprinklers on again and again to get a dose of the cool droplets. The plants got more than their fair share of hydration.

Time, heat, and wet are the perfect recipe for fermentation. In the hothouse garage, the flowers' sweet pollen slowly bubbled into a tangy cocktail laced with ethanol—the active ingredient in booze. The bees took quite a liking. Soon they covered the flowers so thoroughly that pink and purple petals turned black and yellow.

And so, on this day—the day the two beekeepers would eventually be forced to release the chemical spray—they stumbled into an awful scene: hundreds of their precious bees ravenously swarming the spiked stamens while the rest buzzed aimlessly about the pen. If you just happened upon the bees on their wobbly flight, you might miss the difference between sober and tipsy, but to Maeve and Glenn the trouble was obvious. The bees who'd partaken of the flowery hooch were hurtling around the garage like a bunch of regulars stumbling out of a bar at closing time.

The beekeepers were witness to a pattern forged by the changes they'd inscribed in the bees' genes, in concert with nature's complex whims, finished off by the biases and gaps hiding behind their best efforts. Their tweaks to the bees' genes gave those insects a pesky habit: a love for—and a hard time metabolizing—alcohol. Their precious bees were a bunch of drunks.

Though they had yet to track down the source of the trouble, the crisis at hand was clear. Faulty flight paths pose a particular problem. Flight isn't just how bees find their way to food and back; flight paths are also how they communicate. To a teetotaling bee, drunken bees with shaky flights come off as interlopers to be banished from a sober hive. These bees could collapse a colony. It was not what the beekeepers had in mind.

Dejected and sore, the beekeepers retreated to the house to discuss their dwindling options over glasses of chilled wine and plates of Maeve's famous tofu katsu. They pondered whether to get rid of the rabble now or let the bees die on their own, taking time to learn from their errant behavior before the bees passed on.

In the end, the tofu never made it out of the skillet—their dinner interrupted by the hum and tap of drunken bees careening into the windowpanes. They snatched up their canisters of chemicals and stumbled outside to find the same garbled flight patterns they'd discovered in the garage, only now they were spreading across the lawn and toward the trees beyond. Not only had they made wonky bees, but their moment of indecision had somehow released them into the wild.

The two darted across the yard, spraying the air willy-nilly, missing as many bees as they killed. After chasing their creations around the property until their legs gave out, they decided to split up. Maeve ran down toward the garage to tackle the source; Glenn scurried up the dell to raid the house for supplies.

Up at the house, Glenn ransacked the kitchen for anything rotten or sweet. He smashed overripe bananas on a spare cookie sheet, piled brown sugar atop the resulting mush, then unloaded a carton of apple juice across the whole thing.

Now he needed alcohol. He grabbed the stash of a twelve-year-old whiskey they kept around to celebrate their progress. (They'd last opened it when they bred queen Mary.) He poured the remaining half into the pan and stirred the heavy slop around with his palm to make a shimmering amber slop of bananas, sugar, juice, and whiskey. He tossed two glasses on the tray and darted out the back door, cookie sheet in one hand, bee-killing spray in the other.

Down in the garage, the sound of swarming bees was deafening. Maeve plucked a proper gas mask—goggles, breathing nozzle, and all—off the wall. She had to blow and swat to make sure the bees didn't stow away inside as she strapped it over her face. Once the mask was snug, she pumped the chemical sprayer as hard as she could, waving the wand indiscriminately. The cloud of bees crumbled in front of her like a wobbling, turbulent tornado turning into a pile of pebbles. The buzzing got quieter in turn. Soon she could track individual bees circling her head. She took those out too. Then she shoved the business end of the chemical wand into their artificial hive and let loose. More bees poured onto the floor.

On her knees, she picked through the inch-deep pile of carcasses. Stingers brushed across her fingers, rendering them red and welted in minutes. She stopped to survey the carpet of carcasses, searching for signs of movement. Brushing a huge stack of the motionless insects aside, she revealed one large bee laboring across the floor. She covered the crawling bee with the nozzle, pulled the trigger, and didn't let go—pummeling their virgin queen with enough chemical spray to take out a small mammal.

Maeve emerged from the garage with her gas mask, dead bees dotting her shirt like a pilly Christmas sweater. Stepping over the dead bees she'd already laid to rest, she took out anything and everything that flew by: bees, bugs, butterflies—it didn't matter. She kept at it until the sky was quiet and all she could hear was the sound of crickets chirping away in the woods. Soon their song was interrupted by the staccato spurts of her partner's chemical cannister. She followed the hissing sounds back down to the bottom of the dell.

Glenn caught her eye and waved her over to a bench he'd set under the cherry tree. The cookie sheet lay next to him, mushy islands of glistening brown sugar and squashed banana poking above the thick golden liquid. He faced the side of the garage, spray nozzle cocked and aimed at the spot where the tree met the siding, spritzing bees as they wandered from a meandering crack where the tree's wide trunk pushed against the wall of the garage. Meanwhile, bees from around the yard made their way toward the sweet alcoholic nectar. He killed them too.

Maeve sat down and took off her mask. They both stared at the crack the tree had made in the wall and the bees now finding their way out. A long, defeated sigh escaped her lungs followed by, "I'm sure I patched that up."

Glenn put his hand on her shoulder and said two short words, "Things change."

After a moment of silence, Maeve followed up with two words of her own: "Mary's dead."

Glenn leaned back as far as the laws of physics would allow him without sliding off the bench. "Thank god. And thank you."

With the mature queen dead and most of their bees lying motionless on the grass and in the garage, their faulty genetic code was less likely to spread, but the beekeepers weren't out of the woods yet. Their bees were all just like Mary—they too could duplicate themselves. Though the odds had gotten a lot better since the first bee crashed into the window at dinner, they were nowhere near a given.

As for the ones that got away, the two could only hope that the crooked flight paths would be enough for other bees to reject the clones from their hives before Mary's doppelgängers could sneak in and clone themselves.

Glenn pointed his spray nozzle back toward the cherry tree trunk and took out another swath of bees. Then he dropped it and reached beneath the bench for the two brimming glasses.

"I had to use the good whiskey," he said semi-apologetically, "but I siphoned off some for us. It's quite tasty."

They raised their glasses for a toast. The liquid glowed iridescent gold in the late-day sun. With a melancholy clink, they swigged the sweet, cloudy slurry. They sat and nursed their drinks until well after sundown, all the while pumping insecticide at each and every bee they could find. Their dreams of better inverted into a hope that the world would work its magic and help put those dreams to rest. At least until they could come up with a better one.

Though scientists link foraging genes to a taste for alcohol (at least in fruit flies), and there is a South African bee strain with a knack for cloning, complicated behaviors like those in this story won't likely arise from tweaking a few genes.

This story isn't about the ins and outs of genetic manipulation anyway. It's not really about bioengineering at all. Any potent, emergent technology could have stood in as a foil (and biologists themselves express wariness about designing bees). It's about people and the power we unleash into a complex world with the things we create, about how good intentions don't guarantee good outcomes, and about how mistakes come with our wishes. It illustrates the need to add clear-eyed dreams atop our big, good-hearted ones.* (And, we will need every kind of dream we can muster—from grand, visionary dreams to considered, careful ones—if and when things break.)

* Many bioengineers have big, clear-eyed dreams. Some even craft imperfections to stave off issues just like the ones in this story (see page 282).

Picking Up the Pieces When Something Breaks

A big mistake in an even bigger dream was seeded in 1987. It was a momentous occasion, an unparalleled act of global cooperation. Every single country on the planet banded together in pursuit of the ultimate dream: a livable planet.

The Montreal Protocol, ratified on September 16, 1987, provided protection of the ozone layer by phasing out production of chlorofluorocarbons (CFCs). In today's world, where climate change is highly politicized even though it and its anthropogenic (aka, human) causes are well documented scientifically, it's hard to fathom that the only act of universal global collaboration on any topic, ever, was about climate change.

But the 1980s and '90s saw the world band together in shared terror. There was a hole—we all saw it in the satellite images broadcast on classroom TVs and the nightly news—in the ozone layer, the shield in the stratosphere that absorbs the UV rays from the sun. And if we didn't all do our part to help it close, it might mean the end of human existence within a few generations. Life on Earth can't exist without the ozone layer.

We changed our behaviors to save ourselves from crisping to extinction. We were pursuing the dream.

Big-hair lovers around the world adapted away from aerosol cans of hairspray to prevent CFCs from entering the atmosphere. And makers of air conditioners, cars, and refrigerators—where most CFCs were used as coolants—were spurred to replace them with HFCs (hydrofluorocarbons). Swapping that first C for an H means that today's cooling chemicals no longer release chlorine, the key culprit in the ozone hole, into the atmosphere.

Crisis averted! The hole in the ozone layer is healing itself and should be complete by 2050 when the last remaining CFCs have degraded out of the atmosphere.

Crisis averted? Here's the mistake. It turns out that HFCs are a greenhouse gas stronger than carbon dioxide. HFCs keep us cooler but cause our planet to get warmer. An error in the wish.

Everything breaks. So ask yourself: What happens to the broken parts? Sometimes we have systems for fixing breakage (or at least trying to). The Kigali Amendment to the Montreal Protocol, passed in 2016, aims to phase out use of HFCs. Many of the original Montreal Protocol signing countries have adopted it, but not all. What system might you put in place to evaluate and respond to breakage in your own work? What culture of fixing are you in?

In the United States, we tend to fix larger appliances, like refrigerators and washing machines, and some smaller, expensive ones, like mobile phones, to a degree. But for the most part ours is a throwaway culture. The culture of fixing doesn't extend as far as it does in other countries. In 2021, France enabled the first of its kind "repairability index" legislation. It requires electronics manufacturers to label their products with a repairability score built on the following five parameters:

Documentation: How available are technical documents to consumers and repairers?

Disassembly: How easy is it to take apart the product, what tools are needed, and what kinds of fasteners are required to put it back together?

Spare part availability: For how long will the manufacturer make spare parts accessible, and how fast can a consumer get them?

Spare part cost: How expensive are the parts relative to the overall product price?

Specifics: A product-specific catchall category that may include software updates and support services.

What parameters should be in a repairability index for your work? What behavioral shift or business practice might that inspire? The French repairability index is meant to curb the practice of planned obsolescence—things that are designed to be thrown away. But who should govern them? Scores on the French index are currently calculated by manufacturers them-selves. What are the boundaries of trust?

Of course, often when something breaks we destroy or trash it and allow it to degrade, decompose, and rot. Broken parts get sent to landfills. Sometimes we make plans to decommis-sion things—like nuclear reactors—before they break others. Sometimes we recycle, at least in theory, and hopefully in practice. Sometimes we compost, or rather we allow fungi and microbes to compost. There are many ways to deal with broken parts and the things our parts have broken. Some are more admirable than others.

When Everything Goes Right, What Will Go Wrong?

When we interview the finalist applicants to Stanford's Design MS, we ask them to talk us through a project in their portfolio that they're particularly proud of. Then we have them extrapolate: What's the dream? How would you like to see this take hold in the world? They've usually painted a neat and admirable vision. Then we ask the real question: When everything with that project goes right, what will go wrong?*

Imagine that you do whatever you set out to and do it just as you described. What are the second- and third-order implications? How could your project change things for the better—and the worse? What could go wrong?

It's a daunting, name-your-monsters question that requires you to look imperfection in the eye and get comfortable with your discomfort. Nobody wants to envision a world where their creations cause trouble, but it is liberating and fascinating to accept the challenge of dealing with the downsides of your work. Taking responsibility from the start saves the agony of wondering what you are missing.

Asking questions like these doesn't mean our dreams will be error free, but it allows us to think through negative consequences, no matter how far afield they may seem. We don't know what's going to happen with the things we make. But questions like these can make sure we won't shy away from dealing with the errors if (and when) they happen.

* This question is the subject of several stories in this book, like "Hello, Mamas" (page 28); "Veritas™" (page 84); and "Don't Swat!" (page 285).

Gain Literacy in Mischievous Materials

Here is a mantra: You don't need to know the code, but you need to know what the code can do.

Put another way, you don't need to be a technical expert in everything, but you should aim to understand what different technologies and materials can do. You know many materials already. You know that paper can be folded into airplanes and written on with ink. You know that clay can be molded into mugs. You know that light can be captured with sensors and turned into pixels to make photographs. You even know that shared goals, networking, and sticky messaging can be shaped into a protest.

Mediums are what we build with. Everything is made of something, often many things. Many materials are tangible. You can fiddle them in your hands to get a sense for what they can do, like wood, metal, or even digital drawing tools. Cardboard can be bent, scored, rounded, flattened, notched, and connected to other pieces. Even if you don't know how to weld, you likely have a sense that two pieces of metal can be fused together.

But other, newer materials aren't as intuitively transparent. Algorithms and blockchains, synthetic biologies and massive datasets—these are the new materials that makers are using to create our world. They predict our desires and actions online (offline too). They create new medicines, organize currencies, contribute to criminal justice decisions.

These mediums are tricky—we call them "mischievous materials." You can't hold a sample in your hand to get a feel for their power. At times they almost seem alive and creative, pursuing their own ends, scaling swiftly, and continuing to evolve. Most of us don't understand the intricacies of how they work or how to work with them. Their technical complexity has taken many out of the collective of makers. The speed at which they scale and morph and multiply overwhelms our desire to tinker and attempt to participate.

The footprint and the impacts of these mischievous materials are massive, yet only some of us know what the code can do or how it will behave when things go wrong. You can prepare for potential breakdowns by becoming as literate as possible in as many mediums as possible, especially the tricky ones. If you know how a material works, you have a sense for what it can create and how it fails, even if you're not a craftsperson or technical expert.

The biggest issue of all? Only some of us are represented in them. Anyone who's not at least conversational in the language of a material can't speak and won't be heard. Their ideas and experiences won't be represented and can't be created if they can't imagine with the material in mind.

Let's say you've never heard of or seen plastic. If you needed to design a container and didn't know plastic was an option, you wouldn't even consider it. You're illiterate in that material. The same goes for mischievous materials like blockchains. If you don't know, at least at a high level, that they are tools that can fundamentally change the organization of a system—from having a central, governing body to instead having multiple decentralized nodes with multiple new ways of accomplishing tasks and building trust—then you would never consider blockchain as a tool you might use in your next project.

273

Material literacy is even more important when things break. If your refrigerator starts leaking water, you might not know how to fix it yourself, but you can see that there's a problem and call a repairperson, find a DIY tutorial, or even unplug it before that water leaks into your floor and triggers an even larger problem. You can do those things because you can see the problem. But if an algorithm breaks or some synthetic DNA mutates in an unintended way and you don't have any material literacy in those mediums, leaks will spread.

What if everyone could fiddle with algorithms in the same way we can all stretch rubber bands and fling them across the room? What if you had a handheld blockchain that you could run your fingers over to feel what makes it secure? What if we were all literate in the new materials of making and understood how to work with them, shepherd them, fold them? What if we were all part of making them and were all represented by them?

For the future to include room for everybody, now is the time to get literate in the ways it gets made and to help others get literate too. Practice this with the go-to materials you work with: What are they good at? How do they work? If you find yourself mired in technical jargon, level up the question. Ask, "Why is this important?" And then again, "Why is that important?" In no time you'll be talking about materials in terms of what they can do and make happen, not the intricacies of how they work. The more you share this with others, the more you boost their material literacy too.

Here's how to have a material literacy conversation.

274

Tools Plus Time Make Power

Design is as human as talking, maybe more so. It's hard to come by hard evidence of language before the dawn of writing, but most educated guesses say people were speaking at least a few hundred thousand years ago. Evidence of tool-making comes a good two million years *before* that. Our ancestors most likely made things to serve their needs well before they talked about how they did it. Design came first.

Design by everybody lasted for eons, but, in the age of industry and mass media, things began to shift, leaving opportunity for only a select few to create at such large scales. Even outside industrial-scale design, there was a sharp line between creatives and normal folk. Not so much anymore. With the advent of fast, cheap processors, cameras in pockets, and 3D printers, we're all creators again. The tools just look different.

In 2016, Bon Iver released their third album, *22, A Million*. It was a sharp stylistic turn. Their first two albums had a few minor hints of technologist inklings—synth sounds peeking out behind conventional guitar strums—but with titles like "Perth" and "Minnesota, WI," the songs sounded like the traditional acoustic folk fare that made the band famous. *22, A Million* was something else. It was full of synthesizers, auto-tuned vocals, and a slurry of electronic beeps and bloops. This time, songs were named things like "___45____" (underscores included).

Critics mostly loved the new album, but their reviews were laden with phrases like "unexpected departure" and "abstruse reaction." (I had to look up *abstruse*. Ironically, it means "hard to grasp.") They were right to be confused; *22, A Million* is not at all like folk music in the way it sounds. But that's not the point—it is exactly like folk music in the way it got made.

One critic, Will Hermes, summed it up perfectly on NPR's *All Things Considered*: "The more I listened to this record, the more I came to realize . . . electronic music is folk music. Computers are how millions of people around the world make music." These days folk music sounds more like electronic dance music (or the ocean!) than guitar-strumming singer-songwriter protest songs. The guitar used to be the quick way into music. Like it or not, computers are now the easier entry point. It's the same thing—music of the people, by the people, for the people—just in a different package: a motherboard instead of a fretboard.

There's a legend in the hip-hop community that the 1977 New York City brownout kick-started the growth of hip-hop culture. Supposedly, when the lights went out, music stores got broken into and there was more cheap equipment floating around on the street. More equipment meant more tools in the hands of more people. More tools on hand meant more experimentation and faster spread and growth.

In 2018, Daniel Sichel and Eric von Hippel, researchers at Wellesley College and MIT, estimated that personal investment in homespun innovation (like the early days of hip-hop) might account for something like $40 billion in time and money spent and $230 billion worth of tools and things put to use each year (in the United States alone). But no one really takes this value into account. Of all the research and development that goes on to create new products, they estimate that near 30 percent is unaccounted for because everyday people are making it happen on their own and the economists aren't keeping track. This practice is not at all limited to electronic folk music or hip-hop. For example, lifelong diabetic Dana Lewis built a DIY, open-source, artificial pancreas using predictive algorithms and off-the-shelf hardware to create a closed-loop system between her continuous glucose monitor, body, and insulin pump. She's one of many people solving their own problems with their own inventions.

The tools are getting faster and cheaper by the minute—as of now, ownership of smartphones in the United States is well past 80 percent. Soon the bigger question might not be who has the tools, but who has the time? We need to look at time divides in the same way as digital divides and wealth gaps. Scratch the surface of the research on the homespun industry and it's bound to reveal some disparities. Who exactly is inventing at home? Who can afford the time and the space to do it? It's an equity issue.

Other questions linger. What are we really creating? What's easy to make and what isn't? Right now, recording a video or song is simple; not too long ago, that wasn't so. But creating an artificial pancreas is not simple. Should it be? Maybe health care hacking and homespun synthetic biology are new folk arts too.

Learn to Love Constraints

The Cuyahoga River cuts through Ohio like a loopy, U-shaped vein, bisecting both Akron and Cleveland before ending up in Lake Erie. On June 22, 1969, it caught fire. This was not a boat fire on the river. The river itself was in flames. A flaming river is hard to ignore.

Of course, you can't burn a river with water alone. The blazing surface was a filmy cocktail of two parts industrial chemicals and one part raw sewage.

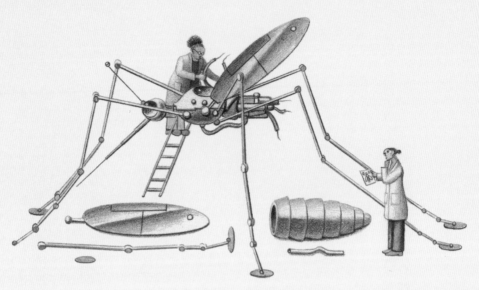

Who has the time to tinker with tools and materials?

As Cuyahoga River fires went, the 1969 fire was far from the worst. Firefighters put an end to it in about twenty minutes. Two bridges got scorched, but they cost only about fifty thousand dollars to fix, a pittance compared with the 1952 fire, which set the city back almost a million and a half. You'd think one or two stinky river fires would have been enough for people to take notice. Not so. There were a baker's dozen even before the one in 1952.

But in 1969, *Time* magazine, a juggernaut with millions of subscribers back then, ran a story on the June fire. Images of two-story flames licking the banks of the river caused an uproar. The photos helped spur a popular uprising that eventually led to what the Environmental Protection Agency later called "an avalanche of water pollution control activities," including the federal Clean Water Act and the EPA itself.

The 1969 Cuyahoga River fire and all the prior ones are examples of a system reaching a limit. That little vein of water could no longer absorb the abuse and pollution. The situation turned from a sad but oddly tolerable problem into a flaming mess of trouble.

Cuyahoga River fire, 1952

When a system like the Cuyahoga reaches its limit, every-thing goes out of whack. There's nothing to do but adjust. A family member gets sick, and you contort your life to take care of them. A fishery gets depleted, and the goal shifts from individual boats trying to pull in a big haul to replenishing the ecosystem. A hole grows in the ozone layer and every country on the planet bands together to help it heal.

Back in 1972, Charles Eames was interviewed by Madame L. Amic, a curator at the Louvre for an exhibit called *Qu'est-ce que le design?* ("What Is Design?"). The result is a delightfully awkward chat. Eames's answers are absurdly short. Most are shorter than the questions. Many are a single word. None are longer than a brief sentence or two, except when she asks him about constraints. Then he gets peculiarly long-winded:

> [Design is] the sum of all constraints. Here is one of the few effective keys to the Design problem: the ability of the Designer to recognize as many of the constraints as possible; [their] willingness and enthusiasm for working within these constraints. Constraints of price, of size, of strength, of balance, of surface, of time, and so forth. Each problem has its own peculiar list.

Truly timeless designs come from an elegant response to constraints. Not responding to constraints makes things stylis-tically fleeting and structurally fragile. Learn to love your limits.

You can see lovely limits at play in the beauty of old warehouses that had to respond to nature to make them livable. Old buildings are made from steel, wood, glass, and brick. Material constraints are what make them feel great. Raw materials like these just naturally go together. The high ceilings and gigantic windows feel good too. They are there because they had to be. Back when they were built, the obvious and often only solution to lighting and ventilation woes was to respond to nature's constraints. Lighting was expensive and often done with dangerous gas. To lower cost and light up the room, factories were fitted with huge windows. To leave room for big windows, they needed tall ceilings. Light and height happen to be lovely and have turned out to be quite desirable (and valuable), but their reason for being was pragmatic.

Here's some promotional copy for United Steel Sash, a factory window framing system sold at the time. The language alone tells you just what a pragmatic matter it was:

> *United Steel Sash flood the interior with daylight, and lighten up the dark corners where filth and waste materials accumulate in dimly lighted factories. Daylight exposes these rubbish piles, and improves the sanitary conditions. Full efficiency of every workman [sic] is assured. . . . With the United Steel Sash a maximum amount of ventilation can be obtained. . . . Good ventilation makes workmen [sic] active and industrious.*

Light to avoid trash piles. Ventilation for industrious workers. That's what created these lovely lofty spaces, now flooded with natural light and cross breezes. To make them useful, the builders had to contort their designs to nature's whims, right in the middle of the industrial era—a moment devoted to transcending nature's grasp. Responding to constraints makes things great. They are the map to, not the enemy of, progress.

More modern techniques, like cheap lighting and climate-controlled air conditioning, allowed builders to transcend natural constraints. What did we end up with? Buildings crisscrossed with low ceilings and fluorescent lights. High ceilings stimulate creative thought. Natural light on our retinas stimulates serotonin, which elevates mood. Natural light on our skin produces vitamin D, which helps the immune system. When we ignore constraints, we ignore natural needs. Fewer constraints give us lesser designs.

We now live in a world that pretends to be free from a lot of natural constraints, even though it's not. We have designs that serve our immediate needs, and while we punt our problems to other parts of the world and further on in time. Natural constraints that are slow to reveal themselves just don't guide and nudge in the same way when we have instant, feel-good solutions in the moment.

The constraints you choose make or break a design's aesthetics, and they make or break your ethics. When you create, what you choose not to do is as important as what you choose to do. The constraints you follow are your ethics; they get built right into the fabric of the world.

Ecological economist Herman Daly put a poetically simple label on the things we might choose to contain but tend to ignore. He called them *bads*, as in "depletion and pollution are costs, they are bads rather than goods." Goods (like goods and services) produce bads (like social strife and contamination). Pretend the bads don't come along with the goods, and natural systems like the Cuyahoga reach their limits.

What constraints might you impose on your own work? Longevity? Inclusivity? Health? Happiness?

Get Ready to Respond

The producer and comedian Lucille Ball once quipped, "Responsibility is just the ability to respond." Her definition is half right; the word comes from the Latin *responsus*, which roughly means "the ability to respond"; it just tends toward verbal things—like having the wits to respond to a question or hold your own in a debate. Still, her twist on the word is not much of a stretch. The slight shift in definition turns responsibility from a burden to a boon. The ability to respond helps you make the most of any situation, ethics aside.

How do we work on our ability to respond when things don't go as planned? *

First and foremost is being brave enough to act but humble enough to adjust. Red Burns, a torchbearer of technology *and* humanity, left us this pearl of wisdom: "Combine that edgy mixture of self-confidence and doubt—enough self-confidence to try new things, enough self-doubt to question." Responses need to come from both actions and words.

Chasing possibilities and acting responsibly sometimes seem like they are in conflict, but we need them both. It would be a shame if we sacrificed potential on the altar of anxiety. We need unapologetic optimism and radical responsibility side by side. We should be building on successes without ignoring the troublesome parts. Even utopias need a sewage system.

* How we respond (and who does it) is always in flux. Back in chapter 2, "Apple Attacks the Amazon" (page 64) digs into that.

Time (or you) can decide whether these overlaps are epiphanies or apophenia.

One way to better our ability to respond? Embrace imperfections—especially if your creations are big, quick, and unwieldy.

Philosophers Paul Virilio and Hannah Arendt pointed to the link between our old friends pace and feelings years ago. Fast is frightening. A roller coaster is a lot more terrifying than a hayride. A stock market crash is scarier than a slow decline. The reasons are reasonable. Fast things can cause more damage; slow things can be easier to respond to. Our emotions can't process fast flows as well as slow flows.

In a *Wall Street Journal* article about how to "fix" social media, NYU professor Clay Shirky suggested something similar when it comes to social networks: "We know that scale and speed make people crazy. We've known this since before the web was invented. Social media is better, for individuals and for the social fabric, if the groups it assembles are smaller, and if the speed at which content moves through it is slower."

The intersection of responsibility and possibility: utopian sewage treatment

Frances Haugen, a data engineer and product manager turned Facebook whistleblower, called for the same in her testimony to Congress, seeking reforms that make "the platforms themselves safer, less twitchy, less reactive, less viral." Twitchy, reactive, and viral are synonyms for too swift. She, Shirky, and others have suggested changes that might make social media less twitchy, like the inability to share a link you haven't read, a time delay between when you post and when something shows up, or as Renée DiResta of Stanford's internet observatory also suggested to the *Wall Street Journal,* "circuit breakers" that automatically kick in to slow overly viral content.

If you make tools that have the unfortunate side effect of stoking outrage, you might not be able to resist wrapping yourself in the warm, responsibility-shielding blanket of "market forces." After all, it really is market forces that make our media twitchy and emotional. Drama gets attention, and attention gets income. The way we made our media market is what makes drama flow.

But market forces also create pollution. It was market forces that pushed chemical companies to pollute the Cuyahoga River—until it burst into flames. Now market forces are polluting our imaginations with emotional outrage. Market forces will always create pollution. Unless pollution is factored into the equation. Unless we include the bads with our goods. Unless we slow to responsibility. Ask yourself: *Do I have the time or tactics to respond if my work breaks?*

The bigger the things are, the harder they can be to control. So, while a single person or even a single company (with a few grand exceptions) can't do it all, if you design products, lead a company, are a parent, or just care, you should be eager to adopt shared constraints that take the bads into account. Cooperative coordination, safety measures, and smart regulation make for a good, thriving, *imperfect* world.

The problem, of course, is that it's hard to break free of the past, even when you want to. Many big companies made big investments in old infrastructure, which might be messy and hard to unwind. People are rightfully skeptical of regulation too. Too much regulatory hoop jumping also drags down our ability to respond. More responsive regulation could be written to adapt to data as it comes in and could have built-in check-ins to tweak the parts that aren't performing.

An article in the 2019 edition of the synthetic biology journal *Nucleic Acids Research* has a matter-of-fact title that feels right for such a no-nonsense publication: "Fail-safe genetic codes designed to intrinsically contain engineered organisms." Led by Jonathan Calles of Stanford University, its abstract begins: "One challenge in engineering organisms is taking responsibility for their behavior over many generations." Delivered in deadpan scientific prose, it's easy to miss just how mind-boggling a sentence that is.

Read that sentence again: "One challenge in engineering organisms is taking responsibility for their behavior over many generations." This is a colossal shift in thinking and doing. It means we are the parents of future beings yet to be conceived. We're evolving organisms, not the other way around. We really are working on the world—or as Drew Endy, one of the paper's coauthors, puts it, "*with* the world"—and not just in it. Like all organisms, the ones we unleash will evolve after we birth them. That is some responsibility.

So the researchers took that constraint into account and designed a way to respond down the road. They solved it with . . . an imperfection. To oversimplify it, they designed a way for the DNA to have trouble evolving—making it nearly impossible for the gene to pass on a mutation, and all but ensuring it will be an evolutionary failure.

This insight is no less of a breakthrough than something that seems sexier and more spectacular, like tinkering with the human genome. It is an imperfect design, on purpose.

The solution to the problem of runaway genes is to make them fragile and imperfect. This is what it can look like to design responsibly—and responsively. (Of course, we'll have to see how these patterns play out and how they will allow us to respond down the road.)

. . . .

Be prepared for things to break. Even if you've done everything right, something will go wrong. Gain as much literacy as you can in materials, particularly the mischievous ones, and share what you learn. Be strategic about the work you take on and both the stakeholders you include and those you leave out. Remember that the constraints you choose to follow are a manifestation of your ethics. Preserve your ability to respond. Use imperfection as protection.

And don't be afraid to investigate what the things you make are bound to make and are destined to break—the unseen potential and the unintended consequences. Look beyond your intended audience and toward anyone and everything that might be touched by your designs. As you do, keep in mind the words of designer, printer, and activist Rick Griffith: "Good design should have no victims." Proceed accordingly.

Don't Swat!

In a world in which we'll need to do a lot of responding, who might we call on to help us heal?

―――――――――――

Jaymon and I hike at his maddeningly delightful, dyslexic eight-year-old ADHDer cadence. Every few steps he procrastinates on getting to our campsite. A furled fern leaf here, a white birch tree with a split trunk that looks like it is dancing there, a bird call he could send right back if standing still. The need to smell every single ponderosa until he can assemble a whole pine tree sundae. His experience of the world is so very different from my own neurotypical one. We are both humans but seem to have an entirely different Umwelt. He taught me patience. Rather, I had to learn patience to help him thrive, to connect with him. And it has opened me up. He has shown me all these different interfaces with the world. Being with him is like a portal to possibility.

Once, when he was a couple of years younger and enjoying endless pushes on a swing in the park, the parent next to me picked up a handful of wood chips from the ground and said to her son, "If I start with ten of these wood chips and add five more, how many do I have?" Her son eagerly shouted out the answer: "Fifteen!" Jaymon stared longingly. He had trouble with seemingly simple operations. Academics were so hard for him until we moved him to a special school just for neurodiverse kids. I caught him on a backswing and whisper-asked if he wanted to talk out how to get to the wood chip answer with me. He shook his head. We kept swinging. Later, when it was just us, he said to me, "Mommy, what I was wondering is how many trees did all these wood chips come from?" That was the duality of Jaymon's mind.

On this hike to Fresca Lake, we're more than taking our time, and I'm sensing more than I would have otherwise. Each leaf-examination stop gives the mosquitoes time to catch up. I let three land on my arm and look closely.

There was a time when most of these were natural mosquitoes. I remember doing this same hike with Mike twenty years before. It was a particularly buggy weekend, and I got bitten by all of them. If I didn't vigorously swing my arms as I walked, I was lunch. There were clouds of them, even when we got to the rocky shore where we set up our tent. Mike didn't have my flavor, or my carbon dioxide plume, or my heat—who knows, but I was always the one who got bitten.

I had such a bad reaction to all the bites on that trip that my arms looked swollen. I think Mike wondered if I'd ever camp again. Here I am, though, attempting to instill the camping bug into our son, or rather, learning to love the outdoors in a way I have never managed to with anyone else.

"Don't swat, Mom!" Jaymon calls to me from the peak of a fallen log.

While staring at the three mosquitoes on my arm, I flinch a little as a high-pitched *zeeee* sound whizzes by my ear. My instinct is still to swat, even though I know that most of these mosquitoes are drones.

His arms rise in triumph. "We need mosquitoes, and they need us!"

I groan at the third-grade curriculum being lorded over me. Mosquitoes are a vital part of the ecosystem, blah blah blah, and we all need to find ways to encourage their repopulation. It's not so simple to unlearn our instincts, though. Adults like me, who grew up in the before times, knew mosquitoes as pests to smash, not to mention carriers of malaria, Zika, dengue, and yellow fever. After a childhood of using DEET (the only thing that ever worked) and citronella candles, it hasn't been easy for me as an adult to switch to protecting them.

"Why do you not like mosquitoes, Mommy?" Jaymon often asks me to repeat stories a few times. The retelling helps him internalize learning. I've already told him this story many times, but I don't mind. At this point he's so familiar with it that he annotates it as we go. I start with natural mosquitoes and disease, and then move into the gene drives of the 2020s.

"Scientists inserted special genes into mosquitoes that prevented them from reproducing, and it worked," I continue.

"It worked too good," he says.

"Yup. They did it first in the Seychelles—a set of islands in the Indian Ocean. They offered themselves as a country to test the technology. And it worked—quickly. Within a couple years, the country was free of the mosquitoes that caused a disease called dengue."

"And then everyone did it?"

"Yes. Everyone thought it was just wonderful, and soon people everywhere were running these gene drives for all kinds of mosquitoes across the planet."

"They got rid of all the mosquitoes?"

"A lot of them. Most of them."

"But that's not good for the plants. We need pollinators! And fish food."

"Yeah, that's right. We moved a little too quickly. It saved a lot of people, but it turns out mosquitoes have a really important role in the ecosystem. So then we tried to bring them back. But it was complicated."

"I think they should put dragon DNA in mosquitoes, that way they can breathe fire when someone tries to swat them." He assumes his best "dragon breathing fire" pose.

"Maybe one day they will."

Jaymon blasts off and sprints down the trail. I take the next twenty seconds of alone time for some deep breaths before the question I know will come next.

"And those new mosquitoes hurt Uncle R, so we don't like them."

Uncle R is Ricky, my brother, a synthetic biologist. When it was clear that the global mosquito population was in peril, he was one of the scientists working to help reverse it. His lab had found a couple of genes to switch off in hopes of improving the hardiness and longevity of the remaining mosquito species. They began breeding them, building up their populations in captivity.

The totally incomprehensible thing to me, to this day, is the way they fed those mosquitoes—they would all stick their arms into the mosquito containers and just let them eat—mosquitoes like human blood more than anything else. It was only once a week that Ricky took a mealtime shift, he swore, and he said scientists had done it this way for years. Yeah, except not on poorly understood synthetic mosquitoes.

"Yeah. He got a lung disease from the synthetic mosquitoes. He was in the hospital for a long time."

"And he talks different now."

Different is one way of phrasing it. Ricky no longer has the lung capacity to speak a sentence longer than three syllables without inhaling; as a result, everything he says sounds urgent and agitated.

"It's because he can't get full deep breaths like you and me."

Turns out Ricky was one of the lucky ones. The synthetic mosquito project was ultimately canceled because it was deemed too risky.

We just can't control nature, especially insects, they said. But the need for more pollinators hadn't abated. Mosquitoes as a food source for other species was trickier to measure. By some accounts, the frogs, spiders, and bats had all adapted, found other prey. Others claimed it was too soon to tell, that this kind of massive food source loss would take years to ripple up the food chain. Pollination, though—this need couldn't wait.

"We're happy the new mosquitoes can't bite him anymore now that they are robots."

"That's right. Most of our mosquitoes today are teeny tiny drones."

The drone mosquito project began accidentally outside Mumbai, on a kitchen table that a family of five used for eating, homework, and everything in between. Part of that in between was a side project done by fifteen- and seventeen-year-old sisters. Using off-the-shelf MicroFly components, they built twenty miniature drones for fun. Each was about as long as three grains of rice. The sisters set up an area of netting in their backyard to prevent them from getting lost. Out of curiosity, they loaded the drones with a reinforcement learning algorithm to see if it would enable the drones to teach themselves to fly around the space without crashing into anything. And it worked. But the drones not only learned to avoid crashing into anything; they also learned to mimic the other flying creatures that had been trapped in the enclosure with them: mosquitoes.

Their creation was adapted and miniaturized by scientists, trained by as many species of natural mosquitoes available, and soon, there we were. A world with billions of mosquito drones.

"Now they are so small, and they pollinate!" He holds out his arm and lets a drone mosquito settle on it. It is the size of half a grain of rice. The drone's proboscis pokes at Jaymon's skin, and he yelps, "No!"

I take his arm and gave it a kiss. The drones also learned from their natural trainers to bite humans, but because they don't have saliva, they don't leave itchy welts or transmit disease.

"Just some robot love. You must taste good to them."

He looks closely at the tiny spot on his arm, staring at it for at least thirty seconds. Then he takes off his backpack and starts rooting around the front pocket.

"Let's keep moving, Jaymon. I don't want to get there too late."

"Give me a second."

He pulls out his compass and waves it over his arm.

"I'm magnetic!"

288

"Let me see."

Sure enough, the compass needle twitches ever so slightly in the proximity of the bite. I take the compass and wave it over my own arm. Twitch, twitch.

"We're all full of metal now, Mommy!" Jaymon says gleefully. "We're robots too."

My own reaction isn't quite as enthusiastic. I reach out and scoop him up. He's always been the best hugger. If the mosquito drones are leaving trace metals strong enough to twitch a compass in our skin and around the environment, who knows what the implications might be? It feels like Ricky all over again. I don't think I have it in me.

I give Jaymon a squeeze. "If we're all robots now, we're going to need you to be our robot leader and show us how to survive."

He nods. "Me and my friends will do it."

––––––––––––––––––––

Mosquitoes have caused a lot of disease, and there are active gene drives to try and control them. This story imagines that we have done so, only to realize later that there are consequences we didn't imagine at the time, such as a need for their pollination services. It isn't a huge leap to imagine microdrones providing that function, but of course there would be consequences to having metallic pollution in our bodies, much as microplastics have now made their way into us and many other species.

Temple Grandin, Greta Thunberg, and many others leverage their neurodiversity for positive change. Our education system isn't built for their ways of learning, but people with an ability to see possibility and pattern where the rest of us can't will be the ones with the epiphanies* that save us all.

* Check out "Whom Do You See?" (page 115) for a swirl of apophenia and epiphany.

A Call to Action
Design for Healing

At this moment, we can choose to harness runaway design or get run over.

At this moment, too.

And this one.

All the while, technology will continue to get more intelligent, more creative, and more like us. And nature will continue to become malleable and more like technology. How we understand, respond to, and create with both is where things will go right, wrong, or something in between. The path ahead necessitates design for healing.

To heal, we must embrace our imperfections—those we know about and those that will reveal themselves in time. We can gather, stare at what humanity has created, notice what we've broken, and decide to design to heal. Even so, we must recognize that simply acknowledging that we need to design for healing won't make it so.

Healing isn't magic. Neither is design work, and we all design. We all contribute to and build the world in some way. Healing takes time, checkups, and examination from all angles, professions, people, and nature. Healing is looking hard at what's gone wrong and what's worked. It's about building on the old, composting and repurposing as needed, and acknowledging what has stood the test of time and what needs replacement. Healing requires some assembly. To heal, we must paint pictures of our futures—those we want to see and those we want to avoid. It takes practice. What exists in the future you want to design? Don't forget that what we make makes us back. How would you like to develop from here? What do you hope for your descendants?

No one person will ever know everything, but together our limited points of view can connect to form a full and beautiful dream. If we stop equating speed = efficiency = value, watch out for the flow of our tricky technologies, and acknowledge the emotions that permeate all of what and how we make, we will find our rhythm. It's a lot. Those intangibles lurk in the fog, creeping in and taking hold when we least expect it. But actionable tactics can help draw them out.

We can sit with our awkward moments until the quirky components reveal design opportunities. We can learn to live with turbulence by deliberately disorienting our day-to-day. We can find new connections between words, languages, pictures, cultures, and materials. We can name our monsters and find timely treasure. We can become literate in the mischievous materials that we make with—and that make themselves. We can build in speed traps and fragility to help us respond when what we make fails.

We can consciously define our constraints. The ones we choose become our ethics in action. Well-chosen constraints are not a burden but a source of harmony and a scaffold for possibility.

Seek Harmony

The best design is harmonious. Harmony can feel intangible and hard to pin down, but you know harmony when you feel it, when you hear it, when you use it. The harmony we're talking about goes by many names. When the things we make:

Are in harmony with our senses, we call it beauty.

Bring harmony to groups of people, we call it culture.

Bring harmony to faulty systems, we call it restoration.

Bring harmony with nature, we call it sustainability.

Make tasks easy to do, we call it intuitive.

Balance power across people and communities, we call it equity.

Are in harmony with our hopes, we call it joy.

In short, when the things we make (or take away) bring harmony to a situation, it feels right and works well. That's good design.

Harmony on a large scale is hard. Often, other pressures are much more potent. Remember, society, nature, and our descendants are rarely welcomed as constraints in what we make. Utilizing them to strive for harmony is a big shift.

Harmony is an example of what physicist Carlo Rovelli called a "happening," the emergent relationships between things that make up any given moment. Harmony is elusive because relationships know few bounds. They go in all directions, don't sit still, and change over time.

Harmony wasn't even on the radar for a good part of the twentieth century. Instead, we made heroic (sometimes tragic) attempts to contain, separate, and sanitize nature's messy ways:

physiques flooded with antibiotics to keep away microbes, sky-scrapers filled with cubicles to up productivity, circuit boards crammed with discrete little transistors to process information. The twentieth century was about reducing things to component parts—stuff made of atoms, bodies made of cells. We tried to make things neat.

Our neatness quest worked pretty well for some people for some time. Cheap food, plentiful products, mighty medicines, bountiful energy, magnificent motherboards, and endless air travel. But it's not harmonious. A lot got broken along the way. Climate change, antibiotic-resistant superbugs, massive inequality, and an overemotional internet.

We're in the middle of a magnificent mingling between people, technology, and nature.* Generative AI chatbots are overlapping our own creative capacities. On-demand gene-tweaking tools like CRISPR-Cas9 are making natural materials work more like technology. So where does that leave us humans? There may be only one direction for us to go: lean toward nature. To do that, we need to embrace the mess.

Nature is not neat. Look no farther than your own gut. It's a stew of acid and waste and bacteria. Your gut microbiome—all the bacteria and things that live in your innards—has more cells than your body and weighs a pound more than your brain. All in all, those diverse bacteria boast a thousand times as many unique genes as we have in the rest of our bodies.

But there is a beauty to it. The ancient Greeks had a notion that mental illness came from too much black bile in the gut. They were onto something, in a way. The gut and brain are intertwined. Gut bacteria have a symbiotic relationship with our brain and mood. Some types of depression have been linked to a reduction in gut bacteria, and studies hint that afflictions from anxiety to Alzheimer's may have a gut-brain link. And we know gut bacteria send signals to our nerves to help with everything from our immune system to our temperament.

In nature, things mingle and mix. Likewise, great design work comes from happenings and harmony, not just things and stuff.

Happenings feel elusive, but that's where we live. While the things we make last for a moment, then break, making and using them can take up the whole of our day-to-day. What we make and do is important; *how* we make and do it is more important still.**

A growing movement in architecture turns the act of design into a moment to nourish and heal the communities it serves. It prioritizes the purpose over the goal and takes the *happening* as seriously as the finished product.

* Really, all three are just one big thing. We're part of nature, and so are the materials that make our technology. For some reason, it just seems to make more sense when we split them up.

** Or as philosophizing engineers Terry Winograd and Fernando Flores wrote in *Understanding Computers and Cognition* in 1986, "We encounter the deep questions of design when we recognize that in designing tools, we are designing ways of being."

293

We find it in the collaboration between law professor and justice activist Bryan Stevenson and architects at MASS Design Group on the National Memorial for Peace and Justice in Montgomery, Alabama. The memorial is filled with suspended columns. Each represents a specific, horrific lynching. To connect the history to the communities upended by these horrors, the designers worked with families and descendants to collect soil from all the sites where the lynchings took place. A second set of columns will eventually be distributed to the communities—one at each site. A process for healing is built right into the monument's making.

Healing is also found in the work of Pritzker prize–winning, Burkinabé-German architect Francis Kéré, who uses simple methods, like mixing concrete and mud, with local materials and local labor to create elegant schools that not only serve the community's needs but also train the community to build for themselves. His buildings and how they are made typify a sustainable collaboration between people and the environment.

Not wasting what we have is another way to heal. In 2022, the world's first "upcycled" skyscraper was built in Sydney,

Vintage skyscraper, upcycled. Sydney, Australia

Kintsugi, the Japanese art of golden repair

Australia. Instead of demolishing and building anew, Danish architecture firm 3XN reused two-thirds of the fifty-year-old AMP Center tower while doubling the usable space by grafting new floors onto the old core. No matter how you slice it, hanging on to the bones of the original building was beneficial: it likely conserved enough carbon during construction to power the building for three years, saved $100 million or so in construction costs, and trimmed nearly a year off the usual construction schedule. And the result is beautiful.

Kintsugi—also called *kintsukuroi* ("golden repair")—is the centuries-old Japanese art of reassembling broken ceramics and lacquerware by filling in cracks and seams with a gold dust—resin mixture. The restored pottery is graced with streaks of gold that call out the brokenness of things and treat cracks as an opportunity for beauty. The result is beautiful too—so beautiful that some people deliberately break their own pottery to do it. The metaphor is a bit worn out and overused, but it's a good one. This is design for healing. Making the most of the cracks. Calling them out rather than casting them aside.

Be a Good Jig

Harmony is not just the result of a project but also a way of working throughout a project, a way of existing. One of the great

295

joys of working with creative people is witnessing the things they make to make the things they make.

Take woodworking. Doing it right requires inventiveness, patience, and rapidly spinning metal blades—with teeth. To navigate this blend of creativity and danger, carpenters make jigs—contraptions cobbled together from scraps and fasteners. Their job is to guide a piece of wood through a saw, lathe, sander, or drill at just the right angle or in just the right way, repeatedly.

There is beauty in enabling others to be beautiful.

Jigs can be beautiful in their own right—jig making is an art of its own—but at their core, they're built to build something else, a thing that makes another thing possible.

Is a dandelion the little golden flower that comes in the spring? Or is it the white billowing sphere of cottony seeds? In *Life and Habit*, nineteenth-century novelist and satirist Samuel Butler quipped, "A hen is only the egg's way of making another egg." Life is a mold for life. Everything is a product and a template. Everything is a jig.

If there is one lesson to take from this book it might be this: Be a good jig.

You already are a jig. The things you make and do go on to make and do. The impacts of what you achieve pale in comparison to what you pass on. All this is a shift from a kind of creativity hell-bent on breaking boundaries toward creative work that is adaptive, responsive, and focused on healing and harmony.

Design belongs to the future. It is always in service of moments to come. Like it or not, the things we create end up there via the most reliable and relentless delivery system there is: the passage of time. We are always on the verge of flying apart and always on the verge of beautiful reassembly.

Bibliography

Introduction

Porter, Katherine Anne. "The Future Is Now." *Mademoiselle,* 1950.

Chapter 1

Bierut, Michael. *Now You See It and Other Essays on Design.* Hudson, N.Y.: Princeton Architectural Press, 2018.

Chatterjee, Rhitu, and Marco Werman. "Mexico City Birds Ward Off Parasites with Cigarette Butts." *The World,* December 5, 2012. https://theworld.org/stories/2012-12-05/mexico-city-birds-ward-parasites-cigarette-butts.

'Cúagiláкv (Jess Housty). "Thriving Together: Salmon, Berries, and People." *Hakai Magazine,* April 27, 2021. https://hakaimagazine.com/features/thriving-together-salmon-berries-and-people.

DeepBrain AI. "Re;memory." Accessed June 18, 2023. https://rememory.deepbrain.io/en.

Haram, Linsey E., James T. Carlton, Luca Centurioni, Mary Crowley, Jan Hafner, Nikolai Maximenko, Cathryn Clarke Murray, et al. "Emergence of a Neopelagic Community through the Establishment of Coastal Species on the High Seas." *Nature Communications* 12, no. 1 (December 2, 2021): 6885. http://dx.doi.org/10.1038/s41467-021-27188-6.

Jacob, François. "Evolution and Tinkering." *Science* 196, no. 4295 (June 10, 1977): 1161–66. https://web.mit.edu/~tkonkle/www/BrainEvolution/Meeting9/Jacob%201977%20Science.pdf.

Kimmerer, Robin Wall. *Braiding Sweetgrass: Indigenous Wisdom, Scientific Knowledge, and the Teachings of Plants.* Minneapolis: Milkweed Editions, 2013.

Lovelock, James E. "Gaia as Seen through the Atmosphere." *Atmospheric Environment (1967)* 6, no. 8 (August 1972): 579–80. http://dx.doi.org/10.1016/0004-6981(72)90076-5.

O'Neil, Cathy. *Weapons of Math Destruction.* New York: Crown, 2016.

Rovelli, Carlo. "All Reality Is Interaction." Interview by Krista Tippett. *On Being with Krista Tippett,* March 16, 2017. Podcast, website, 51:35. https://onbeing.org/programs/carlo-rovelli-all-reality-is-interaction.

Simard, Suzanne. *Finding the Mother Tree: Discovering the Wisdom of the Forest.* New York: Penguin Random House, 2021.

Simard, Suzanne. "How Trees Talk to Each Other." Filmed June 29, 2016, at TEDSummit in Banff, Canada. TED video, 18:10. https://www.ted.com/talks/suzanne_simard_how_trees_talk_to_each_other/transcript.

Talhelm, Thomas. "Cowboy Culture Doesn't Have a Monopoly on Innovation." *Scientific American,* February 28, 2022. https://www.scientificamerican.com/article/cowboy-culture-doesnt-have-a-monopoly-on-innovation/.

Talhelm, Thomas, Xuanning Zhang, Shigehiro Oishi, Chen Shimin, D. Duan, Xuezhao Lan, and Shinobu Kitayama. "Large-Scale Psychological Differences within China Explained by Rice versus Wheat Agriculture." *Science* 344, no. 6184 (May 9, 2014): 603–08. https://doi.org/10.1126/science.1246850.

Chapter 2

Amanpour, Christiane. "How Surveillance Capitalism Is Undermining Democracy." *Amanpour & Co.,* PBS, February 19, 2021. https://www.pbs.org/wnet/amanpour-and-company/video/how-surveillance-capitalism-is-undermining-democracy/.

Anaconda Wire & Cable Company. "It's Always Wiser to Wire Ahead." Advertisement. *Time,* August 27, 1945.

Bohannon, John. "DNA: The Ultimate Hard Drive." *Science,* August 16, 2012. https://www.science.org/content/article/dna-ultimate-hard-drive.

Brand, Stewart. *The Clock of the Long Now: Time and Responsibility.* New York: Basic Books, 1999.

Brand, Stewart, and Paul Saffo. "Pace Layers Thinking." *Long Now Foundation.* Streamed live on January 27, 2015, posted February 22, 2020. YouTube video, 58:04. https://www.youtube.com/watch?v=L7ggrxLabKQ.

Buck, Stephanie. "The First American Settlers Cut Down Millions of Trees to Deliberately Engineer Climate Change." *Timeline,* August 22, 2017. https://timeline.com/american-settlers-climate-change-5b7b68bd9064.

Carrubba, Andrea. "Rotten River: Life on One of the World's Most Polluted Waterways—Photo Essay." *Guardian,* November 2, 2020. https://www.theguardian.com/global-development/2020/nov/02/rotten-river-life-on-one-of-the-worlds-most-polluted-waterways-photo-essay.

Church, George M., Yuan Gao, and Sriram Kosuri. "Next-Generation Digital Information Storage in DNA." *Science* 337, no. 6102 (August 16, 2012): 1628. http://dx.doi.org/10.1126/science.1226355.

Crowther, Thomas W., Henry B. Glick, Kristofer Covey, C. Bettigole, Daniel S. Maynard, Stephen M. Thomas, Jeffrey Robert Smith, et al. "Mapping Tree Density at a Global Scale." *Nature* 525 (September 2, 2015): 201–05. http://dx.doi.org/10.1038/nature14967.

Dana-Farber Cancer Institute. "About the PROMISE Study." Accessed January 6, 2022. https://www.enroll.promisestudy.org/about.

Dodge, Jesse, Taylor Prewitt, Remi Tachet Des Combes, Erika Odmark, Roy Schwartz, Emma Strubell, Alexandra Sasha Luccioni, et al. "Measuring the Carbon Intensity of AI in Cloud Instances." *arXiv* (June 10, 2022): 2206.05229. https://doi.org/10.48550/arXiv.2206.05229.

Haroun, Azmi. "The Viral Flying Tesla Stunt in Los Angeles Follows a 100-Year-Long History of Car Stunts and Troubles on the Street." *Insider,* March 31, 2022. https://www.insider.com/flying-tesla-stands-out-long-history-of-stunts-on-baxter-2022-3.

ICARUS. "The Internet of Animals." *Max-Planck-Gesellschaft.* Accessed August 10, 2023. https://www.icarus.mpg.de/28546/icarus-internet-of-animals.

Lopez, Steve. "Column: On One of L.A.'s Steepest Streets, an App-Driven Frenzy of Spinouts, Confusion and Crashes." *Los Angeles Times,* April 4, 2018. https://www.latimes.com/local/california/la-me-lopez-echo-park-traffic-20180404-story.html.

Office of Energy Efficiency and Renewable Energy (EERE). "Data Centers and Servers." US Department of Energy. Accessed February 8, 2023. https://www.energy.gov/eere/buildings/data-centers-and-servers.

Paci, Patrizia, Clara Mancini, and Bashar Nuseibeh. "The Case for Animal Privacy in the Design of Technologically Supported Environments." *Frontiers in Veterinary Science* 8 (2021): 784794. https://doi.org/10.3389/fvets.2021.784794.

Palmer, Annie. "Apple Now Has $210.6 Billion in Cash on Hand." CNBC, July 30, 2019. https://www.cnbc.com/2019/07/30/apple-now-has-210point6-billion-in-cash-on-hand.html.

Reuters. "Apple Makes History as First $3 Trillion Company amid Tech Stock Surge." July 3, 2023. https://www.reuters.com/technology/global-markets-apple-2023-07-03/.

Schneier, Bruce. *Data and Goliath: The Hidden Battles to Collect Your Data and Control Your World.* New York: W. W. Norton, 2015.

Service, Robert F. "DNA Could Store All of the World's Data in One Room." *Science,* March 2, 2017. https://www.science.org/content/article/dna-could-store-all-worlds-data-one-room.

Shah, Sonia. "Animal Planet." *New York Times Magazine,* January 12, 2021. https://www.nytimes.com/interactive/2021/01/12/magazine/animal-tracking-icarus.html.

Tokumatsu, Gordon. "People Are Still Trying to Replicate the 'Flying Tesla' Stunt in Echo Park." NBC Los Angeles, May 25, 2022. https://www.nbclosangeles.com/news/local/people-are-still-trying-to-replicate-the-flying-tesla-stunt-in-echo-park/2902619.

US Bureau of Labor Statistics. "Productivity." Accessed October 10, 2022. https://www.bls.gov/productivity/home.htm#tables.

Wikipedia. S.v. "Whole Earth Catalog," last modified July 23, 2023, 04:10, https://en.wikipedia.org/wiki/Whole_Earth_Catalog.

Chapter 3

Berners-Lee, Tim. "The Next Web." Filmed February 4, 2009, at TED2009 in Long Beach, Calif. TED video, 16:04. https://www.ted.com/talks/tim_berners_lee_the_next_web.

Brady, William J., Julian A. Wills, John T. Jost, Joshua A. Tucker, and Jay J. Van Bavel. "Emotion Shapes the Diffusion of Moralized Content in Social Networks." *Proceedings of the National Academy of Sciences of the United States of America* 114, no. 28 (June 26, 2017): 7313–18. https://doi.org/10.1073/pnas.1618923114.

Burkeman, Oliver. "Forty Years of the Internet: How the World Changed for Ever." *Guardian,* October 23, 2009. https://www.theguardian.com/technology/2009/oct/23/internet-40-history-arpanet.

Bush, Vannevar. "As We May Think." *Atlantic,* July 1945. https://www.theatlantic.com/magazine/archive/1945/07/as-we-may-think/303881.

Cole, Samantha. "Replika Brings Back Erotic AI Roleplay for Some Users after Outcry." *Motherboard: Tech by Vice,* March 27, 2023. https://www.vice.com/en/article/93k5py/replika-brings-back-erotic-ai-roleplay-for-some-users-after-outcry.

Damasio, Antonio. "The Brain Is a Servant of the Body: Antonio Damasio about Feelings as the Origin of Brain." *ZDF Aspekte,* November 11, 2017. YouTube video, 13:36. https://www.youtube.com/watch?v=x5GFB5NjfYw&t=614s.

Dubner, Stephen J. "Why Is U.S. Media So Negative?" *Freakonomics,* October 6, 2021. Podcast, 51:17. https://freakonomics.com/podcast/why-is-u-s-media-so-negative.

George, Jennifer M., and Erik Dane. "Affect, Emotion, and Decision Making." *Organizational Behavior and Human Decision Processes* 136 (September 2016): 47–55. https://doi.org/10.1016/j.obhdp.2016.06.004.

Gillies, James, and Robert Cailliau. *How the Web Was Born: The Story of the World Wide Web.* Oxford: Oxford University Press, 2000.

Kelly, Kevin. "What Technology Wants." Filmed November 16, 2010, at TEDxSF in San Francisco. YouTube video, 21:00. https://www.youtube.com/watch?v=nF-5CM0zGWY.

Kelly, Kevin. "WIRED's Founding Editor: Wisdom He Wish He Knew with Kevin Kelly." *Faith Driven Entrepreneur,* May 2, 2023. Podcast, 53:27. https://www.faithdrivenentrepreneur.org/podcast-inventory/episode-151-wireds-founding-editor-he-wish-he-knew-with-kevin-kelly.

Krulwich, Robert, and Jad Abumrad. "Willpower and the 'Slacker' Brain." *Radiolab,* NPR, January 26, 2010. https://www.npr.org/2010/01/26/122781981/willpower-and-the-slacker-brain.

Lerner, Jennifer S., and Dacher Keltner. "Beyond Valence: Toward a Model of Emotion-Specific Influences on Judgement and Choice." *Cognition and Emotion* 14, no. 4 (2000): 473–93. http://dx.doi.org/10.1080/026999300402763.

Licklider, J. C. R. "The Intergalactic Computer Network: Topics for Discussion at the Forthcoming Meeting." *Memorandum for Members and Affiliates of the Intergalactic Computer Network,* Advanced Research Projects Agency, April 23, 1963.

Licklider, J. C. R., and Robert W. Taylor. "The Computer as a Communication Device." *Science and Technology,* April 1968. https://internetat50. com/references/Licklider_Taylor_The-Computer-As-A-Communications-Device.pdf.

Longstreth, Richard. "'Stores the Road Passes Through': The Drive-In Markets of the 1920s." *The MIT Press Reader,* December 10, 2020. https://thereader.mitpress.mit.edu/ drive-in-markets-of-the-1920s.

Malik, Om. "Technology and the Moral Dimension." *On My Om* (blog), November 26, 2014. https://om.co/2014/11/26/ technology-and-the-moral-dimension.

Rathje, Steve, Jay J. Van Bavel, and Sander van der Linden. "Out-Group Animosity Drives Engagement on Social Media." *Proceedings of the National Academy of Sciences of the United States of America* 118, no. 26 (June 23, 2021): e2024292118. https://doi.org/10.1073/ pnas.2024292118.

Roose, Kevin. "The Online Search Wars Got Scary. Fast." *The Daily,* February 17, 2023. Podcast, 32:39. https://www.nytimes.com/ 2023/02/17/podcasts/the-daily/the-online-search-wars-got-scary-fast.html.

Sacerdote, Bruce, Ranjan Sehgal, and Molly Cook. "Why Is All COVID-19 News Bad News?" NBER Working Paper Series, Working Paper 28110, National Bureau of Economic Research, Cambridge, Mass., November 2020. https:// www.nber.org/papers/w28110.

Shirky, Clay. "Slow It Down and Make It Smaller." In *How to Fix Social Media. Wall Street Journal,* October 15, 2021, updated October 29, 2021. https://www.wsj.com/articles/ how-to-fix-social-media-11635526928.

Shiv, Baba, and Alexander Fedorikhin. "Heart and Mind in Conflict: The Interplay of Affect and Cognition in Consumer Decision Making." *Journal of Consumer Research* 26, no. 3 (December 1999): 278–92. http://dx.doi. org/10.1086/209563.

Shiv, Baba, and Matt Abrahams. "Feelings First: How Emotion Shapes Our Communication, Decisions, and Experiences." *Insights by Stanford Business,* November 20, 2020. https://www.gsb.stanford.edu/insights/ feelings-first-how-emotion-shapes-communication-decisions-experiences.

Weizenbaum, Joseph. *Computer Power and Human Reason: From Judgment to Calculation.* San Francisco: W. H. Freeman, 1976.

Williams, Evan. "Jon Talks Misinformation with Ev Williams and Dr. Joan Donovan." *The Problem with Jon Stewart,* February 10, 2022. Podcast, 41:34. https://podcasts. apple.com/us/podcast/jon-talks-misinformation-with-ev-williams-and-dr/ id1583132133?i=1000550651240.

Chapter 4

Alais, David, Yiben Xu, Susan G. Wardle, and Jessica Taubert. "A Shared Mechanism for Facial Expression in Human Faces and Face Pareidolia." *Proceedings of the Royal Society B* 288, no. 1954 (July 14, 2021): 20210966. https://doi. org/10.1098/rspb.2021.0966.

Beck, Julie. "This Article Won't Change Your Mind." *Atlantic,* March 13, 2017. https://www. theatlantic.com/science/archive/2017/03/ this-article-wont-change-your-mind/519093.

Benn, Evan S. "How I Found the Virgin Mary Grilled Cheese." *Esquire,* April 12, 2013. https:// www.esquire.com/food-drink/food/a21918/ virgin-mary-grilled-cheese.

Currin, Grant. "Elderly Male Elephants Are the Most Determined to Mate." *National Geographic,* July 2, 2019. https://www. nationalgeographic.com/animals/article/ elephants-older-mating-poaching#close.

Heider, Fritz, and Marianne Simmel. "An Experimental Study of Apparent Behavior." *The American Journal of Psychology* 57, no. 2 (April 1944): 243–59. https://doi. org/10.2307/1416950.

Higuchi, Russell, Barbara Bowman, Mary Freiberger, Oliver A. Ryder, and Allan C. Wilson. "DNA Sequences from the Quagga, an Extinct Member of the Horse Family." *Nature* 312 (November 15, 1984): 282–84. http://dx.doi. org/10.1038/312282a0.

Katchadourian, Nina. "Moss Maps." Accessed June 8, 2022. http://www.ninakatchadourian. com/maps/mossmaps.php.

Kintisch, Eli. "Born to Rewild." *Science* 350, no. 6265 (December 4, 2015): 1148–51. https://doi. org/10.1126/science.350.6265.1148.

Ledgard, Jonathan. "Interspecies Money." In *Breakthrough: The Promise of Frontier Technologies for Sustainable Development,* edited by Homi Kharas, John W. McArthur, and Izumi Ohno, 77–102. Washington, D.C.: The Brookings Institution, 2022.

Le Guin, Ursula K. "The Carrier Bag Theory of Fiction." In *Dancing at the Edge of the World,* 165–70. New York: Grove Press, 1989.

Lindbergh, Anne Morrow. *Hour of Gold, Hour of Lead: Diaries and Letters of Anne Morrow Lindbergh, 1929–1932.* New York: Harcourt Brace Jovanovich, 1973.

Marshall, George. *Don't Even Think about It: Why Our Brains Are Wired to Ignore Climate Change.* New York: Bloomsbury, 2015.

Mezrich, Ben. *Woolly: The True Story of the Quest to Revive History's Most Iconic Extinct Creature.* New York: Simon and Schuster, 2017.

Musk, Elon. "Elon Musk: 'A.I. Doesn't Need to Hate Us to Destroy Us.'" *Sway,* September 28, 2020. Podcast, 48:36. https://www.nytimes. com/2020/09/28/opinion/sway-kara-swisher-elon-musk.html.

NASA Sun & Space (@NASASun). "Say cheese!" Twitter, October 26, 2022, 3:43 p.m., https://twitter.com/NASASun/ status/1585401697819656193.

NASA. "Voyager 1's Pale Blue Dot." *Solar System Exploration.* February 5, 2019, updated February 13, 2020. https://solarsystem.nasa.gov/resources/536/voyager-1s-pale-blue-dot.

NPR staff. "Ever Wonder What a Woolly Mammoth Sounds Like?" *All Things Considered,* NPR, July 23, 2011. https://www.npr.org/2011/07/23/138644143/helping-mammoths-roar-again.

Onoda, Hiroo. *No Surrender: My Thirty-Year War.* Translated by Charles S. Terry. Annapolis, Md.: Naval Institute Press, 1974.

Perelmuter, Zeev. "Doxa versus Epistêmê: A Study in Aristotle's Epistemology and Scientific Thought." PhD diss., University of Toronto, 2002. https://tspace.library.utoronto.ca/handle/1807/121932.

Pew Research Center. "Where Americans Find Meaning in Life." November 20, 2018. https://www.pewresearch.org/religion/2018/11/20/where-americans-find-meaning-in-life.

Porco, Carolyn. "How the Celebrated 'Pale Blue Dot' Image Came to Be." *Scientific American,* February 13, 2020. https://blogs.scientificamerican.com/observations/how-the-celebrated-pale-blue-dot-image-came-to-be.

Porco, Carolyn. "Viewpoint: A Day to Celebrate the Pale Blue Dot." *BBC News,* June 19, 2013. https://www.bbc.com/news/science-environment-22968105.

Public Domain Review. "Ancient Courses: Harold Fisk's Meander Maps of the Mississippi River (1944)." July 20, 2020. https://publicdomainreview.org/collection/maps-of-the-lower-mississippi-harold-fisk.

Raichle, Marcus E., and Debra A. Gusnard. "Appraising the Brain's Energy Budget." *Proceedings of the National Academy of Sciences of the United States of America* 99, no. 16 (July 29, 2002), 10237–39. https://doi.org/10.1073/pnas.172399499.

Revive & Restore. "Wooly Mammoth Revival." Accessed August 13, 2023. https://reviverestore.org/projects/woolly-mammoth.

Stone, Daniel. "See the Mississippi River's Hidden History, Uncovered by Lasers." *National Geographic,* November 7, 2019. https://www.nationalgeographic.com/science/article/mississippi-rivers-hidden-history-uncovered-by-lidar.

Thomas, David. "David Thomas: The World's Most Useless Creatures." *Independent,* December 5, 2011. https://www.independent.co.uk/voices/commentators/david-thomas-the-world-s-most-useless-creatures-6272377.html.

Vedantam, Shankar, Maggie Penman, and Max Nesterak. "Why Our Brains Weren't Made to Deal with Climate Change." *Hidden Brain,* April 19, 2016. Podcast, 24:00. https://www.npr.org/2016/04/18/474685770/why-our-brains-werent-made-to-deal-with-climate-change.

Vergano, Dan. "Woolly Mammoths Wiped Out by Grass Invasion?" *National Geographic,* February 6, 2014. https://www.nationalgeographic.com/animals/article/140205-mammoth-grass-clover-food-ice-age.

Weiss, Sabrina. "The Climate Crisis Has Sparked a Siberian Mammoth Tusk Gold Rush." *Wired,* November 18, 2019. https://www.wired.co.uk/article/mammoth-tusk-hunters-russia-china.

Yong, Ed. "How Animals Perceive the World." *Atlantic,* June 13, 2022. https://www.theatlantic.com/magazine/archive/2022/07/light-noise-pollution-animal-sensory-impact/638446.

Zimov, Sergey A. "Pleistocene Park: Return of the Mammoth's Ecosystem." *Science* 308, no. 5723 (May 6, 2005): 796–98. https://doi.org/10.1126/science.1113442.

Chapter 5

Burns, Red. "Creativity and Technology." *The Education of an E-Designer,* edited by Steven Heller, 102–6. New York: Allworth Press, 2001.

Goodall, Jane. "What It Means to Be Human." *On Being with Krista Tippett,* August 6, 2020. Podcast, 51:10. https://onbeing.org/programs/jane-goodall-what-it-means-to-be-human.

Jacobs, Jane. *The Death and Life of Great American Cities.* New York: Random House, 1961.

Miller, Bennett, dir. *The Cruise.* 1998. Santa Monica, Calif.: Lionsgate Home Entertainment, 2006. DVD, 76 min.

New York Times. "Percival Lowell." November 14, 1916. https://timesmachine.nytimes.com/timesmachine/1916/11/14/301931792.html?pageNumber=10.

Nigg, Joseph. *Sea Monsters: A Voyage around the World's Most Beguiling Map.* Chicago: University of Chicago Press, 2013.

Pearson, Cynthia, and Norbert Delatte. "Collapse of the Quebec Bridge, 1907." *Journal of Performance of Constructed Facilities* 20, no. 1 (February 2006). http://dx.doi.org/10.1061/(ASCE)0887-3828(2006)20:1(84).

Roberts, Jennifer L. "The Power of Patience." *Harvard Magazine,* November–December 2013. https://www.harvardmagazine.com/2013/11/the-power-of-patience.

Rotaru, Victor, Yi Huang, Timmy Li, James Evans, and Ishanu Chattopadhyay. "Event-Level Prediction of Urban Crime Reveals a Signature of Enforcement Bias in US Cities." *Nature Human Behaviour* 6 (June 30, 2022): 1056–68. http://dx.doi.org/10.1038/s41562-022-01372-0.

Schiaparelli, Giovanni, cartographer. *Schiaparelli's Chart of Martian "Canals,"* 1877. In *Astronomy in a Nutshell, the Chief Facts and Principles Explained in Popular Language for the General Reader and for Schools,* by Garrett Putnam Serviss. New York: G. P. Putnam's Sons, 1912. https://commons.wikimedia.org/wiki/File:Astronomy_in_a_nutshell,_the_chief_facts_and_principles_explained_in_popular_language_for_the_general_reader_and_for_schools_(1912)_(14595879027).jpg#file.

Scoles, Sarah. "To Prevent a Martian Plague, NASA Needs to Build a Very Special Lab." *New York Times,* August 31, 2022. https://www.nytimes.com/2022/08/31/science/nasa-lab-mars.html.

Schumacher, Ernest F. *A Guide for the Perplexed.* New York: Harper & Row, 1977.

Suri, Jane Fulton. *Thoughtless Acts? Observations on Intuitive Design.* San Francisco: Chronicle Books, 2005.

Chapter 6

Biomimicry Institute. "Spider-Inspired Silk Company, Spintex, Awarded $100,000 Ray of Hope Prize." Accessed August 19, 2023. https://biomimicry.org/spider-inspired-silk-company-spintex-awarded-100000-ray-of-hope-prize.

Blokh, Daniel. "A Talk with John Bargh about the Common Interests of Art and Social Psychology." *Yale Daily News,* April 24, 2020. https://yaledailynews.com/blog/2020/04/24/a-talk-with-john-bargh-about-the-common-interests-of-art-and-social-psychology.

Boland, Jack. "A Study of How Much My Glasses Party." Class assignment, *The Design of Data* course, April 2020, Stanford University.

Byrne, Cormac, and Rónadh Cox. "Drumming the Waves: Conveying Coastal Geoscience with Rhythm." *EGU General Assembly 2021,* online (April 19–30, 2021): EGU21-1405. https://doi.org/10.5194/egusphere-egu21-1405.

Canine, Craig. "Building a Better Banana." *Smithsonian Magazine,* October 2005. https://www.smithsonianmag.com/science-nature/building-a-better-banana-70543194.

Carter, Carissa. *The Secret Language of Maps: How to Tell Visual Stories with Data.* Emeryville, Calif.: Ten Speed Press, 2022.

Corner, James. "The Agency of Mapping: Speculation, Critique and Invention." In *The Map Reader: Theories of Mapping Practice and Cartographic Representation,* edited by Martin Dodge, Rob Kitchin, and Chris Perkins, 89–101. West Sussex, UK: John Wiley & Sons, 2011. https://onlinelibrary.wiley.com/doi/10.1002/9780470979587.ch12.

Cox, Rónadh. Personal interview. February 2023.

Critical Ecosystem Partnership Fund (CEPF). "Biodiversity Hotspots Defined." Accessed August 25, 2023. https://www.cepf.net/our-work/biodiversity-hotspots/hotspots-defined.

Crow, James Mitchell. "The Concrete Conundrum." *Chemistry World,* March 2008. https://www.rsc.org/images/Construction_tcm18-114530.pdf.

Dahmani, Louisa, and Véronique D. Bohbot. "Habitual Use of GPS Negatively Impacts Spatial Memory during Self-Guided Navigation." *Scientific Reports* 10, no. 6310 (April 14, 2020). https://www.nature.com/articles/s41598-020-62877-0.

Einhorn, Catrin. "Nearly Every Country Signs On to a Sweeping Deal to Protect Nature." *New York Times,* December 19, 2022. https://www.nytimes.com/2022/12/19/climate/biodiversity-cop15-montreal-30x30.html.

Faste, Rolf. "Mind Mapping." *Rolf A. Faste Foundation for Design Creativity,* 1997. http://www.fastefoundation.org/publications/mind_mapping.pdf.

Gentner, Dedre, and Donald R. Gentner. "Flowing Waters or Teeming Crowds: Mental Models of Electricity." In *Mental Models,* edited by Dedre Gentner and Albert L. Stevens, 99–129. Hillsdale, N.J.: Lawrence Erlbaum Associates, 1983.

Godart, Frédéric C., William W. Maddux, Andrew V. Shipilov, and Adam D. Galinsky. "Fashion with a Foreign Flair: Professional Experiences Abroad Facilitate the Creative Innovations of Organizations." *Academy of Management Journal* 58, no. 1 (February 1, 2015): 195–220. http://dx.doi.org/10.5465/amj.2012.0575.

Honduran Foundation for Agricultural Research (FHIA). "Banana and Plantain Program." Accessed August 25, 2023. http://www.fhia.org.hn/html/Programa_de_Banano_y_Platano.html.

Jonkers, Henk M. "Self Healing Concrete: A Biological Approach." In *Self Healing Materials: An Alternative Approach to 20 Centuries of Materials Science,* edited by Sybrand van der Zwaag, 195–204. Dordrecht, the Netherlands: Springer, 2007.

Kambhampaty, Anna Purna. "What We Can Learn from the Near-Death of the Banana." *Time,* November 18, 2019. https://time.com/5730790/banana-panama-disease.

KU Leuven. "When Science Goes Bananas." *KU Leuven Stories,* October 2, 2019. https://stories.kuleuven.be/en/stories/when-science-goes-bananas.

Lagay, Faith. "The Legacy of Humoral Medicine." *AMA Journal of Ethics,* Virtual Mentor 4, no. 7 (July 2002): 206-208. https://journalofethics.ama-assn.org/article/legacy-humoral-medicine/2002-07.

Lakoff, George, and Mark Johnson. *Metaphors We Live By.* Chicago: University of Chicago Press, 1980.

The Language Conservancy. "The Loss of Our Languages." Accessed August 18, 2023. https://languageconservancy.org/language-loss.

Liang, Nathan Sherwood. "The Storm Orchestra." Accessed August 19, 2023. https://nathansherwoodliang.weebly.com/the-storm-orchestra.html.

Lightman, Alan. *Einstein's Dreams.* New York: Vintage Books, 1993.

Lu, Annie. "The Storm Orchestra: An Exploration of Geosciences through Music." *Williams Record,* October 19, 2022. https://williamsrecord.com/461830/arts/the-storm-orchestra-an-exploration-of-geosciences-through-music.

Lupi, Giorgia. "How We Can Find Ourselves in Data." Filmed March 14, 2017, at TEDNYC Design Lab in New York. TED video, 11:04. https://www.ted.com/talks/giorgia_lupi_how_we_can_find_ourselves_in_data.

Maffi, Luisa, ed. *On Biocultural Diversity: Linking Language, Knowledge, and the Environment.* Washington, D.C.: Smithsonian Institution Press, 2001.

McLuhan, Marshall. "A Conversation with Marshall McLuhan." *Voice of America, Perspective Series,* episode 156, June 1, 1966. YouTube video, 31:21. https://www.youtube.com/watch?app=desktop&v=WqIq6UPvNo0.

Montenegro, Maywa, and Terry Glavin. "In Defense of Difference." *Seed Magazine,* October 7, 2008.

Oldale, R. N., and R. A. Barlow, cartographers. *Geologic Map of Cape Cod and the Islands, Massachusetts.* 1986. 1:100,000 scale. Miscellaneous Investigations Series Map I-1763, USGS National Geologic Map Database. https://ngmdb.usgs.gov/Prodesc/proddesc_9902.htm.

Paige, Paul, cartographer. *A Map of Cape Cod.* 1940. East Brewster, Mass. 66 x 89 cm. David Rumsey Map Collection. https://searchworks.stanford.edu/view/11878306.

ProMusa. "Fundación Hondureña de Investigación Agrícola (FHIA)." Updated April 19, 2019. https://www.promusa.org/Fundaci%C3%B3n+Hondure%C3%B1a+de+Investigaci%C3%B3n+Agr%C3%ADcola+-+FHIA.

Sapolsky, Robert M. *Behave: The Biology of Humans at Our Best and Worst.* New York: Penguin Press, 2017.

Solnit, Rebecca. *Infinite City.* Oakland: University of California Press, 2010.

Spencer, Erin. "Why the Mimic Octopus Is the Ultimate Master of Disguise." *Ocean Conservancy,* April 1, 2016. https://oceanconservancy.org/blog/2016/04/01/why-the-mimic-octopus-is-the-ultimate-master-of-disguise.

Tufts University. "Racial Diversity Improves Group Decision Making in Unexpected Ways, according to Tufts University Research." *ScienceDaily,* April 10, 2006. https://www.sciencedaily.com/releases/2006/04/060410162259.htm.

Chapter 7

Abraham, Cresques, cartographer. *The Catalan Atlas.* 1375. Bibliothèque Nationale de France. https://gallica.bnf.fr/ark:/12148/btv1b55002481n/f6.item.

Adams, Gabrielle S., Benjamin A. Converse, Andrew H. Hales, and Leidy E. Klotz. "People Systematically Overlook Subtractive Changes." *Nature* 592 (April 7, 2021): 258–61. https://www.nature.com/articles/s41586-021-03380-y.

Aporta, Claudio, and Eric S. Higgs. "Satellite Culture: Global Positioning Systems, Inuit Wayfinding, and the Need for a New Account of Technology." *Current Anthropology* 46, no. 5 (December 2005): 729–53. http://dx.doi.org/10.1086/432651.

Aubert, Julien. "Geomagnetic Acceleration and Rapid Hydromagnetic Wave Dynamics in Advanced Numerical Simulations of the Geodynamo." *Geophysical Journal International* 214, no. 1 (April 2018): 531–47. http://dx.doi.org/10.1093/gji/ggy161.

BMW Group. "The BMW GINA Light Visionary Model. Innovative Approach and Optical Expression of Creative Freedom." Press release, June 6, 2008. https://www.press.bmwgroup.com/global/article/detail/T0010817EN/the-bmw-gina-light-visionary-model-innovative-approach-and-optical-expression-of-creative-freedom.

Carter, Carissa, Megan Stariha, Ariam Mogos, Kelly Schmutte, Tessa Forshaw, Seamus Harte, and Mark Grundberg. "I Love Algorithms: A Machineless Machine Learning Creation Kit." *Hasso Plattner Institute of Design at Stanford University.* Accessed August 21, 2023. https://dschool.stanford.edu/resources/i-love-algorithms.

Chittka, Lars. "Do Insects Feel Joy and Pain?" *Scientific American,* July 1, 2023. https://www.scientificamerican.com/article/do-insects-feel-joy-and-pain/.

Chrabąszcz, Patryk, Ilya Loshchilov, and Frank Hutter. "Back to Basics: Benchmarking Canonical Evolution Strategies for Playing Atari." *Proceedings of the Twenty-Seventh International Joint Conference on Artificial Intelligence (IJCAI-18),* July 2018, 1419–26. https://doi.org/10.24963/ijcai.2018/197.

Debord, Guy. "Theory of the Dérive." November 1956. *Situationist International Online.* Accessed August 24, 2023. https://www.cddc.vt.edu/sionline/si/theory.html.

Doudna, Jennifer A., and Samuel H. Sternberg. *A Crack in Creation: Gene Editing and the Unthinkable Power to Control Evolution.* New York: Houghton Mifflin Harcourt, 2017.

Lai, Bun. "Invasive Species." *Miya's Sushi.* Accessed August 21, 2023. http://miyassushi.com/invasives.php.

Lambert, Jeff, George Barnstable, Eleanor Minter, Jemima Cooper, and Desmond McEwan. "Taking a One-Week Break from Social Media Improves Well-Being, Depression, and Anxiety: A Randomized Controlled Trial." *Cyberpsychology, Behavior, and Social Networking* 25, no. 5 (May 10, 2022): 287–93. https://doi.org/10.1089/cyber.2021.0324.

Lindala, April E., Leora Lancaster, and Martin Reinhardt. *Decolonizing Diet Project Cookbook.* Marquette, Mich.: Northern Michigan University Press, 2016.

Livermore, Philip W., Rainer Hollerbach, and Christopher C. Finlay. "An Accelerating High-Latitude Jet in Earth's Core." *Nature Geoscience* 10, no. 1 (January 2017): 62–68. http://dx.doi.org/10.1038/ngeo2859.

McLean, Kate. "Sensory Maps." Accessed August 24, 2023. https://sensorymaps.com.

Menzies, Jeremy. "The Ghost Ship of Muni Metro (Part 1)." *SFMTA News & Blog,* July 21, 2016. https://www.sfmta.com/blog/ghost-ship-muni-metro-part-1.

Menzies, Jeremy. "The Ghost Ship of Muni Metro (Part 2)." *SFMTA News & Blog,* August 4, 2016. https://www.sfmta.com/blog/ghost-ship-muni-metro-part-2.

Newman, Lenore. *Lost Feast: Culinary Extinction and the Future of Food.* Toronto, Ontario: ECW Press, 2019.

Nguyen, C. Thi. "Ezra Klein Interviews C. Thi Nguyen." *The Ezra Klein Show.* February 25, 2022. Podcast, 1:13:53. https://www.nytimes.com/2022/02/25/podcasts/transcript-ezra-klein-interviews-c-thi-nguyen.html.

Olsen, Nils, and Mioara Mandea. "Rapidly Changing Flows in the Earth's Core." *Nature Geoscience* 1, no. 6 (June 2008): 390–94. http://dx.doi.org/10.1038/ngeo203.

Ordóñez, Lisa D., Maurice E. Schweitzer, Adam D. Galinsky, and Max H. Bazerman. *Goals Gone Wild: The Systematic Side Effects of Over-Prescribing Goal Setting.* Harvard Business School Working Paper 09-083. Boston: Harvard Business School, 2009. https://www.hbs.edu/ris/Publication%20Files/09-083.pdf.

Reich, Rob, Mehran Sahami, and Jeremy M. Weinstein. *System Error: Where Big Tech Went Wrong and How We Can Reboot.* New York: HarperCollins, 2021.

Rose, Lisa M. *Urban Foraging: Find, Gather, and Cook 50 Wild Plants.* Portland, Ore.: Timber Press, 2022.

Shariat, Jonathan, and Cynthia Savard Saucier. *Tragic Design: The Impact of Bad Product Design and How to Fix It.* Sebastopol, Calif.: O'Reilly Media, 2017.

Sherman, Sean, and Beth Dooley. *The Sioux Chef's Indigenous Kitchen.* Minneapolis: University of Minnesota Press, 2017.

Stevenson, Robert Louis. *Treasure Island.* Calgary, Alberta: Qualitas, 2010.

Venter, Zander Samuel, Kristin Aunan, Sourangsu Chowdhury, and Jos Lelieveld. "COVID-19 Lockdowns Cause Global Air Pollution Declines." *Proceedings of the National Academy of Sciences of the United States of America* 117, no. 32 (July 28, 2020): 18984–90. https://doi.org/10.1073/pnas.2006853117.

Zembrzuski, Thomas J., Jr., and Margaret L. Evans. *Flood of April 4–5, 1987, in Southeastern New York State, with Flood Profiles of Schoharie Creek.* US Geological Survey, Water-Resources Investigations Report 89-4084. Albany, N.Y.: US Geological Survey, 1989. https://pubs.usgs.gov/wri/1989/4084/report.pdf.

Chapter 8

Allyn, Bobby. "Here Are 4 Key Points from the Facebook Whistleblower's Testimony on Capitol Hill." NPR, October 5, 2021. https://www.npr.org/2021/10/05/1043377310/facebook-whistleblower-frances-haugen-congress.

"Amendment to the Montreal Protocol on Substances That Deplete the Ozone Layer." Conclusion date: October 15, 2016. *United Nations Treaty Series Online* 3288, no. 26369 (2019). https://treaties.un.org/doc/Publication/UNTS/No%20Volume/26369/A-26369-080000028048cd90.pdf.

Arendt, Hannah. *The Origins of Totalitarianism.* London: Harcourt, 1973.

Boissoneault, Lorraine. "The Cuyahoga River Caught Fire at Least a Dozen Times, but No One Cared Until 1969." *Smithsonian Magazine*, June 19, 2019. https://www.smithsonianmag.com/history/cuyahoga-river-caught-fire-least-dozen-times-no-one-cared-until-1969-180972444.

Bowman, Anthony G. "Renaissance Man." In *An Eames Anthology: Articles, Film Scripts, Interviews, Letters, Notes, and Speeches,* by Charles Eames and Ray Eames, edited by Daniel Ostroff, 311. New Haven, Conn.: Yale University Press, 2015.

Burns, Red. "Welcome Address to ITP students." In "In Memory of Red Burns," *Creative Leadership* (blog) by John Maeda, August 24, 2013. http://creativeleadership.com/cl/red-burns.html.

Buur, Stine Liv. "What Is Your Definition of 'Design,' Monsieur Eames?" *Vitra*, January 9, 2020. https://www.vitra.com/en-hu/magazine/details/what-is-your-definition-of-design-monsieur-eames.

Calles, Jonathan, Isaac Justice, Detravious Brinkley, Alexa Garcia, and Drew Endy. "Fail-Safe Genetic Codes Designed to Intrinsically Contain Engineered Organisms." *Nucleic Acids Research* 47, no. 19 (November 4, 2019): 10439–51. http://dx.doi.org/10.1093/nar/gkz745.

Carter, Carissa, Scott Doorley, and David Kelley. "Making Mischief." In *Which Side of History? How Technology Is Reshaping Democracy and Our Lives,* edited by James P. Steyer, 254–62. San Francisco: Chronicle Prism, 2020.

Daly, Herman E. "On Economics as a Life Science." *Journal of Political Economy* 76, no. 3 (May–June 1968): 392–406. https://www.jstor.org/stable/1829303.

Diabaté, Abdoulaye. "Results from Months of Monitoring Following the First Release of Non-Gene Drive Genetically Modified Mosquitoes in Africa." *Target Malaria*, March 31, 2021. https://targetmalaria.org/results-from-months-of-monitoring-following-the-first-release-of-non-gene-drive-genetically-modified-mosquitoes-in-africa/.

DiResta, Renee. "Circuit Breakers to Encourage Reflection." In *How to Fix Social Media. Wall Street Journal*, October 15, 2021. https://www.wsj.com/articles/how-to-fix-social-media-11635526928#renee-diresta-circuit-breakers-to-encourage-1d04f057.

Eames, Charles, and Ray Eames, dirs. *Design Q and A.* 1972. Venice, Calif.: Eames Office, 5 min.

Flatow, Ira. "What Your Genes Can Tell You about Your Memory." *Talk of the Nation*, NPR, October 5, 2012. https://www.npr.org/2012/10/05/162372195/what-your-genes-can-tell-you-about-your-memory.

Gates, Bill. "The World's Deadliest Shapeshifter." *GatesNotes* (blog), April 15, 2019. https://www-new.gatesnotes.com/The-worlds-deadliest-shapeshifter.

Griffith, Rick. "Rick Griffith: A Love Letter to Design, a List of Demands, and a Stern Look." *Print*, December 9, 2020. https://www.printmag.com/design-thinking/rick-griffith-a-love-letter-to-design-a-list-of-demands-and-a-stern-look.

Heilweil, Rebecca. "This Woman Designed— and Texts—Her Own Pancreas." *Forbes,* June 15, 2017. https://www.forbes.com/sites/rebeccaheilweil1/2017/06/15/this-woman-designed-and-texts-her-own-pancreas/?sh=3bb0071443b0.

Hermes, Will. "Bon Iver's Latest Is a Soulful Mix of Wood and Microchips." *All Things Considered,* NPR, September 30, 2016. https://www.npr.org/2016/09/30/496062072/bon-ivers-latest-is-a-soulful-mix-of-wood-and-microchips.

Khan, Ruqqaiya. "Can Bees Get Drunk?" *Science ABC,* August 29, 2022. https://www.scienceabc.com/nature/animals/can-bees-get-drunk.html.

Klein, Joanna. "Scientists Find Genes That Let These Bees Reproduce without Males." *New York Times,* June 9, 2016. https://www.nytimes.com/2016/06/10/science/bees-asexual-south-africa.html.

Koivu, Anniina. "The Kazam! Machine." *Vitra,* September 1, 2014. https://www.vitra.com/en-un/magazine/details/the-kazam-machine.

Mars, Roman. "Lights Out." 99% *Invisible,* October 14, 2014. Podcast, 18:09. https://99percentinvisible.org/episode/lights-out.

McA, Alison. "What Happened to the Genetically Engineered Honey Bee?" *American Bee Journal,* March 1, 2018. https://americanbeejournal.com/what-happened-to-the-genetically-engineered-honey-bee.

Ministère de la Transition Écologique. "Decree No. 2020−1757 of December 29, 2020 Relating to the Repairability Index for Electrical and Electronic Equipment." *Journal Officiel de la République Française* no. 0316, Text No. 5, December 31, 2020. https://www.legifrance.gouv.fr/jorf/id/JORFTEXT000042837821.

"Montreal Protocol on Substances That Deplete the Ozone Layer." Conclusion date: September 16, 1987. *United Nations Treaty Series Online* 1522, no. 26369 (1989). https://treaties.un.org/doc/Publication/UNTS/Volume%201522/volume-1522-I-26369-English.pdf.

Oepen, Anne Sophie, Jamie L. Catalano, Reza Azanchi, and Karla R. Kaun. "The *Foraging* Gene Affects Alcohol Sensitivity, Metabolism and Memory in *Drosophila.*" *Journal of Neurogenetics* 35, no. 3 (June 2021): 236−48. https://doi.org/10.1080/01677063.2021.1931178.

Pennisi, Elizabeth. "Mite-Destroying Gut Bacterium Might Help Save Vulnerable Honey Bees." *Science,* January 30, 2020. https://www.science.org/content/article/mite-destroying-gut-bacterium-might-help-save-vulnerable-honey-bees.

Schulte, Christina, Eva Theilenberg, Marion Müller-Borg, Tanja Gempe, and Martin Beye. "Highly Efficient Integration and Expression of *piggyBac*-Derived Cassettes in the Honeybee (*Apis mellifera*)." *Proceedings of the National Academy of Sciences of the United States of America* 111, no. 24 (May 12, 2014): 9003−08. https://doi.org/10.1073/pnas.1402341111.

Sichel, Daniel, and Eric von Hippel. "Household Innovation, R&D, and New Measures of Intangible Capital." NBER Working Paper Series, Working Paper 25599, National Bureau of Economic Research, Cambridge, Mass., February 2019. https://www.nber.org/papers/w25599.

Trussed Concrete Steel Company. *United Steel Sash.* 5th ed. Detroit: Trussed Concrete Steel Co., 1912. https://archive.org/details/UnitedSteelSashFifthEdition/page/n5/mode/2up.

Virilio, Paul. *The Administration of Fear.* Vol. 10 of *Semiotext(e) Intervention Series.* Los Angeles: Semiotext(e), 2012.

Call to Action

Butler, Samuel. *Life and Habit.* Boston: E. P. Dutton, 1879.

Equal Justice Initiative (EJI). "The National Memorial for Peace and Justice." Accessed June 10, 2023. https://museumandmemorial.eji.org/memorial.

Holland, Oscar. "World's First 'Upcycled' Skyscraper Saves Australian Tower from Demolition." CNN, December 6, 2022. https://www.cnn.com/style/article/australia-quay-quarter-tower-skyscraper/index.html.

Moreira, Paulo. "The Inspiring Architect from Burkina Faso Who Lifted World's Biggest Prize." *The Conversation,* March 21, 2022. https://theconversation.com/the-inspiring-architect-from-burkina-faso-who-lifted-worlds-biggest-prize-179685.

Pennisi, Elizabeth. "Meet the Psychobiome." *Science* 368, no. 6491 (May 8, 2020): 570−73. https://doi.org/10.1126/science.368.6491.570.

Acknowledgments

Jenn Brown—this book would not exist without your limitless care, attention, and brilliance.

Charlotte Burgess-Auburn, our partner in crime, thank you for saying what needs to be said, when it needs to be said, and doing it with glee.

Sarah Stein Greenberg, none of this would come to pass without your powerful knack for making things happen and endless intentionality that inspires us to take care in our work.

David Kelley, your influence informs us at every step and makes this place and book possible.

Carolina Perez, your ability to interpret possibilities from our earliest idea kernels and to show us how they connect to other concepts got this book off the ground.

Bernie Roth, for creating space and trust for us to do our best work.

Kate Maher and Drew Endy, thank you for your willingness to support our ideas and nudge them to new places and spaces.

Debbe Stern and Jill Kasser, no one would know about this if it weren't for you. Both of you are guides and partners all the way. We can't thank you enough.

Laurie Moore, Amanda Tiet, David Martinez, Patrick Beaudoin, Karen Engler, and Brad Hennig, thanks for lending your talents to give this work new meaning.

Christy Fletcher, Eric Lupfer, and Cary Goldstein, you made this happen and made sure it lived up to its promise. Thanks for launching us and sticking with us.

To all of our colleagues at the d.school, past, present, and future, thank you for your influence, care, and creativity, especially those who gave us advice: Megan Stariha, Stacey Gray, Lisa Kay Solomon, Leticia Britos Cavagnaro, Kelly Schmutte, Renée Chao, Ariam Mogos, Louie Montoya, Laura McBain, sam seidel, Seamus Yu Harte, Parker Gates, Chitra Venugopal, Justin Ferrell, Thomas Both.

And to those who inspired us along the way: Susie Wise, Barry Svigals, Julian Gorodsky and Courtlandt Butts (harmony); Ashish Goel (antigoals); Ariam Mogos and Megan Stariha (algorithms); Lisa Kay Solomon and Drew Endy (futures); Grace Hawthorne and Dan Klein (genius and curiosity); Sita Syal (engineering ethics); Maya Razon (experiences); Nihir Shah and Hannah Jones (metaphors); Maryanna Rogers, Dave Baggereor and Enrique Allen (media and tools); Scott Witthoft, Sarah Beckman and Michael Barry (noticing); and many others.

Julie Bennett, your keen eye for clarity and willingness to push us beyond our boundaries made this book what it is.

Kelly Booth and Annie Marino, thank you for bringing this book to life in a way that surpassed what we could have imagined.

Sohayla Farman, thank you for keeping us all on track.

Kristi Hein, thank you for making our words sparkle.

Julie Cepler, thanks to you and your team for giving us even more than we asked for.

Armando Veve, your imagination and talent is unsurpassed; thank you for sharing it with us.

From Carissa

To Dante, for sharing your unique ways of looking at the world and for being my guide.

To Desi, for your unwavering confidence in my success and your enthusiasm for possibilities.

To Ty, for being the bedrock that always keeps me upright.

To Steph, for being my creative confidante.

To Mom, for giving me the confidence to take on the world, and to Dad, for continuing to guide me from the other side.

To Kate Maher, for being the colleague, partner, and friend that keeps me coming back.

To David Dethier, Rónadh Cox, and David Rubin, for your mentorship at my most formative moments.

From Scott

To Rachelle, for encouraging me to be my best and helping me when I can't quite pull it off.

To my kids, for all your guidance and wisdom, which is more than mine (despite my thirty-year head start).

To Mom and Dad, for helping me develop gifts and for reminding me to share them.

To Chris, a brother in every way and then some: an inspiration, a mentor, and a companion.

To Jeannie Goddard, everyone's favorite teacher, who saw things I needed that others missed.

To Fabian Wagmister, who showed me that adulthood can be as imaginative as childhood.

To George Kembel, for showing me how much more I have to give and teaching me how to give it.

To Scott Witthoft for teaching me the value of paying attention to the right details.

Index

Image Credits

Page 15, top: Photograph copyright © by Jose1983/iStock
Page 15, middle: Photograph copyright © by amoklv/iStock
Page 15, bottom: Photograph copyright © by Art Wagner/iStock
page 16: Photograph courtesy of Interstate Signways
Page 17: Photograph copyright © by guowei ying/Getty Images
Page 18: Photograph copyright © by AdmantiumStock/Adobe Stock
Page 25: Photograph by Scott Doorley
Page 48: Photograph copyright © by Mario Alvarez/Unsplash
Page 49, top: Photograph copyright © Karan Chawla/Unsplash
Page 49, bottom: Photograph copyright © by Sony Herdiana/iStock
Page 73: Architectural rendering by Frederick Kennedy, Jr.
Page 80: Illustration from a reprint of "As We May Think," by written Vannevar Bush, published in *Life* magazine (September 10, 1945), p. 21
Page 90: Illustration by Roland B. Wilson from "The Computer as a Communication Device," written by J. C. R. Licklider and R. W. Taylor, published in *Science and Technology*, vol. 76 (April 1968): 35
Page 110: Photograph courtesy of Joe Rimkus, Jr.
Page 111: Image copyright © by zmeel/iStock
Page 112, left: *Mississippi River Sheet 7 Lidar* by Daniel Coe, image courtesy of the photographer
Page 112, right: Map by Harold Fisk for the US Army Corps of Engineers
Page 113: Photograph by NASA/JPL-Caltech
Page 114: Photograph by NASA/JPL-Caltech/Space Science Institute
Page 118, top: Photograph by NASA's Goddard Space Flight Center
Page 118, bottom: *Hawaii* from the series "Moss Maps" (1993) by Nina Katchadourian, image courtesy of the artist, Catharine Clark Gallery, and Pace Gallery.
Page 126: Art from "An Experimental Study of Apparent Behavior," written by Fritz Heider and Marianne Simmel, published in the *American Journal of Psychology*, vol. 57, no. 2 (April 1944): 244, copyright © 1936 by the Board of Trustees of the University of Illinois and used with permission of the University of Illinois Press.
Page 185, top: Illustration from the *Carta Marina* (1539) by Olaus Magnus
Page 185, bottom: *Chart the Planet Mars* by Giovanni Schiaparelli
Page 208: *Geologic Map of Cape Cod and the Islands, Massachusetts* (1986) by R. N. Oldale and R.A. Barlow for the US Geological Survey
Page 209: *Map of Cape Cod* by Paul Paige, image courtesy of Boston Rare Maps, Southampton, Massachusetts
Page 212: *Why Mind Map?* by Rolf Faste (1993), image courtesy of the Rolf A. Faste Foundation for Design Creativity
Page 221: Photograph copyright © by Alp Duran/Unsplash
Page 234: Illustration from the *Catalan Atlas* (1375) by Cresques Abraham
Page 237: *Hospital Corridor Smellscape*, copyright © by Kate McLean (2020), Digital Artwork
Page 242: Photograph copyright © by BMW AG
Page 244: *The Buried Ships of Yerba Buena Cove* by Michael Warner, et al. (2017) for the San Francisco Maritime National Historical Park, National Park Service
Page 245: *Map of 'Treasure Island'* by Robert Louis Stevenson (1850–1894)
Page 257: Art copyright © Eames Office LLC (eamesoffice.com), all rights reserved
Page 278: Photograph courtesy of Getty Images, Bettmann Collection.
Page 294: Photograph courtesy of 3XN, photograph copyright © Adam Mørk
Page 295: Photograph copyright © by Marco Montalti/iStock
Page 296: Photograph courtesy of Tom Raffield.
Endpapers: *Photos of real-word glacial retreat processed into generative AI patterns* from the "Crisis Curated" series by Aaron Huey, www.crisiscurated.com. Used with permission of the artist.

Image copyrights, permissions, and credits listed on page 313.

Typefaces: Luzi Type's Messina Serif, Font Bureau's Prensa, HVD Fonts' Fabrikat Mono, and Adobe Fonts' Shift

Library of Congress Cataloging-in-Publication Data is on file with the publisher.

Trade Paperback ISBN: 978-1-9848-5818-4
eBook ISBN: 978-1-9848-5819-1

Printed in China

Acquiring editor: Hannah Rahill | Project editor: Julie Bennett
Designer: Annie Marino | Art director: Kelly Booth
Production designers: Mari Gill and Faith Hague
Production editor: Sohayla Farman
Production manager: Jane Chinn
Copyeditor: Kristi Hein | Proofreader: Lisa Brousseau | Indexer: Ken DellaPenta
Publicist: Natalie Yera | Marketer: Chloe Aryeh
d.school Publicists: Debbe Stern and Jill Kasser
d.school Marketers: Laurie Moore, David Martinez, and Patrick Beaudoin
d.school creative team: Jennifer Brown and Charlotte Burgess-Auburn

10 9 8 7 6 5 4 3 2 1

First Edition